Managing by the Numbers

Managing by the Numbers ___

Absentee Ownership and the Decline of American Industry

CHRISTOPHER MEEK, WARNER WOODWORTH
and W. GIBB DYER, Jr.

Addison-Wesley Publishing Company, Inc.
Reading, Massachusetts   Menlo Park, California   New York
Don Mills, Ontario   Wokingham, England   Amsterdam   Bonn
Sydney   Singapore   Tokyo   Madrid   Bogotá
Santiago   San Juan

Library of Congress Cataloging-in-Publication Data

Meek, Christopher.
  Managing by the numbers: absentee ownership and the
decline of American industry / Christopher Meek, Warner
Woodworth, and W. Gibb Dyer.
   p.   cm.
  Includes index.
  ISBN 0-201-16129-x
  1. Industrial management—United States. 2. Stock
ownership—United States. 3. Consolidation and merger of
corporations—United States. 4. Industrial concentration—
United States. 5. Employee ownership—United States.
I. Woodworth, Warner. II. Dyer, W. Gibb, 1954–   III. Title.
HD70.U5M413 1988   338.7'4'0973—dc19   87-16088

Cover design by Hannus Design Associates
Text design by Joyce Weston
Set in 11 point Trump by Compset, Inc., Beverly, MA

ISBN 0-201-16129-x
ABCDEFGHIJ-DO-898
First printing, January, 1988

Contents

Acknowledgements

We would like to thank the students and support staff at Brigham Young University for their help in researching and preparing this book. Alberto Zarate's research on People Express was particularly valuable as was the assistance of Tony McCauley and Young-Hack Song in studying the history of United States Steel Corporation (today USX). We would also like to thank the School of Management at Brigham Young University for partially funding the research upon which this volume is based. At Addison-Wesley, Scott Shershow and his staff were especially helpful to us, and we greatly appreciate the time and effort Scott put into consulting with us on this book's several drafts. We must also express our heartfelt thanks to the Jamestown Area Labor-Management Committee and William Foote Whyte at Cornell University for generously supporting the development of the Jamestown community history as well as the Digital Equipment Corporation, Lincoln Electric, and the many companies who have helped us gather data and supported our research activities.

Preface

In many ways, this book is the product of a fortuitous intersection of two different approaches to contemporary American business. Since the mid-1970s, two members of our group, Christopher Meek and Warner Woodworth, have been studying troubled industries and helping managers, workers, and local government officials in their efforts to prevent plant closures and reverse the effects of industrial decline. As interventionists, we were not always successful. But we invariably found, at the heart of the problems we studied and tried to solve, the same two interrelated developments, both having to do with corporate ownership and control.

Throughout this book we refer to these developments as *absentee ownership* and *professional management*. By the first term we mean the ownership of companies by shareholders scattered around the nation and the world, or the ownership of individual plants and businesses by other, larger companies themselves owned by such shareholders. The second term refers to the kind of generic manager whose roots are in an MBA program instead of in the factory or on the shop floor of a specific business; the kind of manager who goes "by the numbers," treating workers and businesses alike as little more than financial assets.

Our third coauthor, Gibb Dyer, arrived, although from a different vantage point, at similar conclusions about the impact of absentee ownership and professional management on American industry. Where Meek and Woodworth came at the problem from the back end—that is, from the point of crisis and deterioration—Dyer started at the front end, by tracking successful family-owned companies from their genesis onward. In these historical studies, Dyer repeatedly found that once successful family-owned businesses faltered, losing the loyalty of employees as well as their technological and marketing competitiveness when they began to be influenced by absentee interests and the values and financial techniques of professional managers. In his consulting work with troubled family companies, Dyer, like Meek and Woodworth, found himself advising management to revive the traditions of family ownership, as well as cautioning founders anticipating retirement to consider alternatives to going public.

Our own critique of professional managers and their training stems in large part from our experience as consultants to executives in businesses ranging from small, family owned enterprises to Fortune 500 corporations. We also have taken as well as taught many MBA courses ourselves in programs at the University of Michigan, MIT, Boston College, the University of New Hampshire, and today at Brigham Young University. Thus, the observations we make and the criticisms we express are not merely reckless "shots made from the hip." They have been derived and developed from our several collective years of experience with business students in the classroom, and with professional managers in the "real" business world.

In our work in America's companies and industrial communities, we were amazed at how frequently we heard the same story—the story of a company, once vital and innovative, that lost its competitive edge after the withdrawal of the founding entrepreneurs and the shift to absentee ownership. Middle managers and workers across the country sadly—and sometimes bitterly—told us a similar tale of how professional managers had drained the profits from their companies, once the economic backbone of their communities. More often than not we found that the answer to our efforts to revive troubled companies was not a program of innovation and change but instead a return to the company's historical and cultural roots.

It was not until late 1984 and early 1985 that we realized that our seemingly different and independent work was coming to the same focal point. As we shared our research findings and consulting experiences at departmental meetings, it became clear that the three of us were essentially looking at the same issues from different angles and coming up with similar conclusions. A panel presentation at the 1985 Academy of Management meetings in San Diego further clarified the overlaps of our research when panel commentator Davis Dyer, then of the *Harvard Business Review*, suggested that we expand on our ideas into a book.

It has been fun writing this book, because we realized from the start that it would be controversial and that reactions to it would probably be mixed and emotional. Some readers, perhaps, will be angry with everything we say—and we look forward to their comments and criticism. Other readers will find themselves cheering our analysis of the problem, but they will not agree with our recommended solutions. And at least some readers, we hope, will give serious thought to our analysis of the impact of absentee ownership and professional management on American business, and will consider how our recommendations may be used in their situations. In any case, we look forward to the debate this book may generate.

CHAPTER 1

Changing Patterns of Ownership and Management

Many people see symptoms of malaise afflicting American business, but few agree on the nature and causes of the disease. The popular press daily covers farm foreclosures, bank failures, or industrial plant closings and layoffs. The business community worries aloud about the inability of American firms to compete in a global economy. We are all aware of the problems afflicting our steel industry, of the labor–management conflict in the airline industry, and of the gradual replacement of manufacturing jobs with low-paying service sector employment.

At the same time, academics attempt more sophisticated interpretations of today's troubled business climate. A number of critics suggest that macroeconomic forces are the real cause of America's industrial problems. Some economists, for example, argue that the current crisis stems from inadequate monetary policy. Others call for protective tariffs to halt the decline of American factories and the loss of American jobs. Still others advocate a national industrial policy to curb economic decline and confront future industrial challenges.[1]

At a different level of analysis, other experts suggest our problems are essentially microeconomic, internal to the functioning of the corporation. In one well-known book, for example, William Ouchi reviewed the strengths of Japanese management and articulated the values of a "Theory Z" approach to working by consensus. Peters and Waterman's best-selling *In Search of Excellence* proclaims organizational culture to be the key factor in America's best-run companies. Organizational behaviorists stress the need to improve communications and redesign boring, rigid jobs. Students of industrial relations voice the need for systems of work that generate a high level of employee commitment.[2] Others argue that industry has failed to adapt to the larger technical, social, and economic environment and that a renewal process is essential to future survival.[3]

INDUSTRIAL METAMORPHOSIS: AN HISTORIC SHIFT

All these comments and commentators provide useful insights into our contemporary industrial dilemma. But they ignore the impact of an important historic shift that has occurred in the nature and structure of business organizations. Our research attempts to fill this gap by examining some of the neglected dimensions of industrial evolution and by suggesting promising new directions to be pursued.

Drawing on original historical data collected while studying family-owned businesses, communities, and large corporations, we intend to critique simplistic assumptions that long-term viability will result from "staying close to the customer" or managing "by walking around." When analyzing corporate performance, our data suggest management style and corporate policy cannot be separated from ownership structure and the distribution of power. The "values" and "symbols" that make up what recent commentators call "corporate culture" do not exist outside of a larger social context, nor do they operate independently of ownership, control, and wealth.

Thus, we emphasize two underlying issues as essential explanatory factors in understanding current problems—absentee ownership and professional management. The emergence of today's global marketplace with its diverse and complex transactions has been accompanied by a corresponding increase in the size and complexity of business organizations. Firms which once focused their energies on a specialized segment of the market now have grown to encompass many different products, services, and businesses. What were once closely held or family-owned firms, centered in a particular community and location, have been transformed into publicly traded, multidivisional, conglomerate structures, owning a multitude of enterprises and controlling a bewildering array of economic activity.

As a result of these changes, distant, or "absentee," ownership has come to be the dominant form of ownership, and with this shift in ownership structure a professional managerial class has arisen, trained in the nation's leading business schools, and supposedly qualified to manage any and all businesses. This industrial trend toward distant ownership and professional management has frequently been hailed as progress, but our empirical research has documented its many unanticipated and difficult organizational and industrial problems. The shift to ever-larger structures, absentee ownership and control, and "professional" managers without roots in specific businesses has had serious consequences on many different levels of business and society.

Evolution of American Corporations

Today's business realities can be seen in the context of two hundred years of American corporate history. That history can be divided into four distinct phases:

Phase I (1800s)
Phase II (1917–1930s)
Phase III (1940s–early 1970s)
Phase IV (mid-1970s–1980s)

Each phase is characterized by a particular kind of interaction between organizations and society. In the first half of Phase I, that is, until the mid-nineteenth century, the dominant model for conducting business was the small-scale craft system. This system was made up of local entrepreneurs who established small shops in their own community, contracting with skilled craftspeople to produce a particular product. Trust, mutual respect, and reciprocal reward systems gave technology a human face.

Late in the century, the factory system, mass production, and the assembly line were the products of an industrial revolution. The modern corporation brought new speed and control of production through work simplification and the systematic de-skilling of laborers. Dark, dingy, and unsafe working conditions producing defective and even dangerous products gave rise to legislative reforms in a variety of industries including food processing, meat packing, mining, and drugs. The excesses of the "robber barons" increased public suspicion of big business, leading to the Federal Trade Commission and antitrust legislation. The struggle between private interests and the public good continued well into the twentieth century.

Phase II was the period of the First World War. The common cause of Allied victory led to a temporary reconciliation of private and public interests. A spirit of cooperation among labor, management, and government led to the formation of the War Industries Board and new positive expectations for the future. After the war ended, however, unmet expectations spelled the end of this new-found trust and led to a growing disillusionment with corporate power. The Great Depression of the thirties only accelerated this trend. The increasing threat of corporate power finally provoked government intervention. Roosevelt and the New Deal won benefit programs for the poor and social security systems for the general population. Society affirmed labor's right to organize through unionization, and created the Securities and Exchange Commission to oversee the stock trading. Congress passed a wide variety of consumer legislation to protect consumers and regulate industrial mismanagement.

The end of World War II ushered in Phase III, a period of tremendous success and affluence in American society. Driven forward by the growth of industry, the United States quickly attained the highest Gross National Product, per-capita income, and standard of living in the world. A growing, mostly white, middle class generally agreed that "What's good for General Motors is good for America." Such statements were not even an expression of corporate arrogance: They were a reflection of social fact.

Soon enough, however, a re-emerging public consciousness began again to question corporate America's role in creating or exacerbating problems such as racism, pollution, and the militarization of our economy. Another body of regulatory laws put industry up against the wall. Ralph Nader attacked GM's Corvair as "unsafe at any speed" and launched a populist campaign for consumer protection. The civil rights movement and the Vietnam antiwar effort shook up boardrooms across the country and led to widespread changes in organizational and private life. The Environmental Protection Agency and a host of other government mechanisms changed forever the way we do business in America.

The present phase IV is a situation similar to Phase I, in that we find ourselves now in the middle of a growing struggle between business and society. Since 1975 or so, American business has been turned on its head. A new and unfamiliar global economics has strangled traditional markets where U.S. firms used to make billions in profit. Once, no matter what American managers did, the wave of the economy simply carried them forward. Now we have lost, and continue to lose, entire industries to international competition. A massive foreign trade imbalance has made Americans nervous and European and Third World investors happy.

Meanwhile, many U.S. plants are idle. Excess capacity and declining productivity are blamed for widespread plant closings and massive layoffs. Gigantic mergers absorb more of our business and financial resources while the federal deficit *quadruples*. Ours has become an era of union busting, general decline for the labor movement, and concession bargaining.

The current crisis, argue the doomsayers, will culminate with the demise of corporate America as we now know it, and a stagnant economy like Britain's will replace the boom years of the past. More optimistic futurists like Naisbitt argue that a millennium of technology and service sector success is just around the corner. Such arguments, however, conveniently ignore the low-paying, dead-end reality of most service sector work, as well as the recent tendency for the computer information industry to follow high-tech manufacturing jobs to the Third World.

Whatever our immediate future holds, it is clear that the notorious corporate incidents of the recent past—Three Mile Island, Johns Manville and asbestosis, the Ford Pinto, Union Carbide in Bhopal, the Bendix-Martin Marietta battle, E. F. Hutton, Ivan Boesky and other scandals in the financial community—have taken their toll. A new backlash against corporate America is manifest in the blocking of proposed mergers, in new tax laws, in limitations on the use of Chapter 11 bankruptcy to abrogate labor contracts, and the recent passage of trade and plant-closing legislation in the U.S. Senate. All are signs of growing concern about the role and power of the corporation in American life.

A central thesis of this book is that much of the current crisis facing, indeed engulfing, American industry is rooted in deeply shifting patterns of corporate ownership and management. We sense that a very different, absentee type of ownership structure has created a correspondingly different professional manager. As companies no longer focus their efforts on a particular community, location, or market, so managers no longer feel the need for experience in or allegiance to a particular business. Combined, these two interrelated changes in the nature and practice of American business are profoundly related to the erosion of our industrial infrastructure.

ABSENTEE OWNERSHIP

As we have seen, over a century ago, business was primarily a system of small, craft-based, family-owned enterprises, held together by personal relationships and driven by entrepreneurial skills. The common condition was that owners directly managed and controlled the firm. Often the family held all corporate stock, sat on the board of directors and appointed other board seats as well. By law the board had a fiduciary responsibility to the stockholders, and a basic theoretical goal of maximizing profit.

This rather simple arrangement of ownership and management has been rent asunder by recent historical developments. The emerging American economy is one dominated by absentee-owned companies, enterprises whose real owners are scattered across the nation. Today's megacorporations are enormous, bureaucratic, impersonal systems operated by executives who, all too often, have only their own career and financial interests at heart. These professional managers have been allowed to pursue their own agenda, with all the economic power of a major corporation at their disposal.

This massive change in corporate control has never been fully investigated. Early in this century Thorstein Veblen pointed to a "red line of cleavage" between what he called "absentee owners" and the general population, and warned of a widening split between "haves" and "have-nots" that could eventually result in social and political chaos.[4] Veblen was perhaps the first to observe that there was a difference both in "material interest" and in "sentiment" between owners who operate as local residents, or community-based entrepreneurs with a stewardship over their business, and purely absentee owners who feel no personal allegiance to a distant industrial plant or the community that surrounds it.

Much of the subsequent research on absentee ownership has also focused on the impact of changing patterns of ownership upon community social structure and decision making.[5] Some researchers have also pointed to the significance of the shift in corporate ownership patterns. The notion of managerial control of American business was first proposed by A. A. Berle and Gardiner C. Means who, half a century ago, argued persuasively that the shift toward large-scale corporations was already in full swing.[6] Even at this early date, two hundred big firms dominated the economy, and the founders, families, and entrepreneurs who originally had owned American business were being supplanted by professional managers. Berle and Means found that 44 percent of major companies were subject to managerial control, while an additional 21 percent were controlled by some sort of legal device. Thus, a total of 65 percent of the firms they surveyed were administered by nonowners.

Berle and Means documented the trend, but they had little to say about its implications for markets, for profits, for employees, and for society as a whole. Since their time, this trend has accelerated. A decade ago, Alfred Chandler argued that managers, not merely the market, controlled the economy. As Chandler saw it, Adam Smith's "invisible hand" of the economy really belonged to senior executives who directed the affairs of Wall Street with tight fists.[7] Our own research supports Chandler's view. As we see it today, huge corporations and their managers have become, in effect, the absentee landlords of our society. Corporate power, ownership, and the American economy alike is in the hands of today's managerial elite.

Thus, our investigations have centered on the ways in which this shift toward absentee ownership and professional management directly affects business itself. We suspect that owners who live thousands of miles away from the businesses they control might well be detached and unfeeling about the community where that business happens to be located. We hypothesize that even managers who may be temporarily based in a local community, but who are really seeking a future career elsewhere, may lack a real sense of personal stewardship over the businesses and plants placed in their trust. Is there evidence to support such a view? We think there is.

Likewise we want to explore whether the corporate culture of an absentee-owned company differs markedly from that of the locally owned company. Do workers feel greater alienation from management, and experience less secure, more stressful, working conditions under absentee control? Are there significant organizational changes when a locally based entrepreneur sells out his or her business to a much larger company that has diverse holdings all across the nation or even the world? What effect does this kind of merger or acquisition have on corporate performance, on profits, on morale, and on the company's ability to compete in the world marketplace? We will be trying to answer these and other similar questions in the rest of this book.

Throughout, when using the term "absentee ownership," we will mean not merely geographical distance, but also a psychological and social distancing of the owners and executive managers from the rest of the organization, and a managerial perspective in which subsidiary operations are seen as little more than financial assets. Absentee ownership also includes what we call a kind of technical distance, an inability to understand and appreciate the fine but often significant points of product design, manufacture, and distribution. We will look in more detail at the various forms of "distance" that can arise between management and employees in Chapter 5.

MEGA-MERGERS

Business mergers are not a new phenomenon. At the turn of the century, acquisitions occurred at such a frenzied pace that by 1902 a full third of all manufacturing firms had been consolidated. Out of those mergers came AT&T, Standard Oil, General Electric, Alcoa Aluminum, U.S. Steel, United Fruit, and International Harvester. These large corporations were run by men who were also owners, founders, partners, or members of a key family of stockholders. For example: Swift and Armour of meat packing; Rockefeller of Standard Oil; McCormick's Harvester; Vanderbilt's railroad empire; Carnegie, Morgan, and Schwab of steel.

The situation is vastly different today with ownership diluted, stockholders scattered across the nation, and top executives operating out of some remote office building in a distant state. Those early "industrial giants" seem like dwarfs in today's industrial world. When Andrew Carnegie and J. P. Morgan joined forces to produce the nation's first billion dollar corporation in 1901, it looked like a veritable Goliath. But against the mergers of the 1980s, these early deals pale by comparison. Recently Chevron merged with Gulf for a $13.4

billion price; Texaco acquired Getty Oil for $10.1 billion; Du Pont picked up Conoco for $7.4 billion; U.S. Steel snatched Marathon Oil for $6.5 billion; GE is completing a $6.3 billion acquisition of RCA; Philip Morris took over General Foods for $5.6 billion; Santa Fe became the owner of Southern Pacific for $5.2 billion; and General Motors is finalizing a $5.0 billion marriage with Hughes Aircraft.

The way to climb the Fortune 500 list is no longer a matter of growing from the ground up through excelling in a particular line of business. Rather, today you buy your way up, and everybody is doing it. Nabisco, Texas Air, ABC, Carnation, Bendix, the list goes on. High tech, low tech, energy, medical care—they're all wheeling and dealing, getting bought, fighting off a takeover, or being sold.

The mix of business deals varies. They include mergers, such as the marriage between GE and RCA, and attempted takeovers such as GAF's $4.1 billion fight for Union Carbide, a firm ten times the size of GAF. The list includes friendly marriages such as General Foods and Philip Morris as well as hostile, nasty battles like the fierce takeover attempt of Walt Disney Productions by Saul Steinberg which cost Disney $325 million to block. And although most deals are domestic, some like Crown Zellerbach's acquisition by Sir James Goldsmith are foreign.

The popular mythology is that such merger activity is a "healthy remaking of the economy." In truth, many firms are "borrowing up to their eyeballs," as one executive put it.

The fact is, since the 1960s the wave of merger activity has set record after record. The underlying logic seems to be that, if small is beautiful, then large is luscious, and gargantuan is gorgeous. A direct connection is claimed between massiveness and efficiency.

So the wave has grown, in spite of annual predictions that it would crest each year. In 1975 the first multi-billion-dollar corporate merger occurred. In the 1980s, there have been over sixty such mergers with thirty-six in 1985 alone. In fact, in 1985, 3,284 mergers and acquisitions were completed, amounting to an 18-percent increase over 1984. This was a record eleven per day, involving $179.6 billion in transactions.

In the past five years, sixty-two of the Fortune 500 list of corporations have been consumed by other giants. Burroughs's $4.8 billion takeover of Sperry Corporation in twenty-three days of maneuvering in May of 1986 was only exceeded by GE's devouring of RCA a few months earlier. Billion-dollar deals are literally a weekly occurrence, with the huge dollar transactions dramatically changing the core and complexion of a company's business. For instance, the simple dairy products operations of Beatrice Foods began in 1896 and continued as such until the 1960s. Then professional top managers began to acquire plumbing supplies and mobile home companies as Beatrice enterprises. In 1983 the company spent $2.8 billion for Esmark, a Chicago company which transformed Beatrice into a new conglomerate with over a hundred subsidiaries and 100,000 employees. Today Beatrice owns Samsonite luggage, La Choy Chinese foods, Max Factor cosmetics, Hunt-Wesson foods, Playtex Women's Wear, Swift meats, and Avis car rental. But Beatrice is no longer calling the shots. In late 1985, it was itself swallowed up by Kohlberg Kravis Roberts for $6.1 billion.

Many mergers have just not worked out that well. IBM purchased Rolm for $1.6 billion in 1984, but the two cultures never meshed, and Rolm lost over $100 million last year. Mobil acquired Montgomery Ward, but has lost over $600 million in recent years and is putting the retailer back on the auction block. Others were quick and dirty deals that were rapidly put together and ended almost before they started. People Express acquired Frontier Airlines, which promptly went bankrupt just six months later under a heavy debt load. This then forced People Express to also file for bankruptcy and sell out to Texas Air. Other disastrous mergers took a little longer to unravel. LTV's J & L Steel merged with Republic Steel in 1984, as a model of the great solution for the industry. But their losses only accelerated, forcing the now number-two steel corporation in the nation into Chapter 11 bankruptcy in 1986. Texaco purchased Getty Oil in just seventy-nine hours in January 1984, in a quick power game top executives cheered as dazzling. It has since led to a successful suit by Pennzoil which was in the middle of a merger with Getty at the time. The court's judgment against Texaco was $11.1 billion, which in turn forced the firm to file for protection through Chapter 11 of the federal bankruptcy code.

As a result of this trend, absentee-owned firms are increasingly managed by remote control. Instead of building a business, you merely buy one. Rather than design and develop new plants to expand into new product lines and new markets, companies simply purchase existing products and their markets. Five years ago executives spent $82.6 billion on acquisitions, approximately four times the amount spent on corporate R&D. Why innovate if innovation can be picked up through a stock purchase?

Who benefits from mega-mergers and acquisitions? The obvious winners are the raiders and investment bankers. T. Boone Pickens and his firm, Mesa Petroleum, netted $760 million in a 1983 bid for Gulf Oil, which ultimately ended up being acquired by Chevron. In the same case, Merrill Lynch got $18.9 million, Morgan Stanley $16.5 million, and Salomon Brothers and its bankers picked up $29.6 million. The take-home pay of Drexel's Michael Milken, who specializes in junk bond financing for giant deals, is estimated to have been $50 million in 1986, a hefty sum for a young upwardly mobile professional of the '80s.

The downside of these mega-deals and increasingly large and diverse conglomerates is considerable. While the managerial rhetoric claims these deals bring increasing economies of scale, the reality is more often an unmanageable increase in costs. Mergers may precipitate immense social and economic distress through plant closings and layoffs. Chevron's takeover of Gulf has resulted in the termination of 16,000 of 79,000 jobs between the two firms. Earlier this year Wells Fargo took control of Crocker National for $1.1 billion, making it the tenth largest bank holding company in the nation. Termination notices were given to 1,650 Crocker employees the same day as the acquisition announcement was made, with a warning that 5,000 jobs would disappear in the coming months. The bank plans to close 120 branches in California, forcing two million customers to relocate their place of banking.

The growing wave of acquisitions also builds pressure in the larger economy. Paul Volcker, ex-chairman of the Federal Reserve Board, complained that merger loans "alter the price and availability of credit" as mega-deals sponge up available loans.[8] Mergers swallowed up 33 percent ($19 billion) of available bank loans in 1981 and 22 percent in 1984. The result is fewer dollars for small business as tens of thousands go bankrupt each year, many because of capital shortages. The "healthy" economy of 1985 was accompanied by the demise of 57,067 businesses in America, up 9.6 percent over the previous year.[9] The average consumer pays interest rates which are higher than they would really be if a larger capital pool existed. In short, the public ends up contributing to the exorbitant costs of merger frenzy.

But do mergers benefit stockholders? It all depends, suggests a McKinsey study of 400 acquisitions over the past decade. In reviewing transactions valued at $100 million or more, the study concludes that the benefits go largely to the sellers who are acquired, not the buyers. McKinsey & Co. also reviewed fifty-eight large company mergers that occurred between 1972 and 1983 and concluded that a scant six cases were noteworthy successes.[10]

Similarly, a *Wall Street Journal* article cites a study by the Citizens for Tax Justice, which reveals that, of the twenty-five top acquiring firms in 1985, eleven spent over $40 billion on takeovers. That amount exceeded all they spent on new plants and equipment for the previous two years. In other words, they cut capital expenditures to "squirrel away cash for future takeovers and to sharply raise the pay of their top executives."[11]

INDUSTRIAL CONCENTRATION

The reshuffling of corporate power by absentee-owned firms does not stop within the walls of headquarters of a remote conglomerate. History testifies to increasingly concentrated markets created by large scale mergers and the subsequent grab for control. Indeed, it may be argued that mergers increase market concentration while simultaneously diluting the concentration of ownership. Thus, mergers turn full circle as large, absentee-owned corporations buy up competitors, resulting in tighter market concentration while simultaneously spreading shareholder control more thinly. The evidence is quite convincing since large firms are continually growing in absolute size throughout this century. As concentration grows, these firms gain power to manipulate markets, develop more sophisticated communication systems, accumulate immense resources for expensive advertising, and establish closer linkages between firms through interlocking directorates.

The corporate melting pot has thickened until, by the late 1970s, the Fortune 500, which represent only .02 percent of all U.S. companies, controlled over 80 percent of all manufacturing sales and 75 percent of all profits. The top four companies in each industry dominated 70 percent of rubber tire production, 89 percent of breakfast cereal production, 90 percent of all electric lamp production, 77 percent of greeting card production, 87 percent of all copper production, and 93 percent of all American auto production.[12]

Enterprises in oligopolies not only control production and markets; they own assets. In recent years over 60 percent of the assets of all non-financial corporations were owned by big firms with $250 million or more in assets. By 1977, in manufacturing, the largest two hundred companies controlled 60 percent of all assets, a significant leap upward from 45 percent three decades earlier.[13]

With the continuing movement toward acquisitions in the 1980s, the large corporations grow larger while hundreds of small businesses close down every day of the year. And growing evidence suggests that the bigger a business is, the more lethargic its economic performance. This is not only true of large defense contractors but of other big industries as well. A 1982–83 pilot study, which tracked the performance of companies in eleven different industries with sales up to $1.6 billion annually, suggests that small is indeed beautiful. The data are quite clear that large companies are less productive and provide significantly lower rates of return on investments than medium and small firms.[14]

Decades ago, industrial concentration led to price-fixing and a trust-busting congress that blocked anti-competitive management strategies. Today's absentee-owners are not only surviving, but thriving in a climate of big growth. While the Reagan administration proclaims this to be the Age of the Entrepreneur, a more apt description would be the Age of Increased Industrial Concentration. Deregulation, new financial manipulations, and relaxed government rules regarding corporate anti-trust practices have brought about an accelerated shift toward an increasingly concentrated economy.

Billion-dollar debts make for tremendously high interest payments, meaning more and more earnings are channeled into retiring debt rather than hiring more people, launching new R&D, or investing in new plants and equipment. As the economy slowly pedals backwards, many people wonder about today's managers.

A NEW BREED OF MANAGERS

Originally many managers in American industry were essentially artisans and craftsmen turned entrepreneurs. They grew up as apprentices in shops where they labored with sleeves rolled up and hands dirty. Managerial style was personalized, that of an artisan rooted to traditions of the past. Success was often born of decades of struggle and toil, and new-found wealth often accompanied by sentiments of *noblesse oblige.*

Success came from "sweat equity" and luck. Competence was derived from an individual's track record over long years. Managerial control was maintained through personal influence with one's workers, intuitive business acumen, and an in-depth knowledge and technical expertise in the firm's products and manufacturing process. These managers tended to create a culture that emphasized quality, family, and community. Such a system was clearly not without its faults, but it did generally reward managers who added value to the customer through better goods and services.

Today's manager, by contrast, professes to be a cool, calculating executive who "goes by the numbers" and is more interested in "doing deals" than achieving excellence in a particular industry. Competence is now based on credentials, college degrees, and fast-track career strategies. In fact, contemporary managers usually have a contempt for physical labor. Their hands are clean, their collars are white, and they are dressed-for-success. They seldom have roots in the local communities where their businesses are located. They control the corporation through asset management and high finance, having little shop experience or comprehension of the businesses they oversee. Disdaining the details of manufacturing and distribution, today's professional managers measure success in terms of return-on-investment, executive perks, and their personal investment brackets.

Professional management began to emerge as a "science" after the turn of the century through the writing of Frederick W. Taylor and his disciples who envisioned the firm as a smooth-running machine. Standardization of roles, precise rules, expanding and extending the hierarchy, time and motion studies—all these fused together in the increasingly accepted notion that management should actually be considered a scientific process.

Gradually the professionalization of management caught on, both as ideology and practical methodology. To create professionals, it was reasoned, training was needed. Through education, one could learn the "universal skills" for managing any business and jump from company to company in pursuit of "career success"—higher earnings and status. Self-defined expertise, mobility between companies, and the idea of a career ladder—all these fostered and sustained the illusion that a professional manager could run any and all businesses.

Furthermore, as entrepreneurial and family-owned enterprises were dismantled and their equity diluted, managers became, not really servants of the shareholders, but elites accountable only to themselves. Federal legislation in 1933–

1934 mandated that executives should increase the number of public investors instead of maintaining their allegiance to the original entrepreneur. Such actions legitimized the bifurcation of ownership and control. By the early 1960s, as one study confirms, individuals or families held the majority of stock in only five of the two hundred largest nonfinancial corporations in the nation, and a full 169 of these 200 companies were controlled by professional managers.[15]

In another study, Edward C. Herman traced the extent of slippage in control away from major stockholders to professional managers.[16] Direct owner control of the largest two hundred nonfinancial corporations declined from 45 percent in 1900 to 42 percent by 1929. Between 1929 and 1975 it fell to only 16 percent. Where managers accounted for control in 23.8 percent of the top two hundred in 1900, the figure rose to 40.5 percent by 1929, and has doubled since then.

For decades, this slow shift in the control of industry appeared to be a positive development. Clear definitions of tasks, predictable routines, and high-volume standardized production led to satisfactory business results. Profits increased, fueled by an ever-growing economy.

Now this professionalization of management is accelerating through MBA programs across the nation, but so are the problems of American business. The failure of American industry in the international economy seems to confirm the disappearance of managerial values and skill. The race to enhance "productivity" with new "labor-saving" devices has resulted in a labor-destroying domestic economy and a growing, soon-to-be-permanent underclass of dislocated, under- or unemployed workers.

Today, the managerial specialist can take over a thriving family-owned business and rapidly obliterate three generations of pride and employee loyalty. Traditional business values that have lasted a century are quickly judged to be hopelessly out of date and economically unsound. Professional managers often see workers as abstractions, mere factors in a financial equation. And as professionalization increases, personal accountability decreases. Today's managers retreat from conscience and human interaction to the supposed precision of modern management science and a hard-nosed concentration on the bottom line.

The Role of Business Schools

In academic circles, the professionalization of management started back in 1891 when Joseph Wharton, himself a wealthy businessman, donated $100,000 for the creation of a new school of commerce at the University of Pennsylvania. By 1899, the University of California and the University of Chicago created business programs. NYU and Dartmouth followed the next year, while Harvard lagged behind until 1908. Accounting and commerce law were the educational foundations at first, while finance, marketing, and human relations were added later. By the 1920s, there were management associations, business groups, and consulting firms.

The growth of business schools continued steadily with a sharp increase after World War II. By the mid-1950s an undergraduate degree in business had become the most sought-after major in America. By that time critics of business schools who claimed business education to be nothing more than vocational training had been silenced, and today there are some 650 business schools scattered across the landscape of U.S. higher education.

Graduate studies in business began to expand in the 1970s. In 1977 MBA degrees were awarded to 46,650 students, a six-fold increase from the class of 1965 which consisted of 7,585 MBAs. Presently, there are some 600 MBA programs, although only 204 have been formally accredited. This year's graduation should yield in excess of 70,000 new MBAs, more than a fifth of all master's degrees conferred in the United States.

Questions regarding these young, well-educated, professional managers began to heighten in 1980 with the publication of a celebrated *Harvard Business Review* article by Robert Hayes and William Abernathy.[17] This stinging criticism of business education's new professionals now being churned out caught the nation's MBA programs by surprise and led to a record number of requests for *HBR* reprints. The journal's associate director soon pointed out that the "article received more attention than anything else published in the *Review* (because) the authors were willing to stand up and say the "emperor has no clothes."[18]

Essentially Hayes and Abernathy voiced a rising concern that business schools were employing specialists rather than generalists, individually trained in esoteric academic formulas but not in practical skills and insight. They observed that return on investment in U.S. corporations had been stopped on a plateau since the 1960s, that R&D was declining, and that American managers were preoccupied with servicing existing markets rather than developing new arenas. Today's professional managers, they said, suffered from a short-term perspective, tied only to quarterly financial statements. In managing by the numbers they had "abdicated their strategic responsibilities."

The indictment of new business school graduates became tied to the growing crisis in industry, the recession of the early 1980s which led the media and popular press to sharply criticize managerial training as well. *Forbes, Fortune, Time,* and *Business Week* joined in the growing chorus. A writer for *Esquire* declared, "The disastrous American emphasis on short-term, bottom line management owes less to science classes at Central High than to MBA classes at Harvard."[19] A professor at Chicago's School of Business stated, "We have created a monster . . . the business schools have done more to insure the success of the Japanese and West German invasion of America than any one thing I can think of."[20] Robert Reich condemns today's corporate managers as "paper entrepreneurs"[21] who simply rearrange assets but generate no new wealth.

As Reich also observes, the tens of thousands of U.S. graduates coming out of American business schools stand in sharp contrast to the 3 percent of college graduates in West Germany who have degrees in business administration. The U.S. contrasts similarly with Sweden and Japan. Other countries, currently out-competing us, heavily stress engineering education and knowledge of the manufacturing process. The training of young lawyers, many of whom today join investment banking firms to become the deal makers for today's mega-mergers and takeover battles, accentuates the problem of professionalization. In Japan for instance, only 100 attorneys are trained for every 1,000 engineers. The American case is just the opposite: We educate 1,000 attorneys for every 100 engineers. A large number of European executives learn administration from civil service experience. They exhibit a stronger public concern and orientation and enjoy lower rates of labor relations conflict than do their American counterparts. In many instances their companies also exhibit higher levels of productivity and provide workers with a higher standard of living as well.

Generic Executives

The contemporary professional manager is often a transient who assumes that he or she can walk into any company, in any industry, and manage it well—even turn it around. With a generic logic, professionals attempt to direct departments of engineering, quality control, production, accounting, and legal counsel. Other professionals are brought in as market analysts, investment counselors, and culture consultants.

Today's new breed have seized control of the whole organizational apparatus. Everything needed for bottom line success can be achieved by creating a program, having a committee, conducting a training seminar, or issuing an edict. Financial management is becoming more like financial hocus-pocus—"now you see it, now you don't." The new managers revel in the manipulation of interest expenses, depreciation, tax credits, and junk bonds. They learn ways to massage accounting numbers to show a better profit than is really warranted. Expensive corporate advertising campaigns are designed to raise stock prices instead of market share, while high-priced experts produce glossy and expensive annual reports to impress potential stockholders and create an aura of prestige. Now, not just individual executives but also the whole corporation must dress for success. Image is everything.

The cost of creating and perpetrating this new managerial class is enormous. As professionalism has risen, so has corporate waste. The ratio of supervisors to production workers has increased steadily with the flow of business school graduates as 50,000–70,000 new MBAs enter the workplace each year. In America, there is often one manager for every ten workers, versus one to two hundred in Japan.[22]

Recruiting, hiring, relocating, and initial training on the job for today's new manager costs well over $100,000 per person. Yet once employed, there is no assurance of long-term service. There is little loyalty and little interest in staying in one organization for a career. So the investment is primarily one way. Today's nomad executives are here today and gone tomorrow. As many as one third of today's professionals turn over their jobs annually, requiring a repeat of the massive training costs.[23] The corporate and societal costs of such a system differ considerably from the 12 percent management and office turnover in Europe and 6 percent in Japan.

The separation between ownership and management has fostered an executive elite atop many companies today—individuals obsessed primarily with their own self-preservation. They enjoy discretionary authority to pursue personal interests instead of what might be in the best interest of the company. Adam Smith's early emphasis on managerial virtues of sympathy and prudence has been displaced by the modern manager's own ambition. Current objectives center on escalating salaries, huge bonuses, stock options, and golden parachutes.

Between 1971 and 1981 the compensation of top U.S. executives listed in Standard & Poor's four hundred largest firms grew by 10 percent in real dollars while shareholder value dropped by 2 percent. Perhaps Tom Wolfe had professional managers in mind when he reflected back on the 1970s as the "Me Decade."

The contradiction between what is good for the company

and one's own self-interest is more manifest in times of economic distress. Thus, in the early 1980s, while unemployment in some areas of the country had reached levels as high as 23 percent, companies were hiring over a hundred thousand new MBAs. While workers were taking wage cuts and unions faced concession bargaining, executives were bestowing upon themselves an average 16 percent salary increase, the largest jump in nearly two decades.[24] Such actions raise questions not only of ethics, but of financial judgment as well.

According to the consulting firm of Booz, Allen and Hamilton, Inc., today's chief executives average approximately $750,000 in annual income, including bonuses, triple that of fifteen years ago.[25] This is roughly fifty times the wages of an average factory worker. Self-administered bonuses now account for over half of top management compensation versus a third a decade ago.

Golden parachutes have become another important factor in the picture. For instance, in 1985 Michael Bergerac, chairman of Revlon, found his company taken over by Pantry Pride. He activated a packaged deal of long-term compensation worth $35 million. Other CEOs, VPs, and CFOs from Beatrice, ABC, and Peabody International took their companies to the cleaners with lesser but substantive deals. The top ten parachutists that year won a tidy $60 million.

Of *Business Week*'s 258 corporations listed in the Executive Compensation Scoreboard,[26] last year's average 9 percent increase clearly helped managers cope with inflation of 3.8 percent. While white collar workers got by with 1985 increases of 5.1 percent, 146 executives in America received over a million dollars each. Back in 1980 only four top managers enjoyed seven-digit compensation packages. Last year one had to make over $2.5 million to even qualify among the top twenty-five paid professionals.

Victor Posner, chairman of DWG, headed the list with $12.7 million in 1985. The flamboyant "greenmailer" Pickens paid himself double that amount in 1984. Chrysler's Iacocca claimed in 1985 to be playing catch-up after years of personal sacrifice as he pulled down a hefty $11.4 million, and in 1986 he topped this figure with $20.5 million. The heads of Firestone, DWG, NCR, and MCA each won over $6 million in 1986.

The theory that good professional management deserves to be amply rewarded is suspect when one compares case by case an executive's performance with his or her company's results. In 1984, for instance, Inland Steel suffered a net loss of over $41 million, yet Frank Luerssen, chairman and CEO, enjoyed a 24 percent salary and bonus boost to $423,336. United Airlines was hit with a $48.7 million loss by the end of the year, while its chairman's pay was doubled to $883,000. AMP, Inc.'s net income dropped 40 percent, yet its top executive enjoyed more than a doubling of his income to just under $1 million. And in a classic case of strategic error, Coca-Cola's new "taste" flopped while chairman Robert Goizveta was "rewarded" a hefty $6.4 million in long-term compensation because of his "courage" in trying a new product.[27]

CONSEQUENCES AND IMPLICATIONS

We contend that the growth of large absentee-owned corporations managed by aloof professional managers has exacerbated, if not created, America's massive economic and industrial problems.

As absentee-managed institutions become surrogates for individual stockholders, the nation's ability to generate new wealth drops precipitously. Real median family income grew 37.6 percent in the period 1950–60; 33.9 percent in 1960–70; and only 6.7 percent in 1970–80. The rise of national income per employee has been considerably under that of most other industrialized nations for twenty years. During the 1970s, Japanese workers experienced overall growth of 3.2 percent, France, 3.0 percent, West Germany, 3.0 percent, the United Kingdom 0.8 percent, while the United States slipped to 0.1 percent.[28]

Today's large, bloated corporations have grown, according to the late U.S. Commerce Secretary Malcolm Baldridge, just "too fat, dumb, and happy." Contemporary professionals' large staffs of assistants have created immense burdens on the lower strata of organization. The bigger the company, the fatter the staff. At AT&T, the ratio of staff to production workers in 1958 was seventy-two to one hundred workers. By the mid-1970s it was ninety-nine to one hundred. The recent breakup of AT&T has reduced the ratio somewhat, but the trend toward an increasing managerial proportion has been quite consistent across most industries for decades. High-tech firms are no different. As one writer observed, fully half of the employees at Intel have become managers of some sort or another.[29] In many companies such single acts as hiring a person or purchasing a box of copy paper require hundreds of steps, dozens of forms, and often a committee to complete the task.

Profits in U.S. firms averaged 12.7 percent yearly in the 1960s. By mid-1975 they had dropped to 10 percent, and they have been under that ever since. Productivity has also been declining. American businesses averaged a robust 3 percent in annual productivity increases for a century between 1865 and 1965. Industrial growth then dropped to 2 percent between 1965 and 1973. Later, in the 1970s, the economy experienced less than a 1 percent increase in productivity, and more recently productivity actually slid over into the debit column. Meanwhile, other nations such as Japan continue to grow, in Japan's case at 7.9 percent annually.

The proportion of manufacturing capacity utilized is also declining—from 86 percent in the 1960s to 80 percent in the 1970s, and under 70 percent by the early 1980s. Many firms still suffer from underutilized capacity. Oil and gas companies are now operating at 72.8 percent capacity and utilities at 75 percent. Empty plant space and idle equipment are just a few symptoms of malaise. The steel industry, for example, in spite of closing 140 plants since the 1950s, is still hurting from excess capacity which will eventually be cut out.

Other trends flow in the opposite direction. Unemployment, for example, has grown off and on as larger absentee-owned conglomerates run by new-breed managers have increased. Back in the 1960s, unemployment averaged 4.8 percent, and through the 1970s it was about 6.2 percent. So far in the 1980s it is averaging approximately 7 percent, and it appears that in the future unemployment will be about the same or greater. Rather than figure out how to tap the resources of people and equipment, many professional managers take a meat axe approach to their firms.

While entrepreneurship and innovation are widely touted terms in many circles today, the reality is that big business has become lethargic. The U.S. Patent Office reports that approximately one-third of all patents are issued to individuals and another one-fourth to small companies with less than a hundred employees. While the "little guy" now creates over half of all patents, the giants are generating fewer and fewer innovations and requiring ever longer time frames to produce new ideas and products.

Today's professional managers are often interested only in "quick fixes" so they can then move on to a new deal or a new job. Hence corporate investments in productive assets have diminished in recent decades. A report in *World Business Weekly* (September 15, 1980) shows that U.S. investment as a proportion of GNP lags below other industrialized nations (17.8 percent). Italy invests 21 percent of its GNP, Canada 22.2 percent, France 23.2 percent, West Germany 24.3 percent, and Japan 33 percent.

The National Science Foundation reports that American R&D expenditures have been declining steadily for twenty-five years. In short, our industrial infrastructure of plants and equipment is growing older and more obsolete.

An inability to compete with foreign companies, lack of investment, huge drains on the supply of capital created by mergers and takeover fights, and poor productivity have combined to seriously threaten our economic future. Thus, America's record-shattering trade deficit on current accounts for 1985 was $117 billion, a figure overshadowed by the 1986 deficit which exceeded $141 billion. Now, for the first time since 1914, the United States has become a debtor nation to the tune of some $160 billion dollars, far surpassing the $103 billion owed by Mexico. Real GNP grew a weaker-than-expected

2.2 percent in 1986. American industry is not digging itself out of the hole. The price to be paid for large, debt-laden, absentee-owned firms led by distant professional managers continues to rise.

THIS BOOK

Our own observations and those of other writers have made us deeply concerned about this shift to a new economic and corporate landscape, owned by faceless shareholders and controlled by today's professional managers. We intend in this book to explore the shift to absentee ownership and professional management by examining the dynamics of the process by which that shift has occurred. Using our own historical research, we will analyze the social and economic consequences of these changes for individual companies, for the communities which depend upon those companies, and for entire industries.

We intend to describe three specific cases in detail as a way of clarifying the variety of issues and problems that emerge at each of these levels. Chapter 2 explores the effect of a change in ownership on a large, family-owned manufacturer of materials handling equipment, looking at how a new professional management affected both corporate performance and labor-management relations. Chapter 3 analyzes similar changes at the broader, community level, looking at a gradual shift to absentee ownership and professional management in the small manufacturing town of Jamestown, New York. Here, our research provides compelling evidence that the shift from a locally owned industrial economy, managed by local entrepreneurs and industrialists, to absentee-owned companies run by professionally trained general managers played a critical role in the decline of the region's economy.

At an even higher level, that of an entire industrial sector, Chapter 4 looks at the impact of changes in ownership structures and the new management upon the steel industry. This chapter focuses on the whole industry in the global economic context, but we also give special attention to the U.S. Steel

Company, now a part of USX, as a prototypical case. In all three chapters, the data point to a number of parallel issues and dilemmas which reverberate from the single firm to the level of a national industry.

In Chapter 5, the problems and contradictions illustrated in Chapters 2, 3, and 4 are synthesized into a theoretical framework for visualizing the chain of related changes in companies, communities, and whole industries. Understanding the links between these different levels is critical to appreciating the significance of the overall problem and the appropriateness of potential solutions.

We then proceed to consider some alternative forms of business structure that have emerged in recent years, asking, "What can be done about the deleterious effects of the shifting pattern of ownership and control?" At the level of the individual company, Chapters 6, 7, 8, and 9 spell out specific potential solutions which should be of interest to managers and shareholders alike. These chapters suggest that we must consider changes in both ownership structure and corporate culture, for tinkering with just one side of the organizational equation will result in, at best, an incomplete solution.

At the macroeconomic level, finally, Chapter 10 addresses public policy issues and articulates specific ways in which the state and federal government, labor leaders, and industry executives can engage in joint action to reverse economic decline and move toward a more productive industrial society. This bold agenda for the future, we believe, is the most promising path toward the transformation and revitalization of American industry.

CHAPTER 1 ENDNOTES

1. See Gar Alperovitz and Jeff Faux. *Rebuilding America* (New York: Pantheon, 1984); Ira C. Magaziner and Robert B. Reich. *Minding America's Business* (New York: Vintage, 1983).

2. The standard works referred to here include William G. Ouchi. *Theory Z* (Reading, MA: Addison-Wesley, 1981); Thomas J. Peters and Robert H. Waterman, Jr. *In Search of Excellence: Lessons from America's Best-Run Companies* (New York: Harper & Row, 1982); J. Richard Hackman and

Greg R. Oldham. *Work Redesign* (Reading, Mass.: Addison-Wesley, 1980); Richard E. Walton. "Establishing and Maintaining High Commitment Work Systems." In John R. Kimberly *et al.* (eds.), *Organization Life Cycles* (San Francisco: Jossey-Bass, 1980).

3. Paul R. Lawrence and Davis Dyer. *Renewing American Industry: Organizing for Efficiency and Innovation* (New York: The Free Press, 1983).

4. Thorstein Veblen. *Absentee Ownership and Business Enterprise in Recent Times—The Case of America* (New York: Sentry Press reprint, 1964). Originally published in 1923.

5. See, for example, Ronald J. Pellegrin and Charles H. Coates. "Absentee-owned Corporations and Community Power Structure." *American Journal of Sociology*, vol. 61, 1956, pp. 413–419; R.O. Schulze. "The Role of Economic Dominants in Community Power Structure." *American Sociological Review*, vol. 23, 1958, pp. 3–9; W. Lloyd Warner and J. O. Low. *The Social System of the Modern Factory* (New Haven, Conn.: Yale University Press, 1947).

6. A.A. Berle, Jr., and Gardiner C. Means. *The Modern Corporation and Private Property* (New York: Macmillan, 1932).

7. Alfred D. Chandler, Jr. *The Visible Hand: The Managerial Revolution in American Business* (Cambridge, Mass.: Harvard University Press, 1977).

8. Mike McNamee. "Mergers Chew Up Loans." *U.S.A. Today*, July 11, 1984, p. 1-B.

9. Donald Bradstreet. "Business Failures." *The Wall Street Journal*, March 25, 1986, p. 33.

10. John Greenwald. "Bigger Yes, But Better?" *Time*, August 12, 1985, pp. 34–35.

11. Lee Berton. "Away from Takeovers, to 'Value Accounting.'" *The Wall Street Journal*, April 2, 1986, p. 20.

12. U.S. Department of Commerce. *1977 Census of Manufacturers: Concentration Ratios in Manufacturing* (Washington, D.C.: U.S. Government Printing Office, 1981).

13. Subcommittee on Antitrust and Monopoly. *Mergers and Industrial Concentration*, 95th Congress (Washington, D.C.: U.S. Government Printing Office, 1978).

14. Hay Associates, The Strategic Planning Institute, and the University of Michigan. *Organization and Strategy Information Service: Pilot Program Results*, 1984.

15. Robert J. Larner. "Ownership and Control in the 200 Largest Nonfinancial Corporations, 1929 and 1963." *American Economic Review*, vol. 56, 1966, pp. 777–787.

16. Edward C. Herman. *Corporate Control, Corporate Power* (Cambridge, England: Cambridge University Press, 1981).

17. Robert H. Hayes and William J. Abernathy. "Managing Our Way to Economic Decline." *Harvard Business Review*, July-August 1980, pp. 66–67.

18. Leslie Wayne. "Management Gospel Gone Wrong." *The New York Times,* May 30, 1982.

19. George Leonard. "The Great School Reform Hoax." *Esquire,* April 1984, pp. 47–56.

20. Cited in Peters and Waterman, 1982, p. 35.

21. Robert Reich. *The Next American Frontier* (New York: Penguin, 1983).

22. Estimate in James O'Toole. *Making America Work* (New York: Continuum, 1981).

23. Robert E. Hall. *The Importance of Lifetime Jobs in the U.S. Economy* (Washington, D.C.: National Bureau of Economic Research, 1980).

24. *The New York Times,* December 16, 1981.

25. Robert Johnson. "Big Executive Bonuses Now Come with a Catch: Lots of Criticism." *The Wall Street Journal,* May 15, 1985, Section 2, p. 37.

26. John Byrne. "Executive Pay: How the Boss Did in '85." *Business Week,* May 5, 1986, pp. 48–54.

27. Ibid., p. 51.

28. Lawrence Franko. *European Industrial Policy: Past, Present, and Future* (Brussels: The Conference Board in Europe, 1980).

29. Jeremy Main. "How to Battle Your Own Bureaucracy." *Fortune,* June 29, 1981, pp. 54–58.

The Transformation of the Brown Corporation

I n Chapter 1, we suggested that the movement toward absentee ownership and professional management has significant ramifications for American industry. In this chapter we will begin to examine the effects of this transformation on individual firms by describing how the transition to absentee ownership and professional management affected the Brown Corporation, a medium-sized ($100 million sales) materials handling firm (all names are fictional). The case of the Brown Corporation illustrates how a company's basic values can shift dramatically as local control of ownership and management is lost. But in order to fully understand the impact of absentee ownership and professional management on the Brown Corporation, we must first present the historical context surrounding its founding and development.

HISTORICAL BACKGROUND

The Brown Corporation is located a few blocks south of Main Street in the small town of "Orangeville," in the northeastern United States. The company's green and white buildings are the center of much of the activity in the community. The Brown Corporation employs over five hundred people and brings 14 million payroll dollars into the valley each year. Because of the company's pervasive influence, Orangeville residents see themselves as living in a "company town," with its livelihood and that of the surrounding communities depending on the fortunes of the Brown Corporation.

Orangeville was founded in 1792. Although the first settlers in the valley were primarily farmers, as the village grew craftsmen and artisans began to establish small businesses. One of the most prominent of these new businesses was the English Iron Works, founded by Wilbur English and his family in 1940. The forerunner to the Brown Corporation, the English Iron Works was a gray iron foundry that included a machine shop and planing mill. Iron ore and coal were shipped to Orangeville from Pennsylvania; the finished products were delivered to customers via barge or horse-drawn carriage. The company manufactured a variety of agricultural equipment to be used by farmers in the valley. The iron works prospered for more than eighty years but ran into increasing financial difficulties in the early 1920s. Sales and profits dropped precipitously, and the English family, who had kept the business in the family for three generations, began looking for a potential buyer. They happened to find just the right person in John Brown, Sr., a salesman with whom they had done business for some time.

The Creation of a Family Firm

John Brown, Sr. was born in 1889 in a small town a few miles from Orangeville. Trained as an industrial engineer at a local college, he had worked for a number of firms as a sales engineer. Although he began his career working for others, John had but one goal in mind: He wanted to own and manage his own business. When he heard that the English family was trying to sell their business, he borrowed money from his brother-in-law, found some additional financing from a partner, and bought the faltering iron works for $6,000 in 1922.

Like many entrepreneurs, John, Sr. had a particular philosophy or creed that he espoused in operating the business. While over twenty rules were acknowledged as the core of his philosophy, the essence of these rules concerned hard work, a zest for innovation, and fair play in one's business dealings. John, Sr. carried out his vision with great zeal and his co-workers characterized him as a workaholic. He generally worked seven days a week and would often call his subordinates on Sunday to prepare them for the upcoming week's activities. Following this philosophy during the roaring twenties, the company's sales boomed, reaching over $100,000 by 1929. The number of employees had grown from a handful in 1922 to 100 by 1929.

However, the stock market crash in the fall of that year was to push John, Sr.'s company to the brink of disaster. One by one employees had to be let go until only John, Sr., his trusted assistant, Tim Henson, and a part-time secretary remained. For eight months during 1932 they were the entire work force. During this period many afternoons were spent by John, Sr. and his family driving their Model-T Ford around the valley drumming up business and settling old accounts.

Growth and Expansion

In the 1930s, under the direction of Tim Henson, the company expanded its product line. Hydraulic pumps and lifting equipment could be made at the foundry, and John, Sr. began to see a growing market in this area. World War II brought an increasing demand for lifting and materials handling equipment, and the company prospered during the war years. By 1945 sales had reached $425,000. The work force had increased to sixty.

The early 1940s, however, were not easy for John, Sr. When his absentee partner died, the man's wife, who had inherited his stock, demanded to be seated on the board of directors. Up until this time John, Sr. and his wife had dominated the board. Outsiders were not welcome. A bitter fight developed over who should control the company, and a number of lawsuits followed. Finally, the case was settled out of court in 1945. John, Sr. paid his partner's widow $35,000 for her stock, vowing to never let outsiders gain control of his company.

John, Sr. had two children, John, Jr. and Elaine. Both of them spent many hours at the company—often working weekends and summers doing odd jobs and bookkeeping.

John, Sr. wanted John, Jr. to succeed him as president of the company, and so began grooming him for that position after he returned from military service in 1946. John, Jr. was promoted to sales manager in 1947, which was viewed as a rather quick advancement by company employees. But they never questioned John, Sr.'s prerogative to promote his son. Elaine's husband, Ralph, also worked in the business as John, Sr.'s assistant. There was no rivalry between John, Jr. and Ralph, however, since Ralph was generally seen as lacking leadership abilities and often had to be "taken care of" by the family due to a history of mental illness.

In the late 1940s sales grew rapidly. A new materials handling truck developed by the company's chief engineer increased sales almost twofold. All seemed to be going well, but in November 1948 John, Sr. underwent emergency surgery to remove his appendix. While recovering from this operation he had an attack of pancreatitis. He was given little chance to live. The family was panic stricken, since John, Sr. had not prepared for such an event—he had neglected to do any estate planning and no one was yet prepared to take over the business. Amid these uncertainties the Brown family was prepared to sell the business should John, Sr. die. Miraculously, John, Sr. began to slowly recover, and although he was incapacitated for almost one year he began to once again be involved in the firm's affairs. But his involvement would never be the same. On the advice of his doctor he began to spend the winters in Florida. As John, Sr. began spending more and more time away from the business, the firm entered a transition period that was to last ten years.

Employees who worked for John, Sr. during his tenure as company president viewed him as a "benevolent autocrat." He made all the major decisions. All capital expenditures over fifty dollars had to be approved by him. He and his wife, who kept the company books, kept all important information regarding the firm in the family. Despite this apparent distrust of outsiders, John, Sr. took care of his employees, creating a "family atmosphere" in the firm (albeit a paternalistic family). He took his key employees on fishing trips with him, he sponsored an annual field day and clambake for company employees and their families, and was noted for helping employees with various work and family problems they faced. He also allowed employees to use company equipment for personal use and to take time off from work to go deer hunting.

As he became less involved in the firm's activities, however, the nature of the company began to slowly change. In 1956, primarily for tax advantages and to raise capital, the company's stock was offered for sale to the public. Although the family retained well over 50 percent of the stock, an outsider, the family banker, was added to the board of directors. Moreover, his son, John, Jr., was now making the major decisions.

The Second Generation

In contrast to his father, John, Jr. believed that workers should participate in decision making. His wife had attended a "T" group (sensitivity training) sponsored by the Young Presidents Organization in 1960. She returned from this experience excited to tell her husband about the values learned in the group—trust, openness, and participation. John, Jr. decided to investigate and found himself attending a T-group. From this experience John, Jr. began to develop his own vision regarding the firm—that of creating a "participative culture" where all members of the firm, regardless of position, would be able to influence decisions. To accomplish this goal he began to enlist a number of behavioral science consultants to help him implement the new philosophy. Many company old-timers were bewildered by this dramatic change in leadership style. However, John Brown, Jr. also continued many of his father's traditions, such as the field day and the clambake, and this helped to ease some of the employees' fear of change. Sales climbed from $6 million in 1960 to over $40 million in the early 1970s. John, Sr. was able to witness much of this growth. He died in 1967, having seen his dream fulfilled. He had witnessed the transformation of his small iron works into a major corporation in the space of forty-five years.

THE RISE OF PROFESSIONAL MANAGEMENT

The Arab oil embargo and energy crisis in 1973 and 1974 provided the Brown Corporation with its first major crisis since the Great Depression. Sales slumped and inventories rose dramatically. To turn things around, John, Jr. was encouraged by the board of directors to bring in a manufacturing and inventory control specialist. In the past, they had primarily relied on the family or local talent to manage the firm's problems. They found just such a person in Reed Larson, an experienced manufacturing manager who worked at a large company a few miles from Orangeville.

Creating a "Professional Culture"

The hiring of Reed Larson as Manufacturing Vice-President was to unfold a new chapter in the company's history. Larson, at age 46, having worked in the manufacturing divisions of a number of large corporations, was known for his expertise in production planning and inventory control. Having previously worked at International Telephone and Telegraph (ITT), Larson praised and often seemed to emulate the management style of his former boss, Harold Geneen, who was known as a tough, uncompromising taskmaster. Moreover, while at ITT and in subsequent jobs, Larson had acquired the reputation as a "turn-around guy" who "could make things happen." As Brown's new manufacturing vice-president, Larson moved quickly to implement a more efficient, "professional" production planning and inventory control system. One senior manager recounted the impact of Larson's initial actions to improve manufacturing operations:

> I would think that from the company's standpoint the hiring of Reed Larson was one of the highlights. I think it changed the direction of the company considerably. It was a shake-up. We tended to be a lethargic type of management—business as usual, rather calm—John very much the leader. Reed is a take-over, turn-around kind of guy. He

shook everyone up; he reorganized everyone; he fired a bunch of people who probably should have been fired before, and did all kinds of things to get people really rattling around here. He did a lot of the right things. We had been struggling along. In fact, in 1974–75 we were in the doldrums here. We were in bad shape. We had a tremendous inventory, a very high backlog. One of Reed's first assignments to us was to get that inventory down. We did. We brought down inventory five or six million dollars in a year's time and increased shipments while we were doing it. I think he has brought a lot of new ideas and a lot of fire to the organization.

The effects of Larson's new program were dramatic. In 1975, output per man-hour increased 40 percent. Inventory was reduced by 26 percent, and the number of managerial positions in manufacturing was cut 50 percent, from 58 to 29 through firings, reassignments, and demotions. The total number of employees on the payroll also dropped by more than 25 percent. Consequently, while sales rose by $5 million in 1975 to $52 million, manufacturing costs actually dropped over $1 million from the previous year. Net income also doubled in 1975. In the rest of this chapter we will describe some of the specific changes that were brought about by Reed Larson and the professional managers that followed him.

Changes in Management Style

Not only did Larson's new methods improve the firm's financial situation, but his interpersonal and management style had a major impact as well, according to Brown employees:

Reed is a very "no nonsense" person; he says "Come in, give me the facts, give me the options, and I'll choose. Don't come in and give me a lot of 'I think' or 'I feel'—I don't give a damn what you think or feel—just give me the facts."

Because of Larson's dramatic impact on the firm's performance, his appointment as manufacturing vice-president is seen by managers, clerical workers, and factory workers as the most significant event in the firm in the 1970s:

> Brown employees say "You know, there's AC and BC—Before Christ and After Christ; and here at Brown there's BL and AL—before Larson and everything after Larson. He had 'bloody Fridays' and 'bloody Tuesdays' when he just went out and wiped out half the management and half the people. He just decided he was going to clean house and he did. Boom! It was like the San Andreas fault—one day it's a family-held firm, and the next there's professional management, with emphasis adjusted accordingly. And no one knows for sure if the landscape will be improved or ruined by the earthquakes in their future."

Despite the fact that some Brown employees considered Larson abrasive and authoritarian in stark contrast to John, Jr., there was a "fearful respect" of Larson and his management expertise (to emphasize his "toughness," Larson was nicknamed "Jaws" by lower level employees). The significant growth in profits, which was attributed to Larson's management expertise, increased the amount of money available for profit sharing, and eventually opened up opportunities for advancement and higher salaries.

The Changing Role of the Brown Family

The year 1975 was significant for the Brown family as well. Eleanor Brown, John, Sr.'s wife, died. Soon afterward, Tim Brown, John, Jr.'s second son, joined the business. Tim had spent some time in the armed forces and had obtained an MBA degree. In contrast to the oldest son Mike, Tim was interested in pursuing a managerial career, and so he began to work at Brown as a systems analyst. In 1975 the family only controlled over 30 percent of the shares outstanding, and with the third generation now entering the firm, John, Jr. began to groom his sons as potential leaders for the future.

However, in 1977, John, Jr.'s wife Helen was kidnapped and murdered during a robbery at their home. This sent shock waves through the company and the community, deeply affecting John, Jr. and his children. During the period of time after Helen's death, John turned over much of the responsibility for operating the business to Reed Larson. With Larson in command, the firm continued to grow, with sales reaching an unprecedented $76 million in 1978. As a result of this success, Larson was named president and chief operating officer in 1978. John, Jr. retained the CEO position and board chairmanship. The company had become "Reed Larson's organization." With family influence eroding, one manager said:

> Well, John, Sr. used to be out in the plant. John, Jr. did less of it. Now a whole new set of players are running it—what does that mean? Well, they are just transients, they aren't the Browns!

Sacred Cows Versus the Bottom Line

With Reed Larson firmly established as president, more professional managers began to enter the business until they controlled almost half (43 percent) of the top management positions in the company in 1979. A new addition to the plant increased office space for top management; the work force grew to 1,700 employees; and, because of the firm's rapid growth, one-third of all employees were promoted in 1979.

Reed Larson and the other professional managers stressed competence and efficiency as the guiding criteria in making decisions. Absence for deer hunting was no longer tolerated; company tools could only be used after going through proper channels, job descriptions became more specific, and employees were reprimanded for not operating within their prescribed roles; company objectives became formalized and operationalized so that accountability could be determined. In 1979, for example, twenty corporate objectives and 169 departmental goals were identified and accountability assigned. Three typical examples were:

Reduce service parts back order by $500,000 (Jim Gould).
Add twenty new salespersons to dealer network (Tim Frantz).
Receive orders for (50) Model A products (Bill Spence).

This set of goals and objectives was to help accomplish Reed Larson's primary goal of tripling sales every five years.

In the process of bringing in a set of formal rules, some professionals saw the need to eliminate some of the seemingly inefficient work norms—the Brown Corporation's "sacred cows." As one professional stated:

> There were a lot of perceived sacred cows. I can remember people frequently saying "John Brown would never tolerate that" or "You can't do that because . . ." Well, bullshit.

Another professional described his experience in coming to the Brown Corporation:

> Many people really took it very hard when I came in as a marketing manager. Within about a year or so, I had to transfer or let go most of the employees, and they took this extremely hard because all these people were in their jobs for fifteen or twenty years and the new path was completely different. . . . So that was a shock to a close family. I say "close family" because the problems are closely held: Everybody went out and got drunk together, and everybody closed the place down at the opening of deer season. Of course, when you come in as an outsider you tend to see that as being inefficient. You can't close business, so you say, "No, you can't do it." You have to come in and kill some of these old sacred cows. Like I said, taking the first day of deer season—*that* was a sacred cow. I mean, they shut the place down, just about. That stopped. Also, people would come in at 7 a.m. and leave at 3:30. Well, if you're in marketing you can't do that. You can't tell customers, "I'm sorry, I'm going. I've already put in my eight hours." You start at 8 and work until 5. There was a time I really went through some hard times here trying to change some of the sacred cows.[1]

In the past, another "sacred cow" was the preferential treatment of members of the Brown family. While the professional managers believed that "objective, professional criteria" should be used in making all promotions, they accepted the fact that John Brown, Jr.'s sons, if proven to be competent, should be given some considerations not afforded other managers (given that their father was still the Board Chairman and controlled the largest block of company stock). But as one professional manager put it: "They may be born with silver spoons in their mouths, but we don't have to feed them."

Becoming More Impersonal

As the company continued to grow, and as professional managers began to have increasing influence on the work life of Brown employees, Brown workers felt that the nature of employee–management relationships began to change. During the 1960s and early '70s, meetings between Brown management were frequent, often lasting a half day or more. Moreover, workers were often included in decision making. Meetings now became less frequent, personal contacts much shorter, and often members of various management committees began missing meetings because of a problem that they perceived was more important. These changes were also related to the increase in the number of employees and the increasing complexity of managing the business.

As Brown employees began to see more and more of their co-workers as strangers, they began to characterize the Brown Corporation as an increasingly impersonal place to work. This perception that the company was becoming more impersonal began to be reflected in significant changes in some of the organization's time-worn traditions and rituals. The Brown Chorus, founded in the early '60s and a symbol of pride for both the corporation and the community, was disbanded in 1978. Enrollment continually dropped in the mid-1970s until there were simply not enough interested employees to continue the chorus. Figure 1 illustrates the declining enrollment in the Brown Chorus from 1963 to 1978.

Figure 1. Brown Chorus Membership, 1963–1978

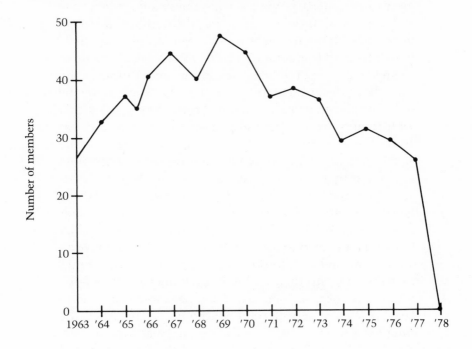

Another major change has been in worker attitudes about length of service pins and the traditional pictures taken with a member of the Brown family when they receive these awards. Workers seem to no longer treasure these rewards as they did in the past. One old-timer, reflecting on these changes in the Brown Corporation, commented:

> John, Sr. used to be out in the plant. He used to know everyone by name. There was a great sense of camaraderie that was possible with a small organization. John, Jr., when I first came here, made a very honest attempt to do that. We had 350 employees when I came here. John was out in the shop a lot more than certainly he is now. He did know most of the people. This gets to the service awards.

In our organization the president or chairman of the board used to present guys with a five-year award—a pin—and after ten years all they do is change the number and so on. In my job I have to know most of the people out there. Now I have to lead John to a guy and say, "you remember so-and-so . . ." and tell John a few things about him so John can talk to the guy. I didn't have to do that back in the old days because that was a tradition started by his dad that John tried to foster. The sad part of it is that as John has gotten away from it we have changed the name of the game. It is no longer a Brown tradition in the sense of a Brown family member (presenting the pin). Now the division manager does it for the five-year award and for the ten-year it is the general manager. Reed gets involved at fifteen years. It takes away the personal thing and the older folks that are retiring now remember that. When I give an award now and talk to the people, one of the first things they do is go into their tool box and bring out the old pictures (with John, Sr.) and say, "I don't know if you remember . . ." We are getting more and more people when the time for a service award comes saying "just send me the pin. I don't want my picture taken." We hear more and more people saying "I don't want the picture taken." In the past they looked forward to it. They would keep it and that is the first thing that they would drag out (to show me).[2]

These two examples of the changing of traditional rituals—the disbanding of the Brown Chorus and the lack of interest in the service award picture—symbolized the inexorable movement away from the close ties that the employees had with the Brown family and the company in general. As Brown employees began to feel less involved and feel less satisfied with the kinds of relationships they had in the firm, they began to focus on other rewards for working. In particular, they became more concerned about higher salaries, bonuses, and benefits. In the past, work was not only a means of making money but a social event as well. With the advent of professional management, money became the driving force behind employee commitment to the firm.

Becoming an Absentee-Owned Firm

As mentioned earlier, the workers cited the company's growth as a major factor contributing to the depersonalization of the workplace. But another, more significant reason in the minds of many was John, Jr.'s move to "Bigtown." After the trauma of his wife's death and his subsequent remarriage a year and a half later in 1978, John, along with his new wife, who had lived most of her life in large cities, decided to build a new home in Bigtown to take advantage of the facilities located there. John's decision to leave Orangeville was treated with great surprise and apprehension by the workers. As one manager reported: "Here is a guy that has lived his entire life in Orangeville and now he is going to Bigtown. They don't understand it no matter what John would say." The old-timers suggest that John's move also signaled a change in the relationship between the family and the workers. Rumors of John "selling out" to outsiders became rampant, and morale suffered as employees feared that the company would become "one of those very formal companies" and "lose their link with the Brown family."

John, Jr.'s move to Bigtown represented a dramatic change in company and community norms established during John, Sr.'s tenure:

> We don't have near as many people that live here and expect their kids to go to school here. Upper level people that come in have not chosen to live in Orangeville. They go somewhere else. A certain few of them have gotten the sense that that is what they ought to do. There has been a kind of pattern set. The fact that Reed and then John moved to the city. And some of their desires are not available here—certain facilities of a city, a country club, the YMCA, churches. And the opposite used to be true. If a top engineer or manager came here and elected to live in Bigtown he would have been frowned on. Now it is the other way around.[3]

After John moved to Bigtown, only one of the eleven men on the board of directors, Bill Johnson, the former engineering

Figure 2. Orangeville Residents on the Board, 1922–1982

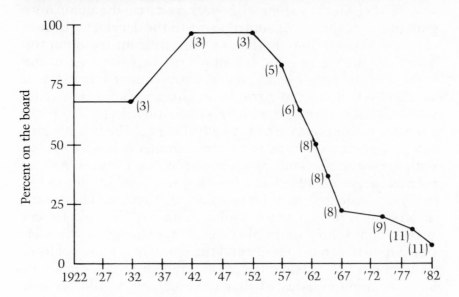

Figures in parentheses indicate total number of board members for that year.

vice-president, lived in Orangeville. Figure 2 illustrates the decline in the number of Orangeville residents on the board of directors. Thus, by 1980, the firm's future was largely in the hands of outside directors, ownership controlled by those removed from the community, and the Brown family's influence had substantially dwindled.

Changes in Career Orientations

The expanding control over the company by "outsiders" seemed to reinforce a prevalent belief among the Orangeville workers that they were slowly losing control of the business to people who were "ladder climbers with little feel for the product." The professional managers, who were generally younger than the local work force, were believed to be more concerned about their own careers than about the company and the community. The workers pointed to the increased turnover in the managerial ranks as evidence of this lack of commitment. The old-timers began to resent this lack of community support:

> In the old days we knew most everybody. I think most everybody lived in Orangeville. New people usually lived in Orangeville. They are getting away from that now as far as the officers are concerned. I understand that because I think it is probably easier to live where you are not part of the community in case you have to fire somebody or when bad things happen. When there are recessions it must be hard for the managers to live in the village. Then, too, they should be supporting the village with their taxes. They used to be very involved. John, Jr. was president of the school board for a long, long time. . . . I think that people who work here should be involved.[4]

But the professional managers were more oriented toward advancing their own careers. As one manager said:

> As long as I'm challenged, I'm here. But I think that somewhere along the line I'm going to come up to a block somewhere. . . . Once you get to a certain level, there's nothing more; *there's nothing more.* The question is, do I settle down and retire here, and say, "Well, I've got a pretty good job and a nice house"? Now I love it because I have my division and my responsibility and I get direction from Reed and he's enlightening to me and it's all mine. If I want to do something, I go and do it, within the budget. It's mine—I do whatever I want. But somewhere along the line, 2, 3, 4, 5 years from now, if I'm still doing that I know I'm going to be bored, then I'm gone. (This manager left the Brown Corporation in 1982, two years after making this statement.)[5]

Changing Emphasis on Technical Innovation

With the introduction of professional businessmen into the firm, Brown engineers became particularly concerned that the firm's reputation for innovation was not going to receive proper attention. As one engineer declared: "They may know business, but they don't have a feel for the product." Another high-ranking engineer reported that research funds were harder to acquire under professional management since the engineers were likely to be asked to justify each new project in terms of its contribution to the "bottom line."

Although assessing the impact of professional management on innovation is difficult, the company has not developed a product that has been well accepted in the marketplace since 1975. A major innovation was introduced in 1981, but sales have been slow. Major innovations have occurred in the 1930s (hydraulic trucks), the late 1940s and early '50s (product "X" trucks), the mid-1960s (the modified "X" truck), and the early 1970s (more flexible "X" trucks and computerized trucks). Although the link between the professionalization of management at the Brown Corporation and innovation is not completely clear, what is clear is that the engineers who have had budgetary controls imposed upon them feel that it is more difficult for them to be innovative in the 1980s.

Layoffs, Competition, and Distrust

In the wake of the company's unprecedented growth and favorable economic forecasts, Reed Larson felt that his goal of tripling sales every five years could only be reached by restructuring the organization. The functional structure was cumbersome, Larson argued, and a streamlined structure of semi-autonomous divisions would be more conducive to a growth strategy. Thus, six divisions, the Model A, Model B, Parts, Major Products, Leasing/Sales, and Corporate divisions, were established in 1979 and 1980. Professional managers often find that reorganization is a good way to eliminate inefficiencies, fire "deadwood," and consolidate their power.

The Model A and B divisions were primarily designed to

manufacture two of the company's major products. The Model A division was located 150 miles from Orangeville and was designed to manufacture the company's most popular truck. The Model B division, located in Canada, produced a less important product line. The Parts division's mandate was to provide all of the company's distributors and customers with parts and to service and maintain products previously sold. This division was established in a converted warehouse sixty miles from Orangeville. The Major Products and Leasing divisions were centered in Orangeville, as was corporate headquarters. The Major Products division manufactured other trucks besides the Model A and was the major supplier of parts to the Model A and Parts divisions. The Leasing division handled all truck leasing arrangements with dealers, while corporate headquarters, headed by John, Jr. and Reed Larson, was designed to coordinate the divisions, provide training, centralize accounting, and provide legal services. With each division specializing in its segment of the business, it was believed that the company would become more proficient in each of these areas, expanding both sales and market share. A secondary goal of this new structure, as stated by top management, was to reduce the dependence of Orangeville residents on the corporation for employment. By moving product lines outside of Orangeville, thereby reducing the number of jobs available for the local population, top management believed the town would not have to rely so heavily on the company to provide jobs during difficult economic times.

The favorable economic forecasts of the late seventies were quickly proven wrong. Orders began to decline in 1980 just as the new divisional structure was created. To cope with the slump in orders, top management decided to ask its 1,729 employees to take early vacations or time off without pay. Then, as orders continued to plummet, the company began experimenting with job sharing and a furlough system. While these actions did slow the decline in profitability, Reed Larson insisted that the divisions attempt to achieve their 1980 goals by working within their allotted budgets. To meet these goals, division managers concluded that the only logical course of action was to begin layoffs; so, in June, 1980, the first major layoff occurred. By October 1980, 237 employees had been laid off. In terms of sheer numbers (rather than in terms of percentages), most of the layoffs occurred in the Major Products division, thus affecting Orangeville employees more than workers in other divisions. In January 1981, 140 more workers were laid off, reducing the number of Brown employees in Orangeville to 860—a 34 percent reduction from the peak level of employment in 1979.

The layoffs fostered some resentment among the Orangeville employees who believed that jobs had been taken away from them by other divisions and that they were absorbing the brunt of the layoffs. The employees were particularly bitter about the Model A division, which they felt "took over 200 jobs with it." As one Orangeville employee stated:

> There is a lot of rivalry [between divisions]. In any manufacturing company you have got the night shift and the day shift. The night shift—it is the day shift's fault. The same thing I see happening between Orangeville and the Model A division. It is not a good feeling. I went up there and felt like [they were saying] "Well, look at us, you are down there and we are growing and we have got this beautiful facility and gorgeous offices." We were looked down on and felt like second-class citizens. Everything was so fantastic up there, everything was so marvelous—they were having so much fun. Five of us went up and we all felt like saying "stow it." They were painting a very beautiful picture for us.

This resentment, extended, although to a lesser degree, to the Parts division, which had not experienced the decline in demand occurring in other divisions. As a manager in the Parts division reported:

> For new orders received, we are booming right now. We are not bringing people back that we laid off in June at this point in time because we are able to handle it a little more efficiently than we were before. But it is different from what is going on in Orangeville. They have a hard time recognizing the fact that business can be booming in Parts

and it is the pits in Orangeville. They don't have anything to build except what they are building for us to ship. They have got that to deal with and they just don't understand why they have to lay off another fifty people and we are hiring or we are replacing somebody that just left. That bugs them and creates some animosity there.

Even the corporate headquarters, located in Orangeville, was not exempt from criticism by employees in the other divisions:

We wonder if they are sacrificing as much as we are. I think that everybody wonders that in the shop. I think they wonder if they are taking much time off without pay. But you wonder if they are making any sacrifices. I know people have said, instead of taking time off why doesn't everybody take a 10-percent cut in their pay, including John, Reed, etc. They would want to know that everybody was doing that.

These feelings of resentment for "corporate" and the other divisions were translated into a variety of behaviors. The Orangeville employees in the Major Products division were often slow to ship parts or equipment to the Parts and Model A divisions. This increased tensions, because these two divisions were unable to operate efficiently without adequate supplies. Eventually the Model A division, unable to secure the necessary parts from Orangeville, was no longer able to produce trucks. The situation became so desperate for the employees in the Model A division that, in the spring of 1981, a group of them drove a truck down to Orangeville on a Sunday afternoon, broke into the warehouse of the Major Products division, loaded the needed parts on their truck, and returned quickly to the Model A plant. Of this event, one top manager explained:

The Model A division was desperate for some parts which were supposed to come out of Orangeville. I don't know the reason why [they took the parts], but that doesn't build very good feelings.

While these actions served to strengthen the feelings of competition and distrust among divisions, there were also beginning to be the same kinds of feelings within divisions. Employees, fearful of being laid off, reported that they were unwilling to "pass up bad news" in fear of its potential impact on their jobs. They also questioned the layoff policies as applied within and between departments, believing that some individuals and departments were not "carrying their load."

In the early 1980s rumors of new layoffs abounded. But little information about them seemed to be conveyed to the workers. Even the Director of Human Resources at Brown revealed his lack of information on the subject when he was quoted in a newspaper report in 1982 as saying, "I can't really put faith in the rumor mill . . . but it is amazing how often the rumors come true . . . they have turned out to be true too often in the past." The rumors, reflecting worker anxiety and uncertainty about the future, became a permanent fixture in the community and organization. In contrast to the relative friendship and trust of earlier times, Brown employees were now seeing one another as adversaries and competitors.

Growth in Union Activity

Capitalizing on worker dissatisfaction, the International Association of Machinists began a drive in 1981 to organize Brown workers. However, one Brown employee spearheading the union drive reported that progress was slow:

> Unionizing workers at the Brown Corporation plant here could take a long time because workers fear losing their jobs. Fear is the company's greatest weapon.

He also noted some significant changes in the company:

> Management/worker relationships at the plant have changed 180 degrees since I began to work eighteen years ago. Workers used to be part of a family. Now you are treated as cogs in the corporate machine, which is reflected in the management philosophy that you have to get mean with these (production workers) and force them to work.

Although this is the view of a disenchanted union activist, all Brown employees, to varying degrees, felt that the company had indeed become more impersonal, less like a family in recent years. But Orangeville employees were suspicious of the union as well, wondering if jobs or certain benefits would be lost were they to be represented by the union. John, Jr. and Reed Larson, however, were worried that a union drive might succeed this time, and prepared a letter in February 1982 to be sent to all employees warning them about some of the potential repercussions if the union drive succeeded. Angered by the letter, union organizers charged the company with unfair labor practices. Despite the union's efforts, Brown employees, fearing for their jobs, only gave the union marginal support, and the union stopped actively organizing in the summer of 1982.

Cost Cutting by Professional Managers

As orders continued to fall, Reed Larson began to look for additional ways to save money without laying off workers. Twenty percent pay cuts and a four-day workweek were tried at the beginning of 1982. By the spring of 1983, however, Larson decided that these measures were not sufficient and developed a plan to close the plants at the Model A and Major Products divisions for a few weeks in the summer of 1982. Layoffs and demotions also continued (even Mike Brown's wife, a Brown employee, was laid off). During plant closing in the summer of 1982, unemployment in the county where Orangeville is located soared above 15 percent.

With layoffs occurring almost weekly, the management resorted to using the "hotline" to announce changes. The hotline is a large bulletin board located in a wing of the Major Products division. Layoffs are announced by putting up a new organization chart on the hotline. If one's name doesn't appear, that person is scheduled to be laid off or demoted. Of the "hotline system" one Orangeville employee remarked:

> They put a notice up on the hotline today which showed
> that a number of jobs had been changed. My boss's job was

changed and now I have a new manager. Everybody wonders what's going to happen to my previous manager. We really don't have a lot of communication about that, but we hope something will happen to let us know what is going on in the near future. The cuts may have been necessary, but this was not a good way to do it. People seem victims of what these higher level people are doing. And when the axe falls, people think of it as being impersonal, cold, and really a hard way of doing things. (They) ask: "What are we all about? Why are we doing this?"

Turnover in the professional managerial ranks also increased in the 1980s. In 1981 and 1982, two of the eleven top officers quit and one retired early. One of the managers who quit took a number of top engineers with him and started his own business to compete against the Brown Corporation. The following is one old-timer's analysis of the higher turnover rate:

> The lack of business and cutbacks [cause] a lot of unrest. Some of the people, fairly young manager types, are ladder climbers and they won't sit still for this kind of thing.

In general, Brown employees accepted the layoffs and plant closings with a rather fatalistic attitude. Two long-term employees seemed to summarize these feelings:

> Amazingly, to me, they are accepting [the layoffs] rather fatalistically. I guess they have decided that there is nothing they can do about it and so why cry over it.

> The older people feel less involved—particularly the hard working people. They don't feel that they can be involved and don't like some of the changes. They believe people are now seen as necessary casualties in management's pursuit of their objectives. They see themselves as innocent bystanders, incapable of controlling their actions and being dominated by a group of individuals whose motives they don't understand.

The tight controls and layoffs imposed by the professional managers created apathy and a feeling of powerlessness among the workers. Such feelings were exacerbated when top management, in an attempt to be participative, did a survey to ask employees whether they favored a four-day week in connection with a certain holiday. Although the employees overwhelmingly favored the four-day week, Reed Larson rejected their input and opted to continue with a five-day week, since it would be more cost effective.

THE BROWN CORPORATION IN THE MID-1980s

In the mid-1980s the company was still experiencing slow sales. Layoffs were still occurring and employees continued to be dissatisfied with many of the changes brought about by the lack of local control of ownership and by the increases in the number of professional managers. For example, one old-timer said that he continues to "keep a low profile" to avoid giving his superiors any reason to fire him or lay him off. Moreover, he stated that

> I don't get personally involved with the boss or other people I work with. The boss doesn't encourage group closeness like in the old days. There's little socializing—the bosses seem more aloof. But we're more independent now than in the past. We can make individual decisions and take responsibility. That can be satisfying.

Another old-timer expressed similar feelings this way:

> When I joined the company in 1962 we were a tight group of friends, very close knit, and we had a lot of fun. We'd often lock arms to solve problems. Lately we don't socialize, we don't know each other or each other's families. There's a lot of competition with each other so we won't catch hell from Reed Larson. We want to look good so we sometimes get into massive fights over $3,000 worth of computer paper. There is a lot of "go to hell, I won't do that for you."

Historically the turnover rate for the company had been quite low, rarely reaching over 2 percent. In 1980 turnover rate reached 3 percent for the first time and rose to over 6 percent for the first four months of 1983. Figure 3 summarizes the company's turnover rate from 1954 to 1983. Executive turnover has also increased.

Figure 3. Turnover of Orangeville Factory Workers and Executive and Office Workers, 1954 through April, 1983

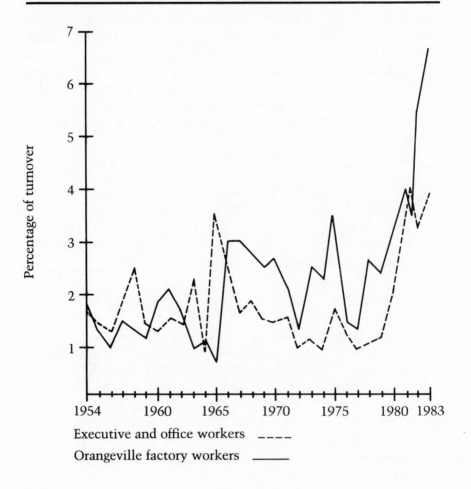

Executive and office workers ----

Orangeville factory workers _____

In commenting on the recent increases in turnover, one professional manager proffered the view:

> There are basically three reasons for the higher turnover. The first is "bad hires." We just hire some people who don't fit. Second, people find opportunities elsewhere so they move on. Third, I think it's becoming a norm. Leaving is a neat thing to do.

The following statement by an old-timer regarding the employees' willingness to leave the Brown Corporation seems to summarize the views of many old-timers:

> When I first joined Brown over fifteen years ago I was wedded to the company. But that's not true now. I'd move for the right job and the right responsibility. My wife's job and the kids are what's keeping me in this area.

Thus, the Brown Corporation had become a "stopping off" point for many employees. They no longer viewed the company as a place to start and end their careers. Despite these problems, there were some employees who had relatively favorable attitudes toward the company. These attitudes seemed to be primarily a result of the Brown employees' acceptance of three views often expressed by top management. These views were: (1) because there are bad economic conditions nationwide, the layoffs were unavoidable; (2) despite lower sales, the company continued to make a profit, profit sharing continued, and the stock price remained high ($32 a share); and (3) many of Brown's competitors were losing money and also had experienced significant layoffs, making the Brown Corporation look good by comparison. Hence, these three beliefs, which were highly publicized at the stockholders meeting in the spring of 1983, served to mitigate against any major unrest by employees and stockholders.

At the stockholders meeting in April of 1983, John, Jr. announced that he would step down as chief executive officer no later than October of 1984 and that Reed Larson was to be named the new CEO. As the result of this announcement, some old-timers were openly worried that if John, Jr. was not present to "hold Reed Larson back" the company would become an increasingly difficult place to work. Rumors of a takeover also fueled the uncertainty felt by the old-timers. John, Jr. said at the stockholders meeting that "we have a price" at which the company would be sold. With rumors of a possible takeover, the company stock soared to $32 a share—the highest in its history. Furthermore, with about 30 percent of the company's 1.3 million shares still in the hands of members of the Brown family, the company, according to one Wall Street analyst, "is a very good target for a takeover."

SUMMARY

The case of the Brown Corporation highlights the potential benefits as well as costs as the firm moved to absentee ownership and professional management. The change clearly had the effect of weeding out incompetent managers, putting more pressure on Brown employees to achieve higher profits, and adding new management tools to aid in decision making. The result was a corporation that was able to increase profits and survive during some very difficult times.

Such changes were not without some costs, however. Employees began to grow apathetic and feel less committed to the business. Competition for promotions increased, as did employee turnover. Distrust and uncertainty pervaded the workplace and rumors were rampant. Union activity had increased as the average employee became more disenchanted with the company. Innovation was often stifled as the professional managers began to impose strict controls over engineering. Finally, the Brown employees had lost sight of the values espoused by John, Sr. and the Brown family. In a sense, they had lost their history—their connection with the past—and this left them without a "vision" to which they could offer their loyalty and dedication.

CHAPTER 2 ENDNOTES

1. Dyer, W. Gibb, Jr. *Cultural Change in Family Forms: Anticipating and Managing Business and Family Transitions.* San Francisco: Jossey-Bass, 1986, p. 108.
2. Ibid., pp. 104–105.
3. Ibid., pp. 106.
4. Ibid.
5. Ibid., pp. 102–103.

CHAPTER 3 ===============

The Industrial Experience in Jamestown, New York

We saw, in the previous chapter, how a change in a corporation's ownership can also profoundly change the corporate culture. In that specific case, control of the Brown Corporation passed from a locally based, committed entrepreneur to professional managers and absentee shareholders; and this change had significant negative consequences for both the corporation and its employees. If this process is repeated in several companies within a single community, then the community as well as the companies may experience the same kind of economic and social deterioration. By following the industrial history of the small manufacturing city of Jamestown, New York, we can illustrate how changes in ownership and management can also have a profound impact on the quality of life within a whole community.

"YANKEE CITY"

We are not the first researchers to take an interest in this issue. Early work by University of Chicago sociologists W. Lloyd Warner and J.O. Low made perhaps the first significant observations of the relationship between absentee ownership and industrial decline.[1] While studying social relations in the city of Newburyport, Massachusetts (they called it "Yankee City" when publishing their research), they observed something which at first was very difficult to explain. During their research, a city-wide strike hit Newburyport's key industry, shoe manufacturing, and, to their surprise, they witnessed local politicians, merchants, and even some manufacturers supporting the striking workers. It seemed incomprehensible that traditional defenders of the establishment as well as petty capitalists should join in with union pickets. As they continued to study the situation, however, the data convinced them that absentee ownership was the true cause of this surprising turn of events.

According to Warner and Low, there had once been a reciprocal relationship between workers and the shoe manufacturing companies. Company owners were also local citizens, and several had been shoemakers themselves at one time. They participated in Newburyport churches, ran for political office, and contributed to local charities, sharing the resources of the local community with their workers and looking to that community as the source of their status and prestige. Thus, according to the researchers, it was ultimately against the company owners' own self-interest to treat their employees unfairly either in terms of wages or conditions of employment. This situation changed, however, as the area's shoe manufacturing factories were bought up by absentee interests.

The new owners did not live in the community, nor did they derive any social or personal benefit from being "good citizens." Similarly, the new professional managers brought in to run the plants had no interest in the social and political life of the community. They preferred to live out of town and looked forward to the day when they could move up the corporate ladder to a position in a major city. Thus, the management of these absentee-owned factories treated the workers in a cool and impersonal manner, avoided friendly interaction, laid off employees at any down-turn of the business, and took a hard stance in collective bargaining with the unions. From the community's point of view, both the owners and the managers of the local companies were strangers, who treated the city and its people with indifference and contempt, and who felt free to cut wages or move plants out of town without any regard for the impact on Newburyport.

The researchers also agreed that the community had lost

what had been a common bond of shared interests between the manufacturers, the workers, and the other residents of the town. Now the local economy was dependent on people with little or no concern for townspeople's welfare. As a result, Newburyport's economic base started gradually to deteriorate. Some factories left town, and citizens who actually had different class interests were forced together in opposition to the callous policies and actions of the shoe industry's absentee owners and professional managers.

Subsequent researchers have criticized Warner and Low for depending too heavily on oral accounts of Newburyport's history, which gave an over-idealistic and simplistic view of industrial life under local ownership.[2] There had been strikes against local owners, and industrial relations had not always been idyllic during this period. Nevertheless, the local economy had been much healthier in those days, and employers and employees had always been able to eventually work out the most difficult of conflicts and return to a peaceful and mutually beneficial relationship. Under local ownership, at least, factories had never been moved out of town, and the merchants, politicians, and manufacturers had not joined the picket lines. So even if the sociologists' reconstruction of history was not entirely accurate, there is certainly some truth to their argument.

In the rest of this chapter, we will be looking at the industrial and economic history of the town of Jamestown, New York. Like Warner and Low's analysis of "Yankee City," our case focuses on the evolution and transformation of this manufacturing community, but our analysis has been built on a variety of data sources not limited to oral history. We too found that, if local ownership was no heaven on earth, absentee ownership did become a kind of economic hell for the town and its residents.

HISTORICAL BACKGROUND

Jamestown is located in the southeastern corner of Chautauqua County, the most southwesterly county in New York

State. Today, Jamestown proper has a population of approximately 40,000, with 60,000 in the greater metropolitan area. The town relies heavily upon manufacturing for its employment base. Although its population is comprised of several different racial and ethnic groups, the principal ethnic groups are Swedish and Italian. The Swedish first immigrated to the area just before the Civil War; the Italians in the 1880s. Both groups played key roles in the economic growth of the community.

The Beginnings of Industrialization

The Jamestown area's first industry, as with most communities, sprang from its immediately exploitable natural resources, specifically its dense timberlands. Prior to the depletion of the area's lumber during the 1840s, it was known to produce an average 100,000 board feet of timber per acre, including white pine, fir, hemlock, and a wide variety of hardwoods.[3]

The first sawmill for the production of salable lumber was built in 1808. By 1830, more than forty million feet of lumber was being cut annually and floated down the Allegheny River on enormous rafts to Pittsburgh.[4] Later, it became apparent that local hardwoods could also be useful in the production of furniture, and the capital that had been accumulated through the sale of softwood lumber helped to spawn the emergence of what would become Jamestown's principal industry, furniture manufacture.

Royal Keyes, a carpenter and joiner who came to the town from Newfane, Vermont in 1815, was the first of Jamestown's furniture makers. Starting as a builder of houses, Keyes gradually began also making and selling simple cabinet furniture in his spare time. Eventually, he erected a two-story shop near where today stand Main and Fourth streets in Jamestown. In 1821, Keyes took on another Yankee, William Breed, as his partner. Three years later, Breed bought out Keyes's share and eventually joined with his brother to transform the shop into a full-time operation. In 1832, the two brothers undertook a major expansion and modernization effort and converted the

business into one of the first water-powered furniture factories to be established in western New York.[5]

Water power also helped to facilitate the development of
what for a while was Jamestown's largest industry, textile
manufacturing. Daniel Hazeltine was responsible for establishing the first of Jamestown's worsted mills. He began his
business in 1816 with the traditional "putting out system" by
contracting with local women to weave cloth, which he, in
turn, dressed and then sold on the market. Eventually he accumulated sufficient capital to begin to mechanize, and rowed
a boat to Pittsburgh where he had the equipment he needed
made. He then rowed the machinery back upstream to Jamestown where he had built a small mill which measured 24 by
26 feet. From these simple beginnings a major industry grew
such that, by the late 1800s, no less than eight textile mills
had been established in the Jamestown area as well as several
small allied mills.[6]

In addition to the lumber, furniture, and textile industries, a variety of other small industrial operations were also
organized during the first half of the 1800s. It was not until
1860, though, that they began to service needs beyond the city
and the immediate region.[7]

Immigration and Industrial Growth After 1860

May 14, 1860, marked a major turning point in Jamestown's history, and from this date forward the city grew from
predominantly an agricultural community into a small but
significant manufacturing center. On this day the last spike
was driven completing the railroad track which placed Jamestown along the route of the Atlantic and Great Western Rail-
way. After more than a decade of hard work, the city's political
and industrial leadership had finally succeeded in establishing
a major transportation link with Pittsburgh and New York
City. This was a day of great jubilation for the entire community, which joined to celebrate while the Jamestown Cor-
onet Band greeted the first train by playing, "Ain't I Glad to
Get Out of the Wilderness."[8]

Once this initial rail link was established, it was followed by several more, as well as by a rapid growth in population and industry. By 1865 the city's population had grown to a figure of 3,155. By the year 1900 this number had increased to 22,892, and Jamestown could boast some 178 factories.[9] Thus, the railroads enabled raw materials and vital energy resources such as coal and oil to be imported inexpensively and, likewise, provided a means for exporting manufactured goods at a low cost so that industrialists could profit from their efforts.[10]

With Jamestown's industrial growth also came many foreign immigrants. As local capitalists of Yankee stock like James Prendergast accumulated sufficient capital from the lumber industry to exploit the new commercial opportunities presented by the railroads, they began to encourage the immigration of skilled workers to help them build their enterprises.[11]

English workers were some of the earliest immigrants to settle in Jamestown. One of the most important individuals to promote English resettlement was William Broadhead. In 1873, Broadhead, in partnership with two other Jamestown industrialists, established the Jamestown Alpaca Mills. Two years later Broadhead left the firm and established a second worsted mill, Broadhead and Sons. Both companies were quite successful and eventually together employed over 2,000 persons. Much of the millwork, as in other mill towns, was performed by local women and children. However, the machinery required to produce worsted cloth had to be imported from England, and in order to maintain the machinery skilled mechanics and machinists were required. Craftsmen of this type were of course located in Great Britain, and therefore entrepreneurs like Broadhead actively recruited their skills into the area.[12] As a result of this practice, there were nearly 2,000 persons of either English birth or parentage in Jamestown by 1920.[13]

Where the English provided the skills for the development of the textile industry, immigrants from Sweden supported the growth of Jamestown's furniture industry. The majority of these immigrants came from Småland and the other southern provinces of Sweden where woodworking skills were widespread and furniture manufacturing highly developed.[14] Thus, during the latter half of the nineteenth century, many Swedish men who were highly skilled in the art of wood furniture making moved to Jamestown from Sweden. As the city moved into the twentieth century and furniture making became more mechanized and metal furniture gained popularity, the skills and work experience of Swedish immigrants shifted in correspondence. Thus, by 1920, the bulk of Swedish immigrants coming into the area were comprised of experienced factory workers and technicians possessing skills as machinists, toolmakers, welders, mechanics, draftsmen, and so forth.[15]

Although the textile mills were the largest industry in Jamestown for many years, this situation began to shift after the turn of the century. By 1900, furniture making had become the second largest industry and employed 1,209 wage earners, in contrast to textile manufacturing's 1,911.[16] Ten years later wood and metal manufacturing had become the dominant industries in Jamestown with a total of 3,814 persons working at forty factories.[17] In fact, by this point, Jamestown had become the nation's second largest center of wood furniture production and first in the manufacture of metallic furniture. This trend continued through the 1930s when 50 of the city's 110 manufacturing concerns were producing either wood or metal furniture.[18]

In light of the impressive growth displayed by the furniture industry, it is not surprising that the Swedes, rather than the English, rose to become Jamestown's dominant ethnic group. In 1850, there were approximately 250 Swedish immigrants residing in the community, and by 1880 this number had climbed to over 3,000. This trend continued on into the 1900s, and Jamestown grew to become America's largest Swedish settlement other than New York City. Thus, by 1920, there were over 15,000 in Jamestown, and in 1930, 22,000 of the city's population of 45,155 could claim Swedish birth or ancestry.[19]

Eventually the worsted mills disappeared from the Jamestown manufacturing scene, as a result of both the Depression and competition from mills in the south that had cheaper labor and material costs. The differential growth in these two industries, however, cannot be solely attributed to these two factors; for furniture manufacturing presented the opportunity for the diffusion of much greater entrepreneurial activity than did textiles. Many of the Swedish immigrants possessed trade skills intrinsic to furniture making and, in many instances, moved into the business on their own. For many years it was possible for immigrant Swedish craftsmen to leave the ranks of wage earners or middle management and start businesses of their own. This was especially true during the nineteenth century, and even well into the 1900s most of the city's factories operated with relatively limited mechanization, involving in the furniture industry tools such as slash saws, band saws, planers, molding sanding machines, and so on. In fact, electric motors were not even introduced into the area's wood furniture factories until after World War I.[20] Thus, because of this situation, the establishment of a new furniture manufacturing concern required substantially less capital than a textile operation (see Table 1).

Because the furniture business required a relatively modest investment, it was therefore not unusual for an individual or a small group of Swedish craftsmen to pool their resources and go into business for themselves. Henry Love estimated that between 1869 and 1939, Swedish immigrants had orga-

Table 1. Industry in Jamestown, New York: Average Capital per Factory, Selected Years

	FURNITURE MILLS	WORSTED MILLS
1855	$ 2,163	$ 16,500
1870	6,664	38,000
1900	73,484	1,242,290

Source: Paul A. Spengler, The Development of the Furniture Industry in Jamestown, New York from 1816 to 1945. Paper presented at the Conference on Local History, SUNY College at Fredonia, New York, 1978, p. 6.

nized no less than 75 wood furniture making concerns in Jamestown.[21] By 1920 at least half of the community's forty wood and metal furniture factories were owned by Swedes as well as a number of other manufacturing concerns outside of the furniture business. In total, Swedish manufacturing, business, and banking leaders constituted at least one-third of Jamestown's economic elite by 1920.[22]

Not surprisingly, Jamestown became in many respects a Swedish cultural island. Residents in neighboring towns referred to Jamestown as "little Sweden." This high degree of ethnic homogeneity and cultural concentration also produced some positive benefits in the business community, at least for Swedish entrepreneurs. For example, in 1919, a group of Swedish businessmen organized Jamestown's Swedish National Bank which was particularly liberal in terms of assisting new and existing local Swedish-owned manufacturing concerns and commercial enterprises.[23]

In the manufacturing community, ethnically based cooperation manifested itself particularly in the wood furniture industry, and up through the 1950s it was not uncommon for local firms in this industry to work together in a variety of areas of common interest. For example, in 1917 the local wood and metal furniture manufacturers established the Jamestown furniture exposition, which was a large multistory showroom building for showing their products to customers.[24] The exposition still exists today. Through the local manufacturing association, the wood furniture companies also worked together on improving their marketing strategies, providing industry-wide educational programs, and reducing transportation costs through joint shipping. In 1958, for example, the Jamestown Area Manufacturers Association sponsored ten different wood industry committees which were responsible for increasing the competitive advantage of local firms over other companies throughout the country. Perhaps one of the most impressive manifestations of this high level of collaboration occurred during World War II. In 1942, nine of the community's wood furniture companies organized a producers' pool for aiding the nation in the war effort.[25]

INDUSTRIAL CONFLICT UNDER LOCAL OWNERSHIP

The extensive interfirm collaboration that resulted from Jamestown's high degree of ethnic homogeneity clearly had some important beneficial effects on the community's industrial development. From the standpoint of labor relations, the impact of this situation was somewhat different over the long run, and, as will be demonstrated, considerable industrial conflict was produced by Jamestown's close-knit and paternalistic economic elite.

The labor movement in Jamestown essentially experienced three separate waves of organizing activity. The first of these involved the Knights, who were active in the community for a period of eight years. The first of the Knights' locals was established in 1883. This first local union was the Cigarmakers Assembly, and, following them, the Weavers, Shoemakers, Woodworkers, and Upholsterers as well as several "mixed" assemblies were formed. At the height of their organizing efforts in Jamestown, the Knights of Labor were able to boast more than 1,000 members and even their own community "Union Labor Party." The factionalism and dissension which developed at the Knights' Richmond Convention in 1886 started a gradual deterioration of the movement in Jamestown as it did elsewhere. After the panic of 1893, all Knights of Labor locals disappeared from the Jamestown area, and the only union left was the Typographers, which was not affiliated with them.[26]

Jamestown's second union organizing wave started in the mid-1890s, and it was led by the American Federation of Labor. On September 26, 1895, the AFL successfully organized its first local, the Metal Polishers Union, at Art Metal Construction Company, which at the time was the largest manufacturer of metallic office furniture in the world. By 1899 they had organized seven more local unions representing various crafts, as well as established an area Central Labor Council. Five years later the Central Labor Council had grown to include fifty member locals which in total represented more than 2,000 workers.[27]

In spite of their clearly aggressive organizing stance, the local AFL leadership was otherwise quite cautious and conservative. They disfavored the use of strike action except as a last resort, and they maintained a tight rein over the area's strike funds. The council insisted on intervening and preferably arbitrating in unresolved disputes before a strike could take place, and if one did occur without their approval all funds were withheld.[28]

The union leaders' conservative attitude can be attributed in part to the fact that, at least in the early 1900s, it was still possible for the exceptional craftsman to set out on his own and become a business leader himself. Indeed, there appears to have been little animosity held toward those individuals who crossed the line from organized labor to capitalist or manager at least during this period. For example, Ernest Cawcroft, who was the editor for Jamestown's labor press, *The Union Advocate,* left the movement to become secretary of the city's Chamber of Commerce.[29] In another case, James Clarey, who had been the chief organizer for the Knights, left the union movement to become a manager for the *Jamestown Evening Journal.*[30] In fact, *The Union Advocate* even went so far as to congratulate Henry Sampson when he resigned as treasurer for the Central Labor Council to become one of the co-owners of the Jamestown Furniture Company.

This conservatism of union leaders, however, was equally matched by that of the local manufacturers. In 1901, the Jamestown Area Manufacturers Association (JAMA) was formed, and, in spite of the positive collaboration previously mentioned, one of the principal reasons this organization was created was to counter union activity and control labor rates. Below, Ernest Cawcroft describes the effectiveness of JAMA and its mode of operation in a statement he made in March of 1907, sometime after he had left the unions to join the Chamber of Commerce.

> The rate of wages in Jamestown may be accurately described as moderate, rather than high or low. The rate had been practically constant for six or seven years. Immediately prior to that, there was a general rise. Increases in

wages in any factory in the Manufacturers Association go
into effect when approved by the association, and the association stands together on all labor matters.[31]

An examination of the census of manufacturers taken
during the early 1900s tends to verify Cawcroft's description.
The wage rates for the average wood furniture worker in
Jamestown, for example, were 20 to 25 percent lower than
those of other workers in the same industry in other New
York State cities during this same period. And this situation
maintained for many years, as can be seen from the following
statement made in 1938 by Russell Rogerson, who was then
a labor attorney for some of Jamestown's largest companies:

> Our cost of labor as compared with large industrial centers
> is relatively low, with the exception of the wood furniture
> industry. Our textile mills are able to employ skilled help
> for approximately 10 to 15 percent less than competing in-
> dustries in New England. The metal industries engaged in
> the manufacture of automobile accessories and structural
> steel equipment enjoy like advantage. Our labor unions
> are active and well established in a part of the industry in
> the town but three of the largest factories employing the
> greatest number of men have no union, several have so-
> called independent unions, and unions affiliated with the
> American Federation of Labor represent the employees in
> most of the metal furniture plants.[32]

Such success at controlling unionization, labor rates, and
in maintaining the local class structure was not, however, carried out without the price of eventually precipitating industrial strife. The extent of the discord produced by this
situation first became drastically apparent in 1919 when the
largest of all Jamestown strikes began. It started with a Machinists local over a demand for higher wages and full union
recognition. These demands, of course, were common to almost every union local in Jamestown, and eventually fifty-six
of the city's factories were struck in sympathy with the Machinists' demands. More than 3,600 workers hit the streets in
support of the Machinists, and the strike lasted the entire

summer. There was no crossing of class lines in this conflict, for it was clearly a battle between what had become an increasingly less mobile working class population and the city's economic and political elite.

As the strike progressed, the Workers International Industrial Union entered the scene, and they began passing out anticapitalist literature and stirring up greater hostility among the town's unskilled and semiskilled workers. The AFL was clearly threatened and frustrated by this situation, and eventually the WIIU's tactics actually damaged the strike; for they created conflict between the predominantly Swedish AFL Machinists and Metal Workers and the Italian workers who had immigrated to the area and taken the lower paying and lesser skilled woodworking and municipal street cleaning jobs. By the end of the summer everyone had returned to work or lost their jobs, and the Machinists had literally been destroyed. The union movement did not reappear with any strength again until the passing of the Wagner Act many years later.[33]

In the mid-1930s the unions began to experience their third and finally successful revival in Jamestown. Bolstered by section 7A of the National Industrial Recovery Act and the Wagner Act in 1935, which made labor's right to organize and bargain collectively legal, the international unions were finally able to gain a foothold in the area. Organizers for the International Association of Machinists (IAM), the United Electrical, Radio and Machine Workers (UE), and the United Furniture Workers of America (UFW) were particularly active from this point forward. Their work was not easy, however, and the National Labor Relations Board had to be called in to settle disputes in at least five of the area's larger metalworking companies, which had successfully avoided recognizing the unions up through the 1940s.[34]

International representatives also found that some of the old conservatism that had characterized the unions during the first two waves of activity still existed. Jamestown's tendency toward being somewhat of a closed system had clearly kept the expectations of the labor force much lower than elsewhere. Art White, one of the key business agents involved in organizing and collective bargaining during the late 1930s and the 1940s, described the situation in the following manner:

> I was the big city boy coming back to the small city and came to wonder what the dickens why couldn't we have stuff like we had in the big city. I used to use the expression, "They must have built a fence around this town." Because it certainly wasn't in step with the outside world and not just in relation to labor. I think you'll find that pattern running pretty near straight through everything. This community wasn't really too forward looking for many years.

A graphic example of what union leaders like White discovered when trying to organize and prepare for bargaining is described below by Art White in a story about when, in 1940, he tried to propose to the members of one IAM local that they include paid vacations among their contract demands.

> I found it even this way among our own people. The IAM was awfully conservative when I first came here. I can tell you an experience I had. I was getting ready to negotiate a contract at Metal Corporation. . . . I suggested to our boys, "I think we ought to ask for five paid holidays." You know I almost got thrown out of that union. I had some of the old Swedes get up and denounce me, "You mean dat we should ask for something we don't do no work for?" I said, "Yes, what is the matter with that." And they said, "We don't do dat here!" I almost got thrown out of that union.

During the latter half of the 1940s the conservatism of the work force began to recede, in part due to the efforts of international representatives like Art White and also because of the raised expectations of younger workers who, during or after World War II, had the opportunity to work in larger industrial cities. Thus, in 1946, there were numerous strikes for higher wages and the addition of benefits considered common practice elsewhere. The fight really started, though, in the 1950s when a virtual revolution broke loose in Jamestown,

Table 2. Strike Activity, Jamestown Manufacturing, 1950–1959

	STRIKES	STRIKE DAYS	AVERAGE NUMBER OF DAYS PER STRIKE
1950	5	156	31.2
1951	3	198	66.0
1952	4	152	38.0
1953	8	176	22.0
1954	1	99	99.0
1955	8	127	15.9
1956	13	492	37.8
1957	10	360	36.0
1958	5	136	27.2
1959	5	90	18.0
Total	49	1986	40.5

Source: New York State Department of Labor, Monthly Work Stoppage Reports, *1949–1959.*

which reached its peak toward the latter half of the decade. The strike activity during this period for Jamestown's manufacturing section is documented in Table 2.

There were both positive and negative consequences that resulted from the strike activity during this period. On the positive side, labor succeeded in bringing wage rates, work rules, and benefits more closely in line with those in other cities. Alaric Bailey, a Jamestown manufacturer during this period, comments about these changes in the following statement made in a labor rate study he conducted in 1956:

> The last issue of the *Labor Market Review,* published by the New York State Department of Labor, reports that the average weekly earning for all New York State production workers in manufacturing was $80.78. The average weekly earning for the same period for the production worker in a Jamestown metal plant was $89.40, and in a Jamestown wood plant it was $77.23 . . .[35]

Bailey also compared fringe benefits in Jamestown with seventeen other major labor market areas surveyed by the

Monthly Labor Review and found the city's industry to be quite competitive.[36]

On the negative side, what might be termed the "labor wars" that took place during most of the 1950s also created a considerable stumbling block to the development of new industry in the area. Nationally, Jamestown became known as a "bad labor" or "strike happy" town, and this discouraged major corporations from building new operations in the area. This was not a significant problem at first, but over time it became one factor among many that almost led to the city's demise.

ABSENTEE OWNERSHIP AND INDUSTRIAL RELATIONS

As the foregoing description illustrates, Jamestown was not by any stretch of the imagination a peaceful or happy industrial town during the period when industry was both owned and managed by local entrepreneurs. Industrial conflict reached nearly a fever pitch toward the close of this era, and animosity and ill feelings ran high. Nonetheless, each camp tended to stay within its own bounds, and the conflict for the most part was internal to the community. This situation began to change during the late 1950s and the 1960s when corporations having headquarters in distant locations began to move into the area by buying up existing plants and companies. Chautauqua Plywood Company was purchased by Magnavox, Curtis Machine Company by the Carborundum Corporation, Conroe Concrete by Marietta Concrete, and Weber-Knapp was purchased by a furniture manufacturing firm in Grand Rapids, Michigan.[37] This shift in ownership patterns continued on through the 1970s, and by 1977 a census conducted by JAMA found that 44 percent (34 firms) of its member companies were divisions or subsidiaries of absentee corporations. It was found that 29 of these operations employed some 6,134 people, or more than 50 percent of the total work force under the employ of JAMA firms.

From the outset, some of these outside interests moved

the firms they purchased to other areas. The Newbrook Machine Corporation and Empire Case Goods, for example, left Jamestown, and the Swanson Machine Company as well as Croft Steel Products were moved to the Deep South where both taxes and wage rates were substantially lower.[38] This trend continued into the late 1960s and early 1970s, and eventually plant closings became a serious economic and employment problem. Before this became apparent, though, absentee ownership at first appeared to have a positive impact on area labor relations.

In many ways the managers brought in by absentee corporations were more progressive than local managers. Thus, initially, the change in ownership brought an infusion of new "professional" managers who had a perspective on industrial relations, contracts, wages, vacations, pensions, etc., molded by their experiences in major cities with standards set by the corporate parent. One former union leader described the situation this way:

> It wasn't until you saw outside industry come into Jamestown that you saw change begin to come gradually. I don't mean a swing over to liberal, but I do mean it started working better. . . . A different type of management developed. A management which was more, perhaps understanding and perhaps had been in other places and I guess I'll have to use the word—more liberal . . . for the most part, in my opinion, I think as the new blood came in and displaced the old regime, I think it was a change for the better.

It is of course not surprising that the managers of the absentee companies were less influenced by local norms governing labor relations, since, unlike their Jamestown counterparts, they were vertically integrated into larger systems, rather than horizontally integrated into the community.[39] Indeed, many chose to even live outside the community, sometimes in the outlying suburbs, and frequently in more distant communities located on Chautauqua Lake or near Erie, Pennsylvania. Thus, much of the old dedication to a collective strategy for controlling Jamestown's labor relations began to deteriorate with the growth of absentee ownership. A former

Jamestown manufacturing manager explained what happened in the following manner:

> When I first came here, we used to have meetings quite often during negotiations. . . . There was nothing illegal about it, but we'd meet for breakfast . . . some of us, and boy we'd go right down the line on what we're offering here, what fringes here, and we totally briefed each other— which in a sense is fair because the unions were doing the same thing. That started to disappear when you got some of the big companies in here because naturally they started to take the attitude that they were a big company . . .

Thus, local labor leaders and community leaders looked upon the labor policies brought in by outside corporations as having a liberalizing influence on area labor-management relations, and therefore they perceived this structural change quite favorably. During the latter half of the 1960s this attitude began to change. As Stanley Lundine, mayor of Jamestown from 1968 through the mid-1970s, described it:

> Outside ownership was really just starting to come in . . . and in this we kind of had the worst of all worlds. What happened was that the locals tended to be mostly old-fashioned types and the ones that came in were the types that saw things as a fight set-up. It was an investment, God dammit! And if it didn't make their 18 percent profit expected on it . . . we'll get rid of it . . . or we'll send a plant manager in there and we don't want any trouble from the union . . .

It thus became clear that local firms owned by outside interests were not only less susceptible to pressures imposed by local manufacturers, but also unresponsive to community concerns with the need for economic and employment stability. A number of wood furniture companies left the area during this period as a consequence of being acquired by outsiders, and a variety of problems developed in absentee-owned metal furniture and other companies in the area.

A majority of Jamestown's manufacturing operations are what is commonly referred to as small batch or job shop operations, and they specialize in the production of unique high-quality products, even to the point of customization. In such operations modern management mass production and bureaucratic innovations often prove counterproductive, given the highly dynamic nature of job shop market and production systems. The management of the outside firms, however, tended to push for increased centralization and a clear-cut separation of functions such as engineering, sales, production management, data processing, and finance. In contrast, a job or small batch operation usually runs more effectively with a rather lean, in-house, multiskilled staff/management group. For example, such operations survive on their ability to obtain both large and small subcontracts, all of which typically involve different demands and specifications. Standardization is virtually impossible, and the "rule of thumb" technique by necessity must govern all phases of the business. Thus, successful bidding for subcontracts typically requires the intuitive abilities of a person or persons who possess a mixture of craft, engineering, production management, and sales expertise. The trick in this situation is to produce bids which successfully integrate such varied and diverse areas of expertise, and the conglomerates generally failed at this miserably by trying to utilize the judgment of separate and highly specialized staffs, many of which were located at some distant corporate headquarters. Similarly, the introduction of mass production manufacturing methods made the typical Jamestown operation a "chaotic mess," since the ability to shift flexibly from one job to another is essential, given the shifting demands and changing time frames that characterize job and small batch businesses.

The ultimate result of the imposition of large corporate firms over Jamestown's job shop businesses was a heavy burden of unnecessary corporate overhead, a confounding of the production process, the introduction of an inaccurate and ineffective bidding process, and eventually a growing disrespect and distrust of management on the part of labor. To the work force, these new managers, who initially appeared progressive, began to seem incompetent at best. Once these problems began to impact each local company's bottom line, and the parent was not realizing their projected return on investment, peaceful labor relations disappeared with an ever-hardening management position at the bargaining table.[40]

Thus, by the mid-1960s, Jamestown's old pattern of union-management conflict began to reappear. Bitter and lengthy strikes ensued, and this time they frequently took place in the absentee-owned plants and companies as Table 3 illustrates. What is most impressive about these figures is the difference in the duration of the strikes. Those that took place in absentee-owned companies tended to last *four times longer* than work stoppages in locally owned companies. Interestingly enough, as the problems in the absentee-owned operations continued, the labor force became increasingly sentimental in their views about the "old days" under paternalistic management. Workers and union leaders interviewd expressed an actual longing for the days when the boss could call them by name, when they knew who the boss really was, and when the company used to sponsor such things as picnics, bowling leagues, and trips to see the fights or football in Buffalo and Pittsburgh.

Perhaps the most dramatic example of this type of situation took place at Art Metal Company, which by the 1960s had grown to become the area's largest employer. During the latter half of the 1960s, the firm, which had gone public, built a new 940,000-square-foot plant in the Jamestown area. The investment, of course, was received positively, but the operation itself, which was designed and developed by outside engineers, attempted to do the impossible. Many different metal furniture products were brought together in one production facility, and an attempt was made to construct the whole facility on assembly line principles. Given the diversity of Art Metal's products and their high-quality nature, the enterprise proved to be a failure. The plant was almost inoperable. Consequently, in an effort to save the company, local citizens, most of which were Art Metal employees, attempted to gain control by purchasing a large block of stock and soliciting the proxy vote. Interestingly, this effort was led by Russell Rog-

Table 3. Strike Statistics, Jamestown Manufacturing, 1962–1972

	LOCALLY OWNED FIRMS[a]		ABSENTEE-OWNED FIRMS[b]		TOTALS	
	STRIKES	STRIKE DAYS	STRIKES	STRIKE DAYS	STRIKES	STRIKE DAYS
1962	3	22	0	0	3	22
1963	1	3	2	169	3	172
1964	0	0	1	12	1	12
1965	2	7	2	12	4	19
1966	3	39	2	41	5	80
1967	0	0	4	263	4	263
1968	3	25	4	95	7	120
1969	5	65	3	228	8	293
1970	1	2	3	101	4	103
1971	1	4	4	78	5	82
1972	1	18	3	62	4	80
Totals	20	185	28	1,061	48	1,246

[a] *Average Days per Strike = 9.3*
[b] *Average Days per Strike = 37.9*
Source: New York State Department of Labor, Monthly Work Stoppage Reports, 1962–1972.

erson, the labor lawyer who had fought so aggressively to keep the union out of Art Metal and other companies during the 1930s and '40s.

The Art Metal situation turned into a very heated battle between Jamestowners and New York interests, and when a proxy fight seemed imminent, the local group tried to save the company by finding what they thought was a friendly buyer. They sold their shares and the firm to Walter Heller and Company of Chicago. The Heller group, however, proved no more successful in running the company than previous management, and, in many ways, things got worse. Many managers came and left the operation over a short period of time, and there was little if any consistency maintained. The union president, for example, complained that almost every time he went to deal with a grievance he found a new personnel manager or a new plant manager when he went to discuss other problems. This situation was further exacerbated by a sharp market drop, and in 1969, Art Metal announced an annual loss of $1,972,000 as compared with a peak profit for the year immediately preceding the sale of the company of $3,976,000 on $51,000,000 in gross sales. In November of 1970 Heller announced a loss of $1,192,000, and along with this released the news that they had sold Art Metal to Tomar Industries of Rochester, New York. Tomar had a reputation as a liquidator, and that is exactly what they did. They sold the equipment, and the trade name was purchased by a New Jersey concern. On June 14, 1970, the company stopped all production and Jamestown lost its largest employer, which at its peak had more than 1,700 employees on the payroll. Even worse, unemployment for the area was approaching the double digit level, and six more plant closings, four by absentee owners, were on the horizon.

CONCLUSION

The case history above both substantiates and contradicts the Warner and Low hypothesis regarding the impact of absentee ownership and control upon industry and the economy at the level of the community. It is clear that, in the long run, many of the same forms of conflict and alienation that were observed in the Yankee City studies also took place in Jamestown, New York. The process, however, was not one of moving from a "happy valley" era of labor peace under local ownership to one of bitter strife under absentee control. The elite arose in Jamestown, and, having once established their societal position, they then sought to defend it by collectively resisting any encroachment upon their power. Once the lines between capitalist and wage earner hardened, as the passage from the latter to the former became increasingly more difficult to traverse, class consciousness, and then class conflict, ensued. Culture and ethnic heritage were not forgotten and loyalties completely set aside, but they likewise did not guarantee an elimination of conflicts of interest.

What appears to be the flow of events, at least in the Jamestown case, is a transition from a relatively fluid local economy in which mobility is possible for many to a more reified society with fairly well defined class interests and limitations. Once a community passes from the latter to the former, industrial conflict can and often does result, and it can be very heated and bitter, as was the case in Jamestown in 1919 and during the late 1940s and 1950s. Such conflict, however, does not necessarily lead to a total loss of reciprocity and influence between the community and industry.

As both capital and product markets grow, the probability that outside interests will acquire local enterprises increases substantially. When this occurs, the immediate effect can in fact be beneficial, since large firms frequently pay higher wages and better financial benefits than do smaller, privately held companies. Nonetheless, the personal relationship that once existed between employer and employee and between firm and community becomes considerably diluted. In the case of the community, this is probably of little importance, as long as the parent and the local operation are performing well financially. In the case of employees, this change probably still has a negative impact upon labor relations regardless of the economic situation. But when the firm is under duress for economic reasons, both the community and the worker are in trouble, because they clearly have no ability to influence the situation. Furthermore, given the difficulties inherent in effectively managing diverse operations in distant geographic areas, it is very likely that some firms which are acquired by absentee interests will in fact experience difficulty because of the introduction of inappropriate management systems and techniques, or simply the imposition of heavy overhead. Whichever is the case, in such situations conflict will develop between employee and company and the company and the community. When this takes place, traditional class lines easily become blurred and the entire community may become united in opposition to absentee owners and their professional managers.

CHAPTER 3 ENDNOTES

1. W. Lloyd Warner and J.O. Low. *The Social System of the Modern Factory—The Strike: A Social Analysis* (Westport, Conn.: Greenwood Press, 1976). Originally published by Yale University Press, 1947.

2. Stephan Thernstrom. "Yankee City Revisited," *American Sociological Review*, vol. 30, no. 2, April 1965, pp. 234–242.

3. Paul A. Spengler. *Yankee, Swedish and Italian Acculturation and Economic Mobility in Jamestown, New York from 1880 to 1920.* Unpublished doctoral dissertation, University of Delaware, Newark, 1977, p. 18.

4. Henry F. Love. "Manufacturing in Chautauqua County." In William J. Doty et al. (eds.), *The Historical Annals of Southwestern New York*, vol. I (New York: Lewis Historical Publishing Co., 1940), p. 324; Spengler, 1977, pp. 36–37; Paul A. Spengler. *The Development of the Furniture Industry in Jamestown, New York from 1816 to 1945.* Paper presented at the *Conference on Local History*, SUNY College at Fredonia, New York, 1978, p. 2.

5. Gilbert W. Hazeltine. *The Early History of the Town of Ellicott* (Jamestown, N.Y.: Journal Printing Co., 1887), pp. 151–152; Love, 1940, p. 325.

6. Love, 1940, p. 328.

7. Spengler, 1978, p. 2.

8. George E. Hammond. "First Agitation for East-West Rail Link Started in Jamestown." *The Jamestown Sun Magazine*, March ɪ ɪ, 1951; Helen G. McMahon. *Chautauqua County: A History* (Buffalo, N.Y.: Henry Stewart, 1958), p. 112; Spengler, 1977, p. 47.

9. U.S. Dept. of the Interior. 12th Census of the U.S.: Manufactures, Part II (Washington, D.C.: U.S. Census Office, 1900), p. 594; 13th Census, 1910, p. 814.

10. Spengler, 1978, p. 5.

11. Love, 1940, p. 328; Spengler, 1977, p. 53.

12. Love, 1940, p. 328.

13. Spengler, 1977, pp. 53–54.

14. Jennie Vimmerstedt. "The Swedish People in Jamestown, New York." In E.G. Westman and E.G. Johnson (eds.), *The Swedish Element in America* (Chicago, Ill.: Swedish-American Biographical Society, 1931), p. 449–454; Spengler, 1977, p. 54.

15. Spengler, 1978, pp. 16–17.

16. 12th Census of the U.S., 1900, p. 1968.

17. Spengler, 1978, p. 11.

18. Ibid.

19. Vimmerstedt, 1931, p. 449; Spengler, 1977, p. 54; Spengler, 1978, p. 16.

20. Spengler, 1978, pp. 7–8.

21. Love, 1940, p. 325.

22. Spengler, 1978, pp. 17–18.

23. Spengler, 1977, p. 219.

24. Love, 1940, p. 327.

25. Jamestown Area Manufacturers' Association. *Application for a Jamestown Wood Furniture War Production Pool.* Unpublished report to the United States Government, The Jamestown Area Manufacturers' Association (Jamestown, New York), 1943.

26. Ernest Cawcroft. The Labor Movement in Chautauqua County. In the *Centennial History of Chautauqua County* (Jamestown, N.Y.: Chautauqua History Company, 1904), p. 174.

27. Ibid., pp. 178–179.

28. Ibid., pp. 176, 179.

29. McMahon, 1958, p. 197.

30. Spengler, 1977, pp. 224–225.

31. McMahon, 1958, p. 197.

32. Spengler, 1977, p. 226.

33. McMahon, 1958, p. 198.

34. Ibid.

35. Ibid., p. 199.

36. Ibid.

37. Spengler, 1978, p. 15.

38. Ibid.

39. Roland L. Warren. *The Community in America* (Chicago, Ill.: Rand McNally, 1963).

40. Michael Gurdon and Christopher Meek. "Problems of Technological Fit: Evidence from the Corporate Takeover of Job Shops." In the *Proceedings of the Southern Academy of Management Meetings* (Mississippi State University: The Southern Management Association, 1980).

CHAPTER 4

The Deepening Crisis in the Steel Industry

So far, we have found that changing patterns of ownership and management had negative consequences both on a specific company and on a whole community. Now we want to explore how the same historical and industrial shift to absentee owners and professional managers permanently transformed the entire steel industry. Similar analyses could be made of various other industries, including textile, rubber, electronics, or even agriculture. Our own research into the recent developments in steel, however, provides a particularly clear example, at this broader level, of the changes we have looked at throughout this book.

AN HISTORICAL OVERVIEW

The methodology for our study of steel includes several years of research into the industry as a whole and the U.S. Steel Corporation (USX) in particular. Our data include company records, media reports, the views of steel analysts and researchers, and interviews with steel company managers, union representatives, and government officials.

Today's steel industry has come a long way from its beginnings. As far back as the late eighteenth century there had been small-scale steel production, typically owned by locally based entrepreneurs who built mills near the town in which the owner resided. By 1860, a mere 748 workers operated the country's thirteen steel mills, producing approximately 12,000 tons of steel annually.[1] Within the next three decades, fueled by demands for steel in the railroad industry and technological changes, production shot up to 4.8 million tons a year.

In this same era, there was also a restructuring of the labor process. Until the turn of the century, the steel industry consisted of two groups of workers. "Skilled" workers were highly respected craftsmen who established agreements with steel owners to be paid a given amount for each ton of steel produced, a wage determined not by the company but according to a sliding scale based on the market. Thus, labor enjoyed a high degree of equality through a cooperative partnership, characterized by mutual respect and a balancing of power. "Unskilled" workers performed primarily heavy labor, as they assisted skilled steelworkers, often through a contract system, in which they were actually hired and paid by the skilled craftsmen themselves, not by the steel owners.

The Amalgamated Association of Iron, Steel, and Tin Workers, the most powerful union in the industry, played a critical role in ensuring skilled steelworkers' control over the production process. At the Homestead mill of the Carnegie Corporation, for example, the 1889 labor contract gave workers control over the division of labor and the pace of production. According to the company's historian,

> Every department and sub-department had its workman's "committee," with a "chairman" and full corps of officers. . . . During the ensuing three years hardly a day passed that a "committee" did not come forward with some demand or grievance. If a man with a desirable job died or left the workers, his position could not be filled without the consent and approval of an Amalgamated committee. . . . [The union was involved in] the matter of apportioning the work, of regulating the terms, of altering the machinery, in short every detail of working the great plant . . .[2]

A number of writers have documented the ensuing struggle, in which employers began to push for increased production through breaking the union's influence, introducing labor-saving technology, and redesigning the structure of work along the lines of Taylor's new "scientific management." Rejecting the traditional argument of a free and open labor market, some writers suggest that the new owners of big steel deliberately sought to overthrow their historically cooperative relationship with steelworkers, eliminate the contract system, disconnect wages from market forces, and destroy the union. Organizational hierarchy and complexity emerged, not as natural social evolution, but precisely as tools to enhance managerial power.[3]

The deal struck between J.P. Morgan and Andrew Carnegie in 1901 led to the first billion-dollar company in America, U.S. Steel Corporation. The new monolith, at the outset, controlled 80 percent of the nation's steel output. Along with the emergence of subsequent big steel companies, U.S. Steel enjoyed dominance in the marketplace, massive profits, and the installation of new technology. The company mined iron ore in Minnesota, dug coal in Kentucky, and extracted limestone in Michigan. Raw materials were transported from company mines by company railroad and water vessels to make steel in hundreds of mills around the country. Their products included sheets and strips, plates and bars, and ore used in everything from tin cans to the structure of the Sears Tower in Chicago.

Historically, U.S. Steel and other major companies were carried along on the wave of the economy, making billions of dollars no matter what their executives did. But the dramatic increase in production throughout the boom years also led, obviously enough, to the building of larger plants, often in distant areas. This development of an absentee-ownership situation moved the industry away from an involvement in local community affairs and a commitment to regional issues toward an exclusive concern with abstract business equations. And, since the mid-1950s, mounting problems have washed away jobs, markets, and profits. Although the nation's economy (GNP) has doubled since 1955, steel production has only risen 17 percent. Over 140 mills have been permanently closed, and the number of steelworkers slashed in half. Now American steel is in crisis, having lost a total of six billion dollars in recent years.

FROM STEEL EXECUTIVES TO MONEY MANAGERS

One of the chief causes of the steel industry's current difficulties is the shortage of capital needed to make massive
investments in new equipment to improve productivity. Investment capital is a scarce resource that tends to flow toward
the most profitable and promising business ventures. The normal criteria for attracting capital investment include cash
flow, debt ratio, earnings per share, and returns on equity.
Measured by these and other tools of financial measurement,
the financial conditions of all the big American steel companies have gone from bad to worse in the last decade. U.S.
Steel's conservative debt-to-equity ratio averaged 33 percent
in 1978; now it has risen to a precarious 60 percent. These
numbers are also typical for the other seven big companies.
Accordingly, the industry's interest expenses for 1982 were
double those of 1981. Such ratios, considered more foolhardy
than aggressive, caused bankers that were traditionally big
lenders to take a very cautious stance toward the steel
industry.

Moreover, since the 1970s, the return on investment for
the steel industry has been less than half the average for U.S.
manufacturers generally. Table 4 illustrates how a similar
trend can be seen with respect to return on equity. The cash
flow for six major U.S. steelmakers has declined steadily since
1978, with a huge drop from minus $7.4 billion to minus $10
billion in 1982. Decreasing profits, mergers, and acquisitions
have diluted earnings per share. The result has been severely
lopsided balance sheets.

The major steel companies say they need capital to mod-
ernize; but, obviously enough, their current financial condition makes them poor candidates for investment. But the real
issue is not so much whether these companies can obtain
sufficient capital, but the way they manage their own capital
resources. Their history of previous capital management suggests what they might really do if they could raise the capital
they claim to need.

When, for example, import restrictions on foreign steel
have been imposed in the past to provide additional capital for

Table 4. Rate of Return on Equity After Taxes: Steel Versus All Manufacturing, 1950–1978

	PRIMARY U.S. IRON AND STEEL FIRMS	ALL U.S. MANUFACTURING
1950	14.3%	15.4%
1951	12.3	12.1
1952	8.5	10.3
1953	10.7	10.5
1954	8.1	9.9
1955	13.5	12.6
1956	12.7	12.2
1957	11.4	11.0
1958	7.2	8.6
1959	8.0	10.4
1960	7.2	9.2
1961	6.2	8.8
1962	5.5	9.8
1963	7.0	10.3
1964	8.8	11.6
1965	9.8	13.0
1966	10.3	13.5
1967	7.7	11.7
1968	7.6	12.1
1969	7.6	11.5
1970	4.3	9.3
1971	4.5	9.7
1972	6.0	10.6
1973	9.5	12.8
1974	16.9	14.9
1975	10.9	11.6
1976	9.0	14.0
1977	3.6	14.2
1978	8.9	15.0

Source: Robert W. Crandall, The U.S. Steel Industry in Recurrent Crisis, *The Brookings Institute, Washington, D.C., 1981, p. 29.*

investment to the industry, evidence shows that these funds were not used for modernization programs. Despite a decade of layoffs, concessions, cost-cutting, deregulation, and tax incentives, industry-wide investment in steel production by 1982 was half of what was invested in 1968.

In fact, the business of making steel is not completely unprofitable, even if it sometimes appears so on paper. Yet to achieve their obvious objective of profit, steel executives are starting to act like money managers, using the same criteria that would be used in the short-term financial markets to determine the appropriate uses for their financial resources. According to these criteria, steel is simply not a good investment. "The only discretionary projects that make any sense," says one steel executive quoted in *Fortune* magazine, "are those offering very handsome returns."[4]

This logic leads to a strategy of diversification through acquisitions and mergers. This diversification is not intended to generate cash flow to assist the company's steel divisions, but rather to enhance the financial position of the parent company. National Intergroup's actions over the past two years illustrate the flight from investing in steel. First, the firm cut its steel-making capacity in half by getting rid of its Weirton Works through an employee buyout. Next, it sold 50 percent of the leftover business to Nippon Kokan Steel of Japan. Next, National announced plans to merge with Bergen Brunswig, a giant pharmaceutical company—a far cry from steel making.

Is $1 billion enough to modernize? Apparently not, according to the American Iron and Steel Institute. It estimates that a thorough program would require $7 billion yearly for a decade in order to become fully up-to-date technologically. Lobbying for government assistance since the 1970s has resulted in various schemes to improve the profit picture. OSHA and EPA regulations were relaxed, higher depreciation allowances were granted, corporate taxes were slashed such that the companies had a net cash flow at the end of 1981 above $4.9 billion. Yet after all these breaks, only two of the

seven largest steel firms increased the level of their investments in steel. The other five actually *decreased* by 9 percent.

A report from the General Accounting Office reveals that
under the Steel Compliance Extension Act, which major steel
companies successfully lobbied for in 1981, only $49 million
has been invested in modernization. This is in sharp contrast
to the $500–$700 million expected in exchange for a three-
year extension in meeting clean air requirements.

U.S. Steel's trade record of not investing in its steel enterprises is an intriguing case of capital management. Back in
1979 the EPA negotiated a consent decree with the company
concerning a number of western Pennsylvania plants. Corporate Chairman David Roderick promised the company would
act aggressively to revitalize its operations, generating a spir-
ited public debate about the firm's sense of social responsibility.[5] Five years later, instead of capital improvements, there
were primarily mill closings. (Two exceptions have been the
new continuous caster installed at Gary, Indiana, and construction of a seamless pipe mill at the Fairfield Works in
Alabama.)

In a widely criticized violation of the spirit of the law,
U.S. Steel used its governmental breaks in an offer to buy Mar-
athon Oil in 1981. This was after Roderick had pledged to use
$500 million in savings gained from the Economic Recovery
Tax Act to initiate massive steel projects.[6]

U.S. Steel's 1983 decision to close part of Pennsylvania's
Fairless Works, significantly eliminating area jobs while im-
porting British steel to be used in its stead, was also problem-
atic. An uproar across the country blocked this action with
accusations that U.S. Steel should change its name to "Foreign Steel, Inc." The steelworkers union claimed that, after
trading concessions for promises of jobs, they were subse-
quently "betrayed" by the deal with Britain. In Congress, the
action was attacked as un-American and a threat to national
security.

Labor costs at U.S. Steel have been cut drastically in the
last several years. Employment reductions of 44,000 workers,
coupled with 9 percent wage concessions, have led to annual

savings of $1.5 billion or 30 percent of total labor costs. In addition, production costs at U.S. Steel have been cut by $45 per ton, almost a 9 percent return of production dollars to the company.

These new investment strategies by the "new breed" of executives at U.S. Steel are considerably different from the corporation's historic pattern. Roderick took the helm of the company in 1979. His predecessors had moved up through the organization's steel operations, but Roderick's previous career had been in finance and portfolio management. Clearly enough, his basic impulse was to invest dollars to maximize returns. As he declared, "U.S. Steel will invest [its] cash flow where it can make money. If that leads to further diversification, so be it."[7]

Thus, U.S. Steel's investments today are a mixed lot. Some are related to its steel business, such as owning five railroads, ocean shipping lines, coal companies, and so on. Non-steel acquisitions are a bit strange—housing construction, cement, plastics and petrochemical industries, the purchase of the nation's second-largest shopping mall, and a hotel at Disney World. The corporation now has less than 25 percent of its assets in the steel business, with over two dozen subsidiaries. The trend toward portfolio management will continue.

> The Corporation seeks to allocate its capital resources selectively to the businesses that best provide opportunities. More than half of the capital budget is currently directed to oil and gas segment projects.[8]

SHIFTING TRADE POLICIES

Another critical aspect of the market situation in the United States is the trade problem with foreign countries. Over the past two decades, imports have made dramatic inroads into the unprotected domestic steel markets.

In the 1950s, imported steel took only 2.3 percent of the U.S. market. In the 1960s the import market share rose to 9.3

percent and in the 1970s to 15.3 percent. By 1984, a record high 26 percent of the U.S. steel market was taken by imports.[9] In the Western states, that figure has been reported to be as high as 50 percent of the market. The American steel industry attributes this high level of market penetration to unfair trade practices such as "aggressive, government-subsidized, mercantilist marketing tactics" which have allegedly been adopted by Japan, the European countries, and, more recently, by the more advanced Third World countries.

One of the tactics foreign producers have been accused of is "dumping," defined as selling a product in a foreign market at a price lower than the price that same product sells for in its home or other export markets. Dumping also refers to selling a product abroad at a price lower than the average cost of production for that product.

As a result of subsidies just for the years 1979–1981, the domestic shipments of American steel firms dropped by 6.5 million tons and gross revenue losses totaled $3.2 billion.[10] William T. Hogan concluded in his book *Steel in the United States* that about 50 percent of the world's total steel production now derives from subsidized or government-owned industry.

Many analysts have called for fair trade legislation in Congress to mitigate the devastating impacts of foreign steel penetration. Instead of tariffs or quotas, however, the Reagan administration has tried to coax foreign steelmakers into voluntary restrictions. These VRAs (Voluntary Restraint Agreements) were initially posed by the White House to not exceed 20.3 percent in imported steel, yet actual implementation has resulted in quotas of 24.5 percent, an additional 4 million tons of steel lost to American producers.

Although the damage done by foreign trade practices to U.S. domestic steel is still considerable, a very real question exists concerning whether or not any trade policy or quota can be effectively established that foreign companies, with help from their governments, cannot find a way around. Regulation cannot succeed without enforcement, but enforcement can only go so far within the limits of current regulatory capabilities. This is particularly so with respect to "voluntary" restrictions now articulated in Washington.

Beyond the difficulty of enforcement are the much more complex and abstract geo-political problems that could result if trade restrictions are too successful. Given the sometimes fragile situations foreign economies are in, if U.S. success comes as a result of policies that reverse the trade disadvantage unfairly, foreign countries will experience increased debt and higher prices for raw materials. In addition, the failure of many of their systems to keep unemployment under control, coupled with a lack of social welfare services, could result in large-scale bankruptcies and social unrest—and the United States would be seen as the culprit.

LABOR ISSUES

After World War II the United Steel Workers of America negotiated pattern-setting agreements with U.S. Steel which were then extended to other major steel manufacturers. Wage rates rose rapidly during the early 1950s, but they slowed during the 1960s due to lack of demand for steel. From 1957 to 1967 wage rates rose about the same as those in other manufacturing industries. But the 1968 contract settlement began a trend which boosted wage rates in the steel industry to 38 percent above other manufacturing industry averages. Between 1973 and 1979, wages in steel mills rose 119 percent compared to a 63 percent rise in the consumer price index. In the early 1970s, a new collective bargaining approach was agreed to by the major steel companies and the USWA. This is referred to as the Experimental Negotiating Agreement (ENA). One result of ENA has been a 71 percent increase in steel wages over national averages as of 1980.

By accepting the ENA, the USWA agreed to give up the right to go on strike in return for a one-time $150 bonus per worker, a 3 percent annual wage increase minimum, and a Cost of Living Agreement based on a percentage of the annual inflation rate. The managerial reasoning behind the ENA has to do with strikes and encroachments made by foreign steel-makers. The ENA was seen as a way to smooth out the demand and minimize layoffs, as well as a way to stop the encroachment of foreign steel in the U.S. market.

But by the time the ENA was put in place, the encroachments being made by foreign producers were built on lower production costs rather than inroads due to labor unrest. This enabled them to compete successfully with U.S. manufacturers—strikes or no strikes. Thus, the faith placed in the ENA appears to have been misguided. It locked the steel industry into escalating wage levels at a time when the wage averages in other U.S. industries were coming into line with those in other countries.

What analysts do not agree on is how significant labor costs are as a production cost factor. From a long-term perspective, the trend seems to be that low labor productivity and inefficient management of limited capital are far more important factors than are wage levels. Yet from a short-term perspective, wage levels, especially under the ENA, are significant. In fact, they are significant enough to make wage concessions and layoffs a widely practiced business move as steel companies try to make their operations more competitive.

Lower wage levels might help cut costs in steel plants enough to contribute to the short-term restoration of competitive productivity levels. But ultimately low labor productivity, primarily due to the lack of capital investment in modern equipment, is the major reason behind the lack of productivity growth and competitiveness in the integrated steel industry. Therefore, one long-term way in which labor costs can make a contribution to productivity growth is through increased capital investment in modern equipment. In light of this conclusion, the extent of short-term labor cost-cutting moves needs to be weighed against the impact that poor labor relations would have on long-term productivity improvement strategies requiring increased cooperation between labor and management.

MANAGING INTO OBLIVION

Changing external factors, such as slack demand and foreign intrusion into domestic markets, have been accompanied by internal changes in the corporate culture of Big Steel. The dominant managerial paradigm in the past, which was essentially defined as steel making, has given way to a new culture which emphasizes diversification, rationalization, and financial performance above all.

As noted earlier, signs of this historical shift include a move away from steel, the lack of capital improvements which would heighten the competitiveness of production, and a slow, sluggish managerial philosophy bent primarily on maintaining control of the domestic steel oligopoly. In contrast to a legacy of progressive labor relations based on mutual self-interest, recent trends have been overtly anti-union. Instead of the traditional emphasis on new technology and plowing of earnings back into the business, most of today's large steel firms reveal a pattern in which historical success has bred stagnation.

U.S. Steel is itself the prototype case. Our study is consistent with the analysis of Lawrence and Dyer,[11] who suggest that over the years the company failed to maintain the optimal level of information complexity. While the environment changed and new problems arose, corporate executives tended to manage by default from the distant corporate suites of Pittsburgh. We also agree with Hayes and Abernathy that top officials in the industry focused on the bottom line and ignored the need for R&D and communication with the shop floor. In their words, the recent managerial trend has become

> analytic detachment rather than the insight that comes from "hands-on" experience and . . . short-term cost reduction rather than the long-term development of technological competitiveness. It is this new managerial gospel . . . that has played a major role in undermining the vigor of American industry.[12]

Officials at U.S. Steel have been seduced by fifty years of success. Lacking the insight to escape executive blindness, they defensively have closed the company off to their difficulties. They have virtually ignored relevant management theory of the past two decades about the need to create a positive motivational climate for employees, attempting instead to create a regime based on a fear of losing one's job and sheer intimidation. The result has been a growing adversarial relationship and worker alienation. The firm has utterly failed at attempts to create innovative marketing strategies. It has struggled uselessly against government EPA and OSHA regulations. Little wonder that a poll of 7,000 executives, financial analysts, and outside corporate directors pronounced U.S. Steel one of the "least admired" companies in the nation when it comes to innovation. Out of a list of the 250 major companies in America, it was ranked number 241, one of the ten worst, alongside the bankrupt asbestos Manville Corporation. Curiously, the study did not even classify the Pittsburgh company among the steel industry, but instead listed it as a petroleum refining company. Even at that, it ranked last on all attributes within that group of ten big companies.[13]

PLANT CLOSINGS AND LAYOFFS

The deepening crisis has affected not only the blast furnace and the boardroom of the steel industry. As in the case of Jamestown, the communities and regional economies are affected as well.

External forces and organizational mismanagement in Big Steel have combined to wreak havoc on local communities, creating severe problems of economic dislocation. The Mahoning Valley houses two important Ohio cities, Youngstown and Warren. The area was once the second-largest steel producer in the country, until a series of mill closings decimated the region.[14] In 1977, Youngstown Sheet and Tube decided to close its Campbell Works and terminate nearly 5,000 jobs. Next, the Brier Hill Works shut its gates in 1979, throwing

1,200 workers into the streets. U.S. Steel's McDonald and Ohio works cut another 3,500 jobs out of the community in 1979–1980. Republic Steel closed its one remaining blast furnace and wiped out approximately a thousand jobs. A *Wall Street Journal* reporter describes how ". . . conditions have run the gamut from bad to desperate . . . not many people in this area believe life is going to get better. Hope seems to be dying . . ."[15]

Back on a single day in late 1979, U.S. Steel announced that it was closing the gates of sixteen operations around the country and eliminating 13,000 jobs. Colt Industries closed Midland, Pennsylvania's Crucible specialty steel plant, in 1982, laying off 5,000 workers. Braddock, Pennsylvania, once the home of U.S. Steel's thriving Edgar Thompson Works, which covered 140 acres and employed 4,400, has seen its civic population dwindle from 22,000 to 6,000. Towns like Ambridge, Pennsylvania, and Cuyahoga, Ohio, have lost their backbone of steel mills and are disintegrating. A nine-year analysis of layoffs in Ohio's steel valley reveals the elimination of 41,500 jobs in that region alone. Lost wages for the 1982 year were calculated to be nearly a billion dollars, suggesting the decade's losses could be in the range of $6–7 billion.[16]

It goes without saying that the labor movement has been hard hit by steel closings. Major steel shutdowns from Bethlehem's Lackawanna, New York, facility to Armco's plate steel mill in Houston have wreaked havoc with local unions. In 1983 in Alabama alone there were 14,635 steelworkers unemployed. USWA president, Lynn Williams, recently testified in Congress that over 600 steelworker local unions were dissolved in only twelve months due to plant closings.[17]

From a high of 571,000 jobs in steel production and maintenance in 1953, employment dropped by 1979 to 342,000. By 1983 the average number of steelworkers was 169,000.[18] Perhaps half of all laid-off steelworkers will never be recalled, even if there is an economic upswing in steel.

In recent months, the shutdown situation has taken an even more severe turn for the worse. The traumatic layoffs of the early 1980s were surpassed in December, 1983, when U.S. Steel announced that, beginning in early 1984, it would shut down six more steel plants completely and reduce operations at twenty-four other facilities, cutting 15,400 jobs in thirteen states. During the past several years, Continental Steel, McLouth, and Wheeling-Pittsburgh have all declared Chapter 11 bankruptcy.

Societal Costs of Shutting Down

The costs of most closings are enormous. Many job losses occur without notice, obliterating the financial lifelines to working families. At a personal level, the impact can be severe. Research reveals that obtaining another job is difficult, and lost wages may never be recouped. One study reports that on the average it takes over twelve months for plant closure victims to secure a new job. In the case of steel closures, two years after a shutdown workers are employed at only 54 percent of their former pay.[19] Many laid-off workers lose their sense of dignity and become demotivated and hopeless. A study by the U.S. Department of Labor suggests that 45 percent of all unemployed workers "eventually withdraw from the labor force."[20]

The costs of plant shutdowns at the macro level of the community and larger society are burdensome, too. It is estimated that at least one-third of the country's unemployment insurance costs of $30 billion a year is required to assist dislocated workers whose jobs have simply disappeared.[21]

Joseph Pershy, an economist at the University of Illinois, has calculated that in that state some 20,000 steelworkers' jobs have been lost since 1979. For every ten jobs in steel not replaced with another basic industry job within five years, an additional seventeen jobs are lost. The prediction was that up to another 34,000 jobs could be eroded as a direct consequence of steel layoffs.

Communities also lose a significant portion of their tax revenues when large firms close. The Ohio River town of Midland, Pennsylvania, used to benefit $750,000 a year in wage taxes from workers at Colt Industries, 80 percent of the town's total budget.

When Colt abandoned its steel operations in 1982, the town's schools and municipal services, such as water, fire protection, and electrical utilities were all drastically impaired. The ripple effect of plant closings washes away other businesses which are dependent on the closed facility. Consumer spending decreases, depressing retail and service industries. Household budgets are reduced and family work roles may shift, causing tensions at home.[22]

The social impact on communities often is borne out in a higher incidence of alcoholism and drug addiction, marital problems, child abuse, crime, divorce, psychological depression, and declining physical health. With respect to the latter, a Johns Hopkins University study using demographic data reveals the pathos associated with a 1 percent rise in national unemployment:

36,887 total deaths
20,240 deaths from cardiovascular diseases
495 deaths from cirrhosis of the liver
920 suicides
648 homicides
4,227 admissions to state mental hospitals
3,340 admissions to state prisons[23]

The economic costs of shutdowns to county, state, and federal government, and thereby the public, are also formidable. A study reported at Congressional hearings on the financial impact of closing the Campbell Steel operations in Youngstown estimated that in the first three years the county would lose $7.8 million in taxes, the state $8 million, and the federal government $15.1 million. Lost wages were predicted to range between $87 and $134 million. Unemployment insurance, trade readjustment assistance, food stamps, and other welfare programs were estimated to cost local and federal governments $33 to $36 million. The combination of lost taxes, lost wages, and required government support makes even one sizable mill shutdown an astronomical expenditure.[24]

The Youngstown experience so far suggests genuine tragedies from plant closings. The number of people seeking help at community crisis centers has doubled, suicide attempts rose 70 percent, child abuse has increased 35 percent, and welfare recipients now exceed one in every six residents.

AFTERWORD

It is now quite clear that whole industries can be damaged by the type of managerial professionalism that is characterized by textbook decisions, short-sighted vision, and questionable practices. In the case of steel, evidence is mounting that American executives are beginning to abandon the industry altogether. Recently U.S. Steel announced its plans to scuttle its Geneva works operation in Utah in order to form a joint venture with Pohang Steel of South Korea. On the social side of the ledger, this action means the closure of a mill which once employed 5,000 steelworkers. The ripple effect is estimated to include thousands of other workers, dozens of small businesses, and a total loss of $560 million annually to Utah's economy as a whole.

Widely dispersed ownership in an industry creates a vacuum of accountability, leaving distant shareholders out of touch with the business and unable to have anything but an abstract feeling for products made. Apparently most owners of steel stock feel that profits, not steel itself, are the major objectives. Or, dispersed as they are, these shareholders simply have no real power to influence corporate interests, giving management full rein in making its own policy. The consequence is, we are now witnessing the de-steeling of the American economy. Perhaps the whole industry will eventually be owned and financed by foreign companies, since they are the only ones willing to put capital into new steel-making technology. Such a shift would raise obvious and profound questions about our foreign policy and national security. Can we retain a strong military defense without control over steel production? We also ask: What are the limitations of an economy if the backbone of steel no longer exists? Can we really survive with an economy based on service? Or, to put it another way, can we afford the apparent economic and human costs of the shift to professional management?

CHAPTER 4 ENDNOTES

1. William T. Hogan. *Steel in the United States: Restructuring to Compete* (Lexington, Mass.: Lexington Books, 1983).

2. James H. Bridge. *Inside History of the Carnegie Steel Corporation* (New York: Aldine, 1903).

3. David Brody. *The Steel Workers in America: The Non-Union Era* (Cambridge, Mass.: Harvard University Press, 1960); Dan Clawson. *Bureaucracy and the Labor Process* (New York: Monthly Review Press, 1980); David Montgomery. "Workers' Control of Machine Production in the Nineteenth Century." *Labor History*, vol. 17, no. 4, Fall 1976, pp. 485–509; Frederick W. Taylor. *The Principles of Scientific Management* (New York: Harper and Brothers, 1947).

4. Edmund Faltermayer. "How Made-in-America Steel Can Survive." *Fortune*, February 13, 1987, pp. 122–130.

5. Leslie Wayne. "U.S. Steel's Corporate Role." *The New York Times*, December 2, 1981, pp. D-1, D-6.

6. Winston Williams. "Hard Choices Face Industry as it Declines." *The New York Times*, November 22, 1981, pp. D-1, D-6.

7. "The New LTV Steel: How Republic Will Fit In." *Business Week*, April 16, 1984, pp. 129–133.

8. United States Steel Corporation, *1982 10-K Report*.

9. Kent Jones. *Politics vs. Economics in World Steel Trade* (London: Allen & Unwin), 1986.

10. *Steel Comments*, November 15, 1982.

11. Paul R. Lawrence and Davis Dyer. *Renewing American Industry: Organizing for Efficiency and Innovation* (New York: The Free Press, 1983).

12. Robert H. Hayes and William J. Abernathy. "Managing Our Way to Economic Decline." *Harvard Business Review*, July-August 1980, pp. 66–77.

13. *Fortune*, July 9, 1984, pp. 50–62.

14. Peter McGrath. "Left Out." *Newsweek*, March 21, 1983, pp. 26–35.

15. James M. Perry. "Idle Mills." *The Wall Street Journal*, January 20, 1983, pp. 1, 14.

16. Ohio Bureau of Employment-Research and Statistics. *Employment Hours and Earnings in Ohio, 1973–1982.*

17. *AFL-CIO News*, March 10, 1984, p. 2.

18. American Iron and Steel Institute. *Annual Statistical Report,* 1983.

19. Plant Closures Project. *Undated mimeo report*, Oakland, California.

20. Sara Fritz. "The Human Tragedy of Unemployment." *U.S. News and World Report*, June 23, 1980, pp. 68–69.

21. Richard Corrigan and Rochelle L. Stanfield. "Casualties of Change." *National Journal*, February 11, 1984, pp. 252–264.

22. Louis A. Ferman. "After the Shutdown." *Industrial and Labor Relations Report*, vol. 18, November 2, 1981.

23. *U.S. News and World Report.* op. cit.

24. *Ninety-Sixth Congress: Plant Closings and Relocations.* Hearing before the Committee on Labor and Human Resources, U.S. Senate, Washington, D.C. 1979.

CHAPTER 5

The Professionalizing of American Industry

I n the three preceding chapters we examined the impact of absentee ownership and professional management upon a single firm, a community, and an entire industry. In this chapter we will summarize what we have learned from these and other cases we have studied. We will describe how this trend away from local ownership and entrepreneurial management control has affected the ability of American industries to compete in a global economy, and how it has literally transformed and laid waste many of America's industrial communities.

THE DISTANCING PROCESS

Before we analyze the effects of this complex historical and industrial shift, however, we want to further describe the characteristics and conditions that make up what we call an "absentee" form of ownership and a "professional" form of management. We developed some working definitions of these terms in Chapter 1 to give the reader a general idea of the issues we have been studying. We can define these terms more clearly now that we have seen them at work in a number of concrete situations.

At the heart of the historical developments we have described is, we believe, a "distancing" process that eventually separates a company's employees from its owners and managers, creating a growing sense of conflict and stress. This distancing process occurs along four principal dimensions.

Psychological Distance

Many things separate people from each other, and no two individuals have precisely the same motives, beliefs, needs and ways of reasoning. This "psychological distance" between any two people decreases as they interact with one another in a common setting. Through interaction, people grow more similar in their way of thinking, or at least gain a shared understanding and appreciation of their respective differences. Certainly this happens in a good marriage or a good partnership, and it can also happen between fellow employees of a company, especially one owned and managed at the local community level. When, however, a company is controlled by absentee owners and managed by professionals from distant corporate offices—who have no intention of settling in the community—a tremendous psychological distance arises between the company's employees and its owners and managers.

Absentee owners and professional managers have a very different frame of reference from their employees, and they seldom see the company and its problems as the employees see them. Moreover, the owners and managers usually have markedly different goals for the company. Mistrust, confusion, and conflict grow between owners, managers, and employees in proportion to these differences. But psychological distance is not an absolute genetic or biological condition. It is the consequence of profoundly different social experiences and technical expertise, compounded by the simple geographical distance that often separates employees from the corporate managers and owners.

Social Distance

Even in locally owned companies, the founding owner-managers usually become members of a social and economic elite in which their employees do not participate. As we saw in the Jamestown case, the conflict can become intense when a community's elite chooses to defend their own piece of the economic and social pie against their employees' growing demands for more. But in spite of the conflict that can result from class divisions, a mutual respect and a sense of interdependence tend to continue between employee and manager as long as a company remains locally owned and managed; for both sides realize they will lose their social and economic status within the community if the company fails.

Professional managers and absentee owners, by contrast, are rarely rooted in the communities where their plants or subsidiaries operate, and where their employees live. They lack ties to local cultural traditions and social relationships. Although the *employees* of an absentee-owned corporation have no doubt that they depend upon the company and its managers for their income, this viewpoint is rarely reciprocated. Once a company passes out of local control, the social and cultural bonds between managers and employees are severed. Employee values, beliefs, and roles remain tied to the local community, and defined by bonds of social and economic interdependence. The company's owners and managers, conversely, are tied to a national or even transnational corporate network, and bound by professional and financial interests. The original owner/managers may have lived and worked in a different social stratum of the local social structure; but absentee owners and professional managers are part of a totally different social world. They do not depend upon the respect of lower- and middle-level employees to maintain their positions of prestige and power within the company and the broader world of business and finance.

Technical Distance

Today's professional managers seldom have more than a general understanding or appreciation of the technical side of the businesses they manage; and shareholders or absentee owners usually have no understanding at all. This situation, complicating the effects of social distance, we call "technical distance." Local managers and employees have a "close-to-the-ground" understanding of the company. They have many years of experience with the products or services which have been the firm's mainstay, and they understand the details of production and distribution to the point that it is "second nature."

By contrast, professional managers usually rely on administrative and financial skills to propel them from position to position and company to company on their way up the corporate and intercorporate ladders. The stockholders who have purchased their shares as a financial investment seldom have either an interest in or a need to know the technical details of the companies they control. Professional managers rarely stay in one position long enough to develop any real technical understanding, even though for them such understanding may be critical to the company's profitability and survival. Given such limited firm-specific knowledge, absentee owners and professional managers tend to fall back upon cruder yardsticks to measure a company's value. Financial measures such as "earnings per share," "return on investment," and "stock price" become the exclusive tests of a company's value.

Geographical Distance

Absentee owners and professional managers are also often distant in the simplest possible sense from their employees and the communities in which they do business. Obviously enough, when a company is owned by a far-flung and diverse body of public stockholders, or by a small group of distant investors, such owners will have little understanding or appreciation for the problems, needs, and concerns of a branch plant or subsidiary located hundreds or thousands of miles away. But this geographical separation is not simply the result of a company being acquired by a parent corporation headquartered somewhere else. Today's professional managers can artificially create geographical distance by trying to cater to their own social interests and tastes.

For example, we studied a rubber hose manufacturing company, whose president, vice-presidents, and marketing staff attempted to run the business from offices in Palo Alto,

California, although its operations and the bulk of its small work force of approximately 150 employees were located in the tiny central Utah town of Nephi. The headquarters of the company's conglomerate parent was in New York City, while the majority of the company's customers were in the oil-producing areas of Texas or the industrial centers of the Midwest and Northeast. In other words, there was no business reason to select Palo Alto for their corporate headquarters. Management did so simply because the Bay Area better suited their preferences in lifestyle and climate than did central Utah. As a result, the company paid a heavy price in additional overhead, conflict with its employees, and misunderstanding with its customers.

Even in less extreme cases, managers often still create geographic distance between themselves and their employees. When professional managers find themselves assigned to a rural plant or subsidiary, they often choose to purchase a home in a nearby town or city more suited to their cosmopolitan tastes. Even if the distance from the manager's residence to the company's operation is a mere twenty to thirty miles, the message communicated to the employees is that both they and their community are "backward." Typical professional managers often further verify this perception with comments that stir up resentment and anger. One manager, for example, told us in an interview:

> The reason I drive a hundred miles roundtrip from home to work and back everyday is because I've got to be around some other intelligent and competent professionals or I'll go crazy. I mean these folks here think this place is heaven, the greatest city on earth, but their schools are way behind and their greatest cultural event is the high school play. Besides my wife absolutely refuses to live here. She said that she'd divorce me before she would waste away here with these country bumpkins. She grew up in Boston and living in this place is like being banished to Siberia. . . . If you talked to her I'm sure she'd tell you that in her opinion this place is really f__ked, and as soon as a promotion comes up you can bet your life we'll take it . . .

Attitudes like this are more the norm than the exception. When they combine with the values and orientation of professional managers, who have been trained and socialized in the MBA programs of this country, the potential for company deterioration and internal conflict is multiplied many times over.

THE ROLE OF THE PROFESSIONAL MANAGER

In our studies of the professional managers who direct the affairs of absentee-owned companies, we have found, as did Hayes and Abernathy,[1] that these managers tend to see their role and purpose to be "managing assets" rather than building profitable companies that increase their market share over time. Because of this "financial orientation" they focus their attention and energies on making short-term gains by managing their collection of companies as if they were a stock portfolio. They use debt to spur company growth through mergers and acquisitions, and they improve corporate performance in the short run by "stock buybacks" and the "restructuring of assets." For these new professional managers the "financial transaction" or the "deal" has become the mechanism for achieving professional success rather than managerial prowess and technical sophistication in the business. And it is not unusual for them to so burden a corporation with debt resulting from their insatiable appetite for capital to fund mergers, acquisitions, and stock buybacks that the company eventually collapses. But hopefully they will have made their mark and moved on to new corporations and new deals before this occurs. It is the companies, communities, and unemployed workers they leave abandoned in their wake that suffer from this "new style" of management, not the professional managers themselves.

This perspective has its origins in the professional training that these men and women receive—often in the MBA programs of the leading business schools of this nation, where they develop a career orientation which emphasizes finance and short-term results. They see themselves as highly mobile professionals, as "deal makers" who are also capable of managing any company in any industry because of their general management expertise. Therefore they tend to feel little if any long-term attachment to their current employer. In fact, it is typical of today's professional manager to look upon his or her present position as nothing more than a stepping stone to greater rewards and opportunities at another organization. This orientation consequently encourages the professional manager to try and look good in the short run through financial manipulations that boost today's stock price rather than through carefully thought out change and effort aimed at yielding sustained profits and sales growth over a time horizon of five to ten years. Thinking further ahead than this could anger the firm's absentee owners, who are concerned only with the present value of their shares, and thereby result in derailing the professional manager's "fast-track" career.

Thus, modern professional management is characterized by sophisticated financial and administrative skills, a value orientation almost exclusively devoted to the promotion of self-interest, and a focus on getting quick results and immediate rewards. It is this combination that can prove so deadly to the long-term success and viability of industry.

BEFORE THE SHIFT: THE "VALUE-DRIVEN FIRM"

Our studies of many organizations in a variety of industries have shown that the ownership structure and management strategies which characterize the absentee-owned and professionally managed business are very different from those that are common when a company is first organized and during the years that it remains a locally owned organization. Like the Brown Corporation, many organizations are founded by a single entrepreneur or a small group of entrepreneurs who begin with a very specific "dream" or "vision" of what the new company should be like and the values it should represent to its employees, customers, and the local community.

Tied closely to this vision are a body of technical skills and values which the founder has gained through many years of work and experience. Always the founder considers these skills to be central to the company's ultimate success. Financing is not unimportant, but it is really the founding entrepreneur's or entrepreneurial group's "vision" for the company, steeped in a concrete set of technical and social values and skills, that provides the driving force behind the firm's progress. The following description, provided by M.I.T. social scientist Ed Schein, of one company and entrepreneur which he studied, helps to graphically illustrate this point:

> Founder A, who built a large chain of supermarkets and department stores, was the dominant ideological force in the company until he died in his seventies. He assumed that his organization could be dominant in the market and that his primary mission was to supply his customers with a quality, reliable product. When A was operating only a corner store with his wife, he built customer relations through a credit policy that displayed trust in the customer, and he always took products back if the customer was not satisfied. Further, he assumed that stores had to be attractive and spotless, and that the only way to ensure this was by close personal supervision. He would frequently show up at all his stores to check into small details. Since he assumed that only close supervision would teach subordinates the right skills, he expected all his store managers to be very visible and very much on top of their jobs.
>
> A's theory about how to grow and win against his competition was to be innovative, so he encouraged his managers to try new approaches, to bring in consulting help, to engage in extensive training, and to feel free to experiment with new technologies. His view of truth and reality was to find it wherever one could and, therefore, to be open to one's environment and never take it for granted that one had all the answers. If new things worked, A encouraged their adoption.

Measuring results and fixing problems was, for A, an intensely personal matter. In addition to using traditional business measures, he went to the stores and, if he saw things not to his liking, immediately insisted that they be corrected. He trusted managers who operated on the basis of similar kinds of assumptions and clearly had favorites to whom he delegated more.[2]

Similar to the entrepreneur and his company described above, most companies take on, very literally, the character of the founder or the founding group. The firm is the founder's "baby" and its culture an extension of his or her personality, values, and beliefs. It is because of this relationship that a company during its early growth years can especially be called "value driven." The founder's values and beliefs become the firm's core values and beliefs—an ideology adopted by employees who in effect become the entrepreneur's "adopted children." Many company founders assume a paternalistic role and "take care" of their employees in return for their loyalty and obedience. Employees at companies like Levi Strauss, Digital Equipment Company, and Hewlett-Packard tell stories of how these firms' founders would extend help and support to them during periods of personal crisis and trouble.

In companies such as these, the founding entrepreneur managed to institutionalize his or her own values within the context of the corporate culture. This merging of values and beliefs holds the company together and enables employees to work cooperatively, frequently with extreme dedication, for both their own and the company's benefit. However, once the combined powers of the founder's business acumen and ideology leave the company, the effect can be devastating. This double loss usually figures strongly in the deterioration of a company that has become absentee owned.

Indeed, absentee ownership is frequently the precursor of the disintegration of both a corporation's ideology and its technical competence. Both are essential to the continuing vitality of a company, and the loss of either or both leaves the company adrift, a ship without its rudder. When this occurs, employees may even try to rescue the firm by keeping it alive in what they believe to be the founder's image. What happened at Disney studios after the death of its founder Walt Disney provides a graphic example of this phenomenon. As *Newsweek* magazine described it:

> For the past few years, Disney has been running more like a Mickey Mouse watch with a rusty mainspring—repairing it will take some powerful doing. Such box office dogs as *Tron* and last year's disastrous *Something Wicked This Way Comes* have cost the company a staggering $75 million. Attendance has been disappointing at the theme parks, and the flagship, California's Disneyland, was hit by a strike of 1,800 workers last week . . .
>
> Disney's basic problem is that it has never adjusted to the death of founder Walt Disney back in 1966. When Walt was alive, says animator Don Bluth, who led a walkout of other animators five years ago, "it was like a benevolent dictatorship. The moment the benevolent dictator is taken away, it's a pack of wolves." "Often," says one former executive, "if there were projects under discussion, people would say, "Walt wouldn't do that." As movie analyst Dennis Forst of Bateman Eichler puts it, "Walt was a real genius. He was running the company 15 years after his death."
>
> . . . That kind of management led to some rather bizarre occurrences on the Disney lot. At one point, conservative, old-line employees held a prayer meeting to protest a decision to make the PG-rated movie "Splash". . .[3]

Sociologists often use the term "anomie" to characterize conditions such as these: a situation of "normlessness" or social chaos. As at Disney, a situation in which chaos combines with rigid adherence to the founding ideology, without any rationally developed business strategy, is a common result of the shift to absentee ownership and professional management.

THE FORMS OF ABSENTEE OWNERSHIP

Table 5 lists some of the different forms of absentee ownership, arranged by the degree of distancing between owner and employee. As this table illustrates, a company need not even be shifted to the hands of investors outside the initial founding family or group to become, in effect, absentee owned.

The Disinterested or Incompetent Heir

After the death or retirement of the founding entrepreneur, a company sometimes begins to develop the kind of problems we have looked at throughout this book. For the founder's heirs or successors often have not gone to that "school of hard knocks" which shaped the founder's vision and established his or her tenacity against all odds. The founders themselves, after achieving their own financial success, usually do not even expect their children to go through the same hardships as they did. Their acquired wealth provides their offspring with the opportunity to gain education and cultural opportunities at top schools in major metropolitan areas. Consequently, the heir may not know the business nearly as well as the founder; and, when the heir assumes the mantle of leadership, it is likely that he or she will lack the technical ability required to fill the founder's shoes. For obvious reasons, this situation often leads to the introduction of professional management to fill the roles which the heir proves incapable of filling. The heir may even turn over the management of the firm to such an extent that no presence at all is felt in the daily affairs of the company. Warner and Low's *The Social System of the Modern Factory* describes such a situation in one community's major shoe manufacturing company, which had recently been turned over to the founder's son:

> Cabot Pierce . . . seemed to take no very active part in the management of the shoe business. "Cabot Pierce is all

Table 5. Types of Absentee Ownership

	DYNAMICS OF INVOLVEMENT
Heir to founder	Founder dies or retires and the firm is taken over by disinterested heir.
Parent corporation	Company is sold to another corporation or investor group for the purpose of recovering initial investment and accrued value.
Public shareholder	Capital needs for expansion exceed the firm's capacity to generate capital through its own cash flow, so the company seeks external investment. Founding group seeks to get out of business and recover invested capital and accrued value.
Venture capital	Investment capital beyond that of founding entrepreneur(s) is provided by a venture capital investor in a start-up or expansion situation.

continued on next page

right but hasn't any say," said a shoe worker. "Cabot Pierce has no brains. He has been to about six schools, but he didn't learn anything. His father took him in, but he couldn't seem to amount to much. He used to take the men away from their work to play cards with them. When his father discovered it he scolded the men and didn't say anything to Cabot. . . . I think he won't last very long on this job."[4]

Because of Cabot Pierce's inability to manage the affairs of his father's company, he was eventually completely di-

Table 5. Types of Absentee Ownership (cont.)

Institutional investor	The trust department of a major financial institution uses pension or mutual funds to purchase substantial blocks of stock or bonds on the public market or as a venture capital investment.
Corporate raider	Through bank loans and the sale of high-risk/high-return bonds ("junk bonds"), a trader/raider purchases large blocks of a stock to reap gains either through forcing a buyback or by taking over and restructuring undervalued assets.
Risk arbitrageur	Trader who piggybacks on takeover bids with the hope of reaping huge gains along with the raider.

vorced from the operation of the firm. This situation is not uncommon. Similar problems plagued Disney enterprises and eventually seem to fall upon all companies. If not in the second then during the third generation of family owners. Indeed, many founders, when faced with the prospect of trying to pass the company on to their children, simply feel there is no other choice than to place the firm in the hands of outside professionals. The executive secretary to the heir apparent of a food and brewing company in the Detroit area graphically described this situation in the following interview:

> Herb just never measured up to his father. He graduated from the University of Michigan with honors, but he studied philosophy. He really didn't know anything about the

business or even business in general when his father brought him on. He was impractical, arrogant, and listened to no one. He made lots of mistakes and didn't seem to learn from any of them. His father finally realized this, and he started sending him out of town whenever there were any big problems or important decisions to be made. The family had a lot of money, and Herb had gotten in to big game hunting. The walls of his office were covered with the heads of all kinds of animals. So anyway his Dad would just send him off to Alaska or British Columbia to go big game hunting whenever anything important came along. That way he wasn't around to screw things up.

Situations like this are common, and when they occur the firm begins to become, in effect, absentee owned. An heir need not have poor judgment or a weak character to precipitate the shift to absentee ownership and its attendant problems. Simply the process of acquiring an education and becoming socialized outside the confines of the firm and the local community can lead to similar difficulties. An heir or heirs who have been educated at major universities, who have developed social ties and acquired cultural tastes different from their parents, can also produce the conditions of absentee ownership. Frequently, after having undergone such a socialization experience, the heirs simply have no desire to pursue the business interests of their father or mother. The owner and founder of a garment manufacturing concern in southeast Massachusetts explained this situation in the following manner:

My children are just not interested in the family business. I've spent my life eating, sleeping, and breathing the apparel business. What can I say, it's my life, but it isn't my children's life. They have no interest in building up this company or in spending their life in these dirty, stuffy shops. My son went to an ivy league school and so did my daughter. I never even went to college. My son he's a lawyer now and my daughter married a doctor. They like to spend their time doing other things—sail boat racing on the Cape, going to the Bahamas and Europe. They like the cultural and social amenities of the big city, and they like their leisure. I never had time for leisure. My whole life has been work, work, work, and I've loved it. But since my kids don't feel the same as I do I'm going to have to find a buyer for this company or get someone to manage it for the family.

Even if a founder's children do not force the introduction of professional management, thereby becoming absentee owners themselves, or the sale of the company to outsiders, they can, even if they choose to run the business themselves, transform it into an organization which suffers from the problems of absentee ownership and professional management. The benefits which a founder's children reap from the family's wealth result, ironically, in less attachment to the firm, less concern for its employees, and less interest in the impact of their business decisions upon their prestige and stature within the community. In other words, the transition to a new generation after the founder can also produce a distance between the company's owners and its employees and the community. To such heirs the company becomes primarily a financial resource which supports their lifestyle, and provides capital for pursuing other business interests. A senior manager at a firm in Jamestown, New York, which had once been one of the chief manufacturers of elevators in the eastern United States, describes this situation:

> When the son owned this company, he used it as a "cash cow" for financing getting into other businesses. He really didn't understand the company, and he didn't have much interest in it until we started losing money. Over the years we made a lot of money for his family, and when he finally took over from his father he started using the cash flow from this business to build a mini-conglomerate. His current hot scheme is selling pre-fab housing to oil-rich Arab countries. He bought and sold several different companies. Some of them were successful and some weren't. Eventually, he took so much money out and put so little in that

we started to really suffer. We weren't replacing equipment or even repairing it properly, and he kind of let sales just take care of itself. We lived on our reputation. Labor problems got worse and worse, costs went sky high, and sales kept going down, down, down. We almost ended up in bankruptcy, but he got out just in time by selling the company to some top managers and local investors.

Thus, when an owner/manager's heirs lack the ability and expertise to manage the business, or simply do not share the founders' interest in and sense of responsibility toward the business, then the firm can suffer from the same distancing problems that occur when a company is acquired by another corporation or goes public. In the event that the founder or his or her heirs want to get out of the business, selling out to another corporation or going public are the usual options.

Selling Out to Outside Interests

Becoming absentee owned by selling a company to outside interests principally occurs in one of two ways. The owner can either sell the company to a group of investors or choose to sell the firm off to another corporation. If sold to an investor group with substantial experience in the same industry, the match can prove to be quite good, especially if the group is already in the community or chooses to join the community and manage the business themselves. In the case of the former elevator manufacturer described above, the new ownership proved to be far superior because the dominant investors were also managers who lived in the community and had many years of experience in the industry. In this instance, the new owners became a second founding group who rebuilt the badly deteriorated company. More often, however, an investor group lacks the technical expertise necessary to operate a company effectively in the long run; therefore the firm again becomes relegated to the status of a "cash cow," valued primarily as a source of short-term funding for other more lucrative investments. In one case we studied, the Wilson Stove Company (a disguised case), the owner sold his successful wood and coal burning stove manufacturing concern five times. Each time he sold it, the new management drove the firm to the brink of bankruptcy because of technical incompetence. Mr. Wilson, the founder, could not bear to see the business that he had built over a lifetime suddenly disappear, so he came to the company's rescue each time. We might fault Wilson for having poor judgment in selecting new owners, but, in fact, it can be extremely difficult to find new owners who understand the business and share the founder's commitment to the company and its employees.

The acquisition of one company by another can take basically three different forms. When a corporation buys another company with the idea of using it as either a supplier or a channel of distribution, it is known as *vertical integration.* In this case, the acquired company can count on being maintained as an integral part of the overall business, at least if it performs its function according to expectations. Nevertheless, vertical integration is not without the problems associated with absentee ownership. For the employees of the acquired company, the change from being an independent entity to a service unit for a parent corporation often feels like a relegation to "slave" status. Although the managers of the parent corporation know what they want from the purchased company, they still may not know how to manage and operate it effectively. Furthermore, since the acquired firm may change from being a "profit center" to being a "cost center" within the overall corporate structure, there may be pressure to reduce costs, including wages and capital investment.

When a company is acquired to complement the parent's dominant product lines and open up new markets, this is known as *horizontal integration.* In this case, the acquired company has the potential to play a central or even dominant role in the parent's business. Because the parent is already in the same industry, the acquired firm may also benefit from the commonality of technology and management. Nevertheless, these benefits can at times be deceiving; for there may in fact be substantial differences between a parent and a subsidiary occupying different market niches in the same industry. Direct application of the methods and techniques used by the parent may prove to be unacceptable at the acquired firm. A manager at a subsidiary of one of the world's largest manufacturers of metal office furniture described it this way:

> When we were acquired . . . they thought that they could come in and transform us into the same kind of operation they have . . . where their headquarters is located. I remember one of the engineers that they sent down here used to say, "We're going to change this place so we'll have desks and files popping out the back door just like popcorn, just like it is back home." What he and other people . . . failed to realize was that our business is different. We make what you call "A" grade furniture, and they make "C" and "B" grade furniture. You know the kind of stuff you buy at Sears. They're a big outfit, and they mass produce the furniture that they make. They make only a few styles and have only a few colors . . . An assembly line type of outfit, and they can afford to be because they sell millions, or at least thousands, of the same thing day in and day out.
>
> Our sales are a lot less . . . but we cater to a different segment of the market. People who buy furniture from us have to know that if they want a lavender filing cabinet they can get it or if they hand us a Navajo blanket to upholster their chairs we'll be willing to do it. We've got hundreds of different options for accommodating our customers, and we charge a high price for giving it to them. I guess our parent corporation thought that when they bought us we would make a nice complement to their low price-low end furniture, but when they thought they could organize us like them with the same controls and trying to put in assembly lines they were wrong. They created a lot of confusion around here, we ended up building inventories we shouldn't have built up and then selling a lot of furniture off as salvage because nobody wanted to buy the stuff we had in stock. They want their own special requirements.

Technological and organizational mismatching such as this played a key role in dragging down the subsidiary's profitability and increasing its costs. Then, in an effort to reduce costs, instead of adapting to the technical requirements of a new market, the parent sought to keep wage and salary increases at a minimum. As a result, the labor-management conflict, which had already developed due to chaotic production and shortages of parts, worsened dramatically. The result was a nine-week strike, the longest in the company's history.

Following either vertical or horizontal integration of two companies, the problems of social distance can also prove to be particularly acute. The acquired firm, because it plays a minor role in the overall business of the parent, can become a virtual training site for managers and professionals who will eventually assume corporate jobs and positions in the primary business. Such companies can become identified as places where young managers make their mark and then move on to "bigger and better things." Such a situation particularly exacerbates the problem of social distance and also encourages managers to "ride roughshod" on the local troops in an effort to establish themselves in the corporation. In the case cited above, it was not uncommon for managers to enter and leave the firm for other corporate locations on a monthly basis; and in a small rural Pennsylvania community, known for its stability and traditional ways, this did not settle well. And when the firm suffered serious financial problems a new top manager was sent in to "shape the place up or get rid of it." In order to feel comfortable about whipping the subsidiary into shape, the new leader chose to buy a home many miles away from the community where he did not have to interact with laid-off workers and the managers he had purged from the system.

The third basic form of acquisition consists of the simple purchase of a smaller company by a conglomerate. This is typically a worse fate for a company than being purchased by a competitor, a supplier, or another firm in the same industry. Conglomerates represent the prototypical example of absentee ownership and professional management. They acquire new companies primarily as investments, and the financial return supplied by an acquired company is its only measure of value and success. In the same way, the management strategies of conglomerates involve primarily the manipulation of assets. When an acquired firm fails to meet the corporate requirements for return on investment, it is often quickly liquidated. The goal of a conglomerate manager is not to build companies or gain market position in an industry, but rather to shift and deploy assets to maximize the return on investment in the immediate future. For example, when the Herkimer Library Bureau in upstate New York, a manufacturer of library furniture which was founded by the inventor of the Dewey Decimal System, failed to produce the 22 percent return expected by Sperry Rand, its conglomerate owner, the parent, was ready to put it on the chopping block. Although the company was not "unprofitable," it was just "not profitable enough."

Obviously, when a firm is acquired by a conglomerate, the degree of distance between the parent and it is tremendous, and such distance contributes to a high rate of failure in terms of effective integration of the acquisition. Michael Porter recently found, for example, in a study of diversification strategies at 33 major firms, during the years between 1950 and 1986, that some 74 percent of all acquisitions made by these companies into totally new and unrelated fields were later divested or shut down. The picture was better, but not glowing, for other acquisitions. Porter found that approximately 50 percent of all acquisitions made by such giants as ITT, W.R. Grace, Xerox, General Foods, Exxon, and so forth, into new but related industries were also divested, and 60 percent of those made into entirely new fields were eventually divested or closed.[5]

Going Public

Public ownership is really the precursor of all the subsequent categories of absentee ownership (except venture capital, though even this form of ownership can include institutional investors). Going public opens a Pandora's box of the kind of problems we have been discussing. Companies go public when the founder or the founder's heirs want to get out of the business or when rapid growth has resulted in a need for capital to fund expansion. On the one hand, a founder may choose to go public to get his or her "sweat equity" out of the company and cash out the increase in the company's value that has accrued over the years. On the other hand, some companies grow so rapidly that their capital requirements far surpass the limits of their internal cash flows. When this happens, taking the company public often appears to be the only way to maintain competitiveness. Whatever the reason, when a firm goes public the ownership changes hands, from a founder who has been deeply involved in and committed to the business to a group of outsiders who have different values and no attachment whatsoever to the company. For the public stockholders, their share of the corporation is an economic investment in the strictest sense of the word. The company is an asset to be managed, and if it fails to produce the return expected through dividends, rising stock prices, and stock splits, then for the public shareholder the decision is clear that another investment should be exploited.

The publicly traded firm is the bastion of the professional manager, and as a firm's stockholders become larger and more diffuse, the pressure on these managers to rely on financial manipulation to produce short-term gains becomes immense. In the case of Levi Strauss, for example, the company experienced a major financial crisis shortly after the Haas family took the firm public. Feeling pressure from stockholders, the board of directors brought in Robert Grohman, who had been a high-ranking officer at Playtex and B.V.D. and Company, to turn the company around. Immediately a number of managers were fired, and Grohman took steps to put the company on strict financial controls. Some company old-timers felt that this new management style was like a "heart transplant." The company no longer had the "feel" of being a family. While the financial performance of the firm did improve, some of the basic Levi Strauss values were challenged by this new management style, which was supported by the public shareholders. Recently, however, the Haas family took the company private again, which may be a sign that the family is attempting to eliminate the pressures of outside investors and return the firm to some of its original ideals.

Venture Capital

Our fourth category of absentee owner is a relatively new form which has achieved its greatest popularity and prominence during the past ten to fifteen years. Venture capital, unlike the other forms of absentee ownership discussed so far, can be involved from the time a company is first formed. When an entrepreneur or inventor seeks to develop a new business or expand an existing firm, but lacks sufficient capital or the collateral necessary for securing bank financing, the venture capitalist can be an invaluable partner. Venture capital has been a critical resource for what have become some of the biggest names in high technology. Until recently, there have been few problems between venture capitalists and the entrepreneurs with whom they developed partnerships. One of the first U.S. venture capitalists, General Georges F. Doriot, exemplified the ideal venture capital partner in the early days of this unique branch of investment activity. Doriot was a retired brigadier general from the United States Army and a distinguished professor at Harvard Business School. In 1946, Doriot founded American Research and Development Corp. (ARD), one of the first venture capital companies:

> Backed by Yankee financiers, Doriot began scouring the depressed New England countryside, looking for business and technological talent. One of the high points of that search came in 1957, when he was contacted by a young engineer and entrepreneur named Kenneth Olsen, who had an idea for something called an "interactive computer." By that, he meant a computer with which a user could communicate directly via a keyboard or terminal, rather than punchcards. . . . Olsen wanted to start a company to develop and produce the device.
>
> On the face of it, his prospects seemed bleak. He had no prior business experience, and nobody but IBM Corp. was

making money on computers anyway. But Doriot saw the opportunity and persuaded ARD's board to invest $70,000 in Olsen's fledgling company, which became Digital Equipment Corp. (DEC). Headquarters were set up in an old woolen mill in Maynard, MA . . . on the second floor, with a narrow stairway and no elevator. Such was Doriot's style. He believed that with too much money, a company's founder might "start buying Cadillacs, 50-room mansions, go skiing in summer and swimming in winter . . ."

Over the next fourteen years, Doriot worked to help build the company. He stayed in close touch with Olsen, advising him on a wide variety of matters, always pushing him to focus on long-term development. Doriot even became upset the year that DEC reported a profit because he feared the company was not spending enough on research and development. In the end, however, everyone profited. By 1971, ARD's initial investment of $70,000 was worth an estimated $350 million.[6]

Such a long-term relationship with an entrepreneur was not unusual for Doriot or other early venture capitalists. Doriot and ARD worked many years with numerous companies including Ionics, the water treatment company; Cordis, the manufacturer of pacemakers; Teradyne, an electronic testing equipment maker; and the pharmaceutical company, Cooper Laboratories. The typical average annual return on such ventures was around 15 percent, but Doriot and venture capitalists like him claimed that this was only a side benefit and not their central goal. Doriot once said, "I don't consider a speculator—in my definition of the word—constructive. . . . I am building men and companies."[7]

Doriot's venture capital philosophy has in recent years given way to something he had considered an impediment to enterprise—speculation. Impressed with successes such as Digital Equipment, Federal Express, and Apple Computer, a variety of different investment groups have entered the venture capital field with new values and very different goals. Large-scale financial institutions, pension funds, investment banks, and insurance companies have been lured by annual returns that have reached levels as high as 40 to 60 percent. Consequently, the pool of available venture capital in the United States grew from only $39 million in 1977 to $4.1 billion by 1983.[8] The availability of such a large pool of capital has tempted many high tech entrepreneurs to establish partnerships which they later regretted. In contrast to tough-minded venture capitalists like Doriot, committed to long-term results, the new breed seek to pump huge amounts of money into new firms with the hope of precipitating an early public offering and large returns. Central to this perspective is the MBA outlook that sees business management as the manipulation of assets. Wayne Erickson, one of the founders of a now successful software firm, Microrim, describes what he encountered when trying to get started:

> Just because they had MBA's from Stanford or Harvard, they thought they knew everything about everything. . . . Their approach was pretty much antagonistic. "Why don't you do that?" they would say. They wanted us to redo everything we had done, and most of them didn't know anything about writing software. I felt I had been nursing this baby and they were telling me that they didn't like the way the baby looked. But the fact is that we had done some things right . . .
>
> I remember sitting in this high-rise in San Francisco, talking to this young venture capitalist, and thinking, "This guy is so precious, he's such a nerd. I don't want him on our board, telling us what to do. . . ." We were sick of haughty disdain. Maybe we wouldn't go silk stocking, but we didn't care. We were going to find a different route.[9]

As a result of encounters like this, many entrepreneurs have chosen to "rough it out" on their own and avoid the help of venture capitalists. Many companies that have chosen to accept such help have proven to be dismal failures, including Osborne Computer, Fortune Systems, Victor Technologies, Pizza Time Theatre, Vector Graphic, Xonics, Evotek, Visi-Corp, and Diasonics. Under the speculative pressure imposed by the new venture capitalist groups, whose eyes remain fixed on their return on investment and the firm's stock price, the conflicts and alienation produced by absentee ownership proceed at an accelerated pace. Indeed, the company begins with the problems that other companies experience only many years after their formation. As one middle manager explained during an interview:

> I feel like we're in a pressure cooker. The venture capitalists run the show around here, and they don't care about our future. All they care about is their big returns. It's like we're all under the gun to accomplish an impossible goal which if it's reached will probably lead to this company's demise when the venture capitalists get their money out . . .

Institutional Investors

As noted above, institutional investors have become major players in venture capital markets, and their orientation toward short-term speculation has produced major problems. The impact of their involvement in the securities markets has been even more pervasive and devastating. Their influence has become so great because institutional investors, principally mutual and pension funds, involve over $1 trillion in corporate holdings, which means that the money managers of these funds control over 60 percent of all publicly traded corporate stocks and bonds. These money managers have pushed the short-term financial perspective to unheard of extremes as the following excerpt from *Business Week* serves to illustrate:

> Money managers themselves are increasingly judged on their quarterly results. Now that computers tot up each trade and track overall fund returns, even their weekly and daily results can be tallied and compared with those of their peers. Because they are judged on their short-term performance, money managers seek the highest yield in the shortest time. Their success comes from beating, or at least matching, their competitors' record, and it matters little whether results are derived from improved earn-

ings by the companies in their portfolios or from premiums that accompany takeovers or breakups of those companies.[10]

Because of this situation, Leon G. Cooperman, a partner at Goldman, Sachs and Company, says, "I don't think any company can afford a long-term investment today unless its managers own 51 percent of it."[11] Obviously, under such conditions, the problems of distance between owner and employee are intensified. The pressure of substantial institutional shareholders upon management, like the pressure of venture capitalists on a new firm, forces managers and boards of directors to rivet their attention to short-run profits and the company's share prices. Investment in long-term potential is exchanged for short-term gains. As *Business Week* explained:

> Just as fund managers cull their portfolios of low-return investments, so chief executives must cull their businesses of low-return operations. The process is known as "redeployment of assets." But it is a corporate triage: A few operations are nurtured, the rest are given up.
>
> Thus, for example, Bell & Howell Co. is out of the instrumentation business. Warner Communications Inc. has sold Atari Inc. Westinghouse Electric Corp. is looking for partners for its robotics business because its management expects that the division will take two to three years to become profitable.[12]

These conditions are carried even further when the power of institutional investors is combined with the strategy and tactics of corporate raiders and risk arbitrageurs. The combination of these forces can literally wreck a successful corporation.

Corporate Raiders and Risk Arbitrageurs

Our last two categories of absentee owners go together, with the risk arbitrageur following along behind the raider like the pilot fish that attaches itself to a shark and then consumes whatever is left over after a kill. Ours is not a pretty analogy, but the impact of the activities of corporate raiders upon companies and the communities in which those firms exist is also less than beautiful. The tactics of raiders such as T. Boone Pickens, Carl Icahn, or the British gentleman Sir James Goldsmith are essentially the same. The raider carefully studies the balance sheets and stock prices of publicly traded companies to identify a company with substantially undervalued stock. Once identified, the company is targeted for a takeover. Risk arbitrageurs keep their ears to the ground for such activity, and if a takeover effort is set in motion they and other institutional investors will jump in, hoping to make substantial gains from either a corporate stock buyback or a lucrative tender offer made by the raider.

Corporate raiders and takeover artists have one of two goals. Either they acquire the firm and dismember it by selling off the parts—which have been determined to have greater aggregate value than the market price at which the firm's stock is trading—or they "greenmail" the company's management, who are forced to buy back the raider's shares at a premium price. In either case the raider stands to make substantial returns on his or her investment. Conversely, the company targeted for a raid or hostile takeover attempt typically suffers great losses regardless of the outcome.

If the firm's management and board of directors decides to fight the takeover attempt, then tremendous resources are expended on both legal fees and debt in order to effect a defense. Substantial sums of money may be borrowed for the purpose of buying back shares to guarantee a defeat of any tender offer put forward by a raider. Similarly, if management and the board of directors choose to pay off the raider with greenmail, again substantial funds may be borrowed and expended for this purpose. Ronald O. Perelman and Revlon, for example, made a hefty profit of $39 million in greenmail from Gillette as a settlement to halt a hostile takeover, and James Goldsmith made a $90 million profit when Goodyear Tire and

Rubber paid $621 million for shares he had acquired in a recent raid.[13] Carl Icahn, a virtual unknown in the world of Wall Street before the late 1970s, made $10 million in greenmail payments from B.F. Goodrich in 1984, and only a year later made another $35 million from Phillips Petroleum.[14]

Such "rape and run" tactics are the more common result of a hostile takeover attempt than a successful acquisition. Whatever the result, the attempt often cripples the target company by causing it to incur such a heavy debt load that it has trouble sustaining itself afterward without either selling off or liquidating important assets to pay for the cost of the fight. As a result of hostile takeovers, U.S. corporations lost some $78 billion in equity in 1984, and added over $169 billion in new debt.[15] One company alone, Unocal, issued some $4.1 billion in debt securities in that year alone in order to fend off a takeover by T. Boone Pickens. Even if a takeover proves to be successful, the company is still weighted down with tremendous debt incurred by the raider in pursuing the takeover effort. And when the target firm's assets are sold off or liquidated, and its operations shut down to meet the costs of servicing debt repayment, jobs are lost and communities devastated. It is not surprising, therefore, that in many cases workers and entire communities have participated in efforts to fend off hostile takeovers by corporate raiders. At Dan River, employees and managers supported an employee buyout of the company in order to avert a takeover by Carl Icahn. Similarly, the employees of Marathon Oil Company joined together with the rest of the community and its leaders in the staging of demonstrations and rallies in protest of a hostile takeover. Congressional representatives from Ohio attacked James Goldsmith in special public hearings when he attempted his raid on Goodyear. Similarly, in Bartlesville, Oklahoma, the headquarters of Phillips Petroleum, residents printed and wore "Boone Buster" T-shirts in protest of T. Boone Pickens's attempt to take over their major employer, and a popular area restaurant called "Marie's" began selling "T-Boone steaks."[16]

THE IMPACT OF ABSENTEE OWNERSHIP
ON COMMUNITIES

In Chapter 3, we presented the history of Jamestown, New York to illustrate what happens to a community when absentee ownership predominates. While the Jamestown study helps to illustrate several of the dynamics of absentee ownership, other writers have also examined this problem from a number of different perspectives.

Early Community Studies

Serious study of the effects of absentee ownership on a community began with the Yankee City studies of Warner and Low, sociologists at the University of Chicago. As we noted in Chapter 3, Warner and Low's interest in the relationship between ownership structure and firm–community relations was stimulated by a citywide strike that hit Newburyport, Massachusetts' shoe manufacturing industry while they were studying the community life of the city. To their surprise, they witnessed local politicians, merchants, and other business leaders support the cause of the striking workers.

This unexpected crossing of traditional class lines became more comprehensible as the research team began to observe differences in the way that absentee and locally owned companies related to the community and their employees. What they discovered was that, as control over Newburyport industry had shifted into absentee hands, the management of these operations had become alienated from the concerns and daily workings of the community. The policies and actions of these organizations had gradually become disconnected from the needs of the local area and oriented primarily toward making profits for the parent firms located elsewhere.

Thus, what Warner and Low observed in the strike was a rebellion on the part of not only workers but also other community residents against the forces that had assumed power over the local economy and over which they had lost all peaceful means of influence. Local manufacturers, as members of the community, had found it necessary to maintain some level of reciprocity in their relationships with their employees and the community. The interests of the local owners were tied directly with the interests of the community. In contrast, the managers of the absentee-owned firms were apparently oblivious to community needs, and often so removed from community affairs that the old informal communication channels through which the community had previously influenced industry all but disappeared. Warner and Low illustrate this new set of business–community relations by comparing the managers of locally owned companies with managers at absentee-owned firms:

> The vertical extension of its managerial hierarchy and the absentee control of factory C also made its relations with the community of Yankee City (Newburyport) much different from those of factories A and B. Typically, the managers and supervisory staffs of the locally owned, independent factories (like A and B) are native Yankees; frequently, they were born and grew up in Yankee City. They are thus involved in the general social life of the community, belonging to various associations, clubs, and other organizations. They subscribe to many general community attitudes which impinge upon their working relations, frequently causing them to modify working behavior away from that which would follow the single-minded dictates of the profit-making logic. Their life in the factory is not divorced from life in the community outside of working hours. Part of the motivation that determines their business behavior is the desire that fellow townsmen regard them as upright and fair businessmen who treat their employees properly. Such desires frequently militate against their acting strictly in accordance with the profit-making logic; business advantages are sometimes sacrificed because the manager (or owner) places greater value on community prestige than he does on increasing factory earnings by some means which would endanger that prestige.

In the case of absentee-controlled shoe factory C, however, there is little business need for the manager to participate in community activities. He can operate the factory in strict accordance with the orders of the main office more easily, in fact, if he does not take part, either as an individual or as a representative of the factory, in local associational activities. If he does involve the factory in community activities, he involves it and the larger enterprise of which it is a part in community responsibilities and subjects it to community pressure and control. This is precisely what the top officials of the large enterprise do not want. They want the factory to be as free as possible of community pressures so that its operations can be dictated in strict accordance with the profit-making logic. *This would even allow them, if it seemed desirable, to move their factory to another community.*[17]

Since the Yankee City studies, many other studies, including our study of Jamestown, New York, have further clarified how absentee ownership alters the structure of community–industry relationships.[18] It has become clear that the involvement of industrial leaders in community politics and affairs changes both in degree and orientation with the transition to absentee ownership. These changes are summarized in Table 6.

Roland Warren helps us to understand this change in orientation by pointing to the major change in key reference groups, or "significant others," for management which attends the transition to absentee ownership. Locally owned and managed firms become "horizontally integrated" into the community because their leadership depends upon the mutual support and acceptance of their peers in the locality as well as of their employees. Therefore, the owner/managers of such firms must give careful consideration to the impact that their "business decisions" have upon the welfare and opinions of the people with whom they share the community and its resources. In contrast, the principal reference system for top management of an absentee-owned company or plant is the larger corporation, and consequently the expectations and de-

Table 6. The Effects of Industry Ownership on a Community

COMMUNITY CHARACTERISTIC	LOCAL OWNERSHIP	ABSENTEE OWNERSHIP
Relationship between political and economic power and decision making	Unitary	Bifurcated
Integration of industry	Horizontal	Vertical
Focus of control over industry	Local	Corporate headquarters
Economic significance of firm's performance controlling management/ownership	Major source of income	Speculative—one of a number of investments
Social significance of firm's performance to controlling management/ownership	Central to individual and family status, prestige, and identity	Peripheral
Dominant professional reference system for top management	Peers within community	Corporate superiors
Motivational orientation of firm toward social and political community involvement	Instrumental and affective	Instrumental

mands that come from corporate superiors must be given priority over any community considerations.[19] Thus, whether representing the "company" means staying out of community affairs entirely or aggressively defending corporate interests, this is the role that the management of an absentee-owned operation "must" play. To do otherwise would be career suicide.

The ultimate result of this shift in alliances and orientation for a community's industrial leadership is the development of what Robert Schulze refers to as a "bifurcation of power."[20] The unitary relationship that once existed between economic, social, and political roles is broken. The people who manage the economic base of the community and control these resources become a group separate and apart from the broader interests of the community. Thus, the people whose future and security are tied to the community and who are the key actors involved in advancing and protecting its social and political life lose influence over local economic affairs. Consequently, when the desires and the interests of these two groups move in opposing directions, conflict is likely to ensue and the crossing of class lines becomes possible. As we saw in the case of Jamestown, there were more strikes and strikes of longer duration in those firms that were absentee owned. Similarly, one of the major reasons behind the major strike at the USX company is the alienation from this new giant conglomerate that the employees and their families feel. Workers feel powerless because they disagree with corporate management about the company's long-term interests.

In summary, the transition to absentee ownership can create deep divisions in a community. The interests of absentee owners and their managers often differ from the community's goals. Labor unrest, the loss of political influence on the part of the community, and feelings of exploitation are created. Moreover, we frequently find that absentee owners can affect the livelihood of communities by closing plants and businesses down or by laying off workers unless they receive concessions from their employees and the community. To counteract these actions, company employees and the community may threaten to strike or take over the plant, based on the doctrine of "eminent domain." In this hostile climate, the community can be racked with economic uncertainty and conflict.

ABSENTEE OWNERSHIP AND INDUSTRY BEHAVIOR

In Chapter 4 we described how absentee ownership and professional management affected the steel industry. In this section we will attempt to outline some general trends that we see in those industries that have made the movement to absentee ownership, and whose organizations are predominantly led by professional managers. We will focus on six of the more significant changes.

Merger Mania

Absentee ownership often comes about as a result of a merger or an acquisition. Thus, those industries that have absentee ownership tend to be comprised of conglomerates. "Growth via diversification" is seen as a viable success strategy; hence, "merger fever" spreads through the industry. The efforts of such conglomerates are largely directed toward taking over other firms or preventing other firms from acquiring them. This leads firms in the industry to become less concerned with adding value to the customer through innovation and new products than they are with finding new companies to acquire.

Creating Corporate Pyramid Schemes

As usually understood, a "pyramid scheme" is a type of business strategy where someone sells a particular good or service to a buyer who must then turn around and find other buyers in order to receive any real benefit. In a successful scheme, the process of "signing up" new buyers can result in huge profits for those on top of the pyramid. Such schemes are deemed to be illegal because those at the bottom receive little or no benefit. Indeed, the whole strategy is based on the assumption that there will always be one more "sucker" to join the scheme at an ever-lower level.

In absentee-owned industries, we find a grander and entirely legal version of the pyramid scheme. Companies attempt to buy other companies solely to "turn them around" quickly and sell them to another buyer. To accomplish this turnaround, the acquiring firm often sells off assets, fires employees, and reduces overhead—all in an effort to make the company look good on paper. The motive behind such actions is *not* to create synergy between the two companies and produce a better product or service. Instead, the strategy is to pay as little for the firm as possible, make the company look good financially, and then sell the business to another buyer at a profit. Here too the assumption is that "there's a sucker born every minute." The result of such pyramid schemes is the creation and preservation of many organizations that add little value to the economy.

Shift in Corporate Power

In absentee-owned industries, the power to make decisions and influence an industry also shifts dramatically. Since the important decisions often involve mergers or acquisitions, bankers and attorneys become key decision makers. "Legal strategies" for effecting or avoiding takeovers replace "corporate strategies" for improving market share and organizational performance. Key decisions are left in the hands of people who may understand the legal and financial implications of a given course of action, but who have little or no understanding of a company's products or markets.

New Debt Structures

The acquisition strategies of absentee-owned firms require a tremendous amount of cash. Companies often rely on debt to accomplish their goals. Hence, we tend to find many absentee-owned firms with very high debt and high interest charges that must be serviced. To service this debt, the firm often must take funds away from other pursuits such as research and development. During difficult times, selling assets, laying off workers, or asking for wage and benefit concessions are the typical strategies used to keep the firm solvent. The weight of debt can make it extraordinarily difficult for an industry to remain competitive in the global marketplace. Competitors in other countries with more favorable financial structures have a significant competitive advantage.

Trading Assets

As we have seen, professional managers of the USX company are more "money managers" than knowledgeable steel men. As asset managers, they attempt to improve the portfolio of assets they are managing. Assets are bought and sold, acquired, and divested to improve the financial picture of the company. While this is not an unimportant function, the asset managers often neglect one important idea—they must add value to the assets they are managing. When assets are merely shuffled around within one industry, growth and development is stifled. Recently, the leaders of many U.S. firms have decided to move their manufacturing operations overseas where labor is cheap and unions virtually nonexistent. While this movement may indeed mean cheaper goods, it certainly does not further the development of the industry in the United States. Jobs are shipped overseas where new plants, many of them containing the latest innovations, are superior to the aging facilities found in the United States. Under such conditions, it becomes difficult for the industry to survive and thrive within the borders of the United States.

Conflict in Industrial Relations

As we have also seen, management–employee relations worsen with the advent of absentee ownership and professional management. Because the owners do not feel tied to any particular firm, or even to an industry, they attempt to extract as large a profit as possible at any price to labor. If the "asset" doesn't yield the expected return, they are likely to "dispose" of it. Under these conditions, the professional managers usually take a hard line approach when it comes to union–management negotiations. More often than not, the union will be asked to give back wages and benefits in return for job security. Thus, the stage is set for strikes, lockouts, and other labor strife.

SUMMARY

In this chapter, we have described a wide variety of changes that take place in organizations, in industries, and in communities when absentee owners and professional managers come to predominate. We find an increasing distance between owners and employees, and a focus on short-term financial gains at the expense of long-term profitability. Innovation becomes more difficult to achieve, labor–management relations deteriorate, and the company becomes alienated from the needs of the community.

As we see it, the trend is clear. It is not an optimistic picture for American industry. But there is nothing inevitable or unavoidable about the transformations we are currently witnessing. In the following chapters of this book, we intend to present a number of specific alternatives to reverse the negative trend and its consequences, which require significant changes in ownership structures and in management values.

CHAPTER 5 ENDNOTES

1. Robert H. Hayes and William J. Abernathy. "Managing Our Way to Economic Decline." *Harvard Business Review*, July-August 1980, pp. 66–77.

2. Edgar H. Schein. "The Role of the Founder in Creating Organizational Culture." *Organizational Dynamics*, vol. 12, no. 2, Summer 1983, p. 17.

3. Tom Nicholson and Peter McAlvey. "Saving the Magic Kingdom." *Newsweek*, October 8, 1984, p. 44.

4. W. Lloyd Warner and J.O. Low. *The Social System of the Modern Factory* (Westport, Conn.: Greenwood Press, 1976). Originally published by Yale University Press, 1947, pp. 144–145.

5. Michael E. Porter. "Competitive Advantage to Corporate Strategy." *Harvard Business Review*, May-June 1987, no. 3, p. 43–59.

6. Joel Kotkin. "Why Smart Companies Are Saying No to Venture Capital." *Inc Magazine*, vol. 6, no. 8, August 1984, pp. 67–68.

7. Ibid., p. 68.

8. Ibid., p. 66.

9. Ibid., pp. 65–66.

10. "Will Money Managers Wreck the Economy?" *Business Week*, August 13, 1984, pp. 88–89.

11. Ibid., p. 87.

12. Ibid., pp. 92–93.

13. "A Flurry of Greenmail." *Business Week*, December 8, 1986, pp. 32–33.

14. "Carl Icahn: Raider or Manager?" *Business Week*, October 27, 1986, p. 99.

15. "The Casino Society." *Business Week*, December 16, 1985, p. 81.

16. "The Oklahoma Town That's at Pickens' Mercy." *Business Week*, December 24, 1984, p. 27.

17. Warner and Low, 1976, pp. 118–119.

18. See, for example, Roland J. Pellegrin and Charles H. Coates. "Absentee-Owned Corporations and Community Power Structure." *The American Journal of Sociology*, vol. 61, no. 2, March 1956, pp. 413–419; Robert O. Schulze. "The Role of Economic Dominants in Community Power Structure." *American Sociological Review*, vol. 23, no. 1, February 1958, pp. 3–9; Robert O. Schulze. "The Bifurcation of Power in a Satellite." In Morris Janowitz, ed., *Community Political Systems* (Glencoe, Ill.: The Free Press, 1961), pp. 19–80; Norton E. Long. "The Corporation, Its Satellites and the Local Community." In E.S. Mason, ed., *The Corporation in Modern Society* (Cambridge, Mass.: Harvard University Press, 1959), pp. 202–217; and Robert Mills French. "Economic Change and Community Power Structure: Transition in Cornucopia." In Michael Aiken and Paul E. Mott, eds., *The Structure of Community Power* (New York: Random House), pp. 181–192.

20. Schulze, 1958 and 1961.

CHAPTER 6 ═══════════════════════

De-Absenteeing the Corporation

When a successful corporation makes the move toward absentee ownership and professional management, something vital to that corporation's success—its *value-driven culture*—may be gradually or abruptly lost. The company becomes an object of speculation, an asset managed with other assets by financially minded managers; and its employees, even its lower and middle managers, are reduced to one more factor in the performance of the asset. Such changes tend to destablize the company and alienate the people who work in it. Under the more extreme forms of absentee ownership, the enterprise becomes a "black box," with its employees, its technology, and the experience and knowledge necessary to manage them sealed inside, completely inaccessible to the company's ownership and top management. This sad state of affairs is, as we have seen, itself the root of America's industrial and economic decline.

Thus, we see a tremendous need to consider and implement alternative industrial ownership structures, structures capable of reducing some of these problems and ensuring the survival of a value-driven corporate culture. When an organization passes on from its entrepreneurial founders, it must consider ownership options other than going public or selling out to other interests, with all their negative consequences. At the same time, it must avoid the political conflict and loss of motivation that come with government ownership. America should be trying to foster new forms of industrial ownership which build a partnership between labor and management and stimulate both social responsibility and profitability. We must encourage the strengths and minimize the harmful aspects of the capitalist system, tempering our desire for long-term growth, employee job security, and the economic vitality of the communities where American companies do business. Many entrepreneurs, even those in the kinds of high-growth, high-tech industries that have been pushed by venture capital into going public throughout the 1980s, are themselves now coming to this realization. A recent article in *Inc. Magazine* describes what happened to one entrepreneur who resisted the lure of big bucks and decided to forego going public:

> Over the past few years, the fever has subsided as the industry slumped. And many of the founders and entrepreneurs who had decided to cash out now find themselves tossed aside like so much excess baggage, often by the same investment bankers who had fawned over them and convinced them of the glories of going public.
>
> Jerry Rochte might have suffered the same fate. Back in 1983, his Cavro Scientific Instruments Inc., in Sunnyvale, Calif., would have been an ideal candidate for an IPO, a $5-million company with sales of precision liquid-handling instruments that had been growing 30 percent annually since 1972. But a year later, disaster struck. The company's largest customer, Syva Co., . . . cut its order drastically, and sales dropped 50 percent.
>
> Rochte envisions what this debacle would have done to a public company. "The demand from shareholders would have been to cut back the business," he figures. "With our sales down by half, the demand would have been to lay off workers or get rid of facilities." But as the CEO of a private company, Rochte's highest priority was not to boost the fading bottom line, but to find new customers. Cutting back key sales and development staff might have improved earnings for a few months, but at the expense of undermining the company's ability to bounce back from the doldrums.

"When you're public, the financial people take over," Rochte says. "You end up focusing on today's numbers as the be-all and end-all. Companies lose their identities; they are simply chips on a board. And you forget profits aren't everything. Survival is everything."

To survive, Rochte covered his operating losses with $2 million from retained earnings and launched a new sales drive, which soon turned the company around. Today, Syva represents only 10 percent to 15 percent of total sales, down from 70 percent in 1984, while the number of other clients has increased sixfold. Sales this year are expected to climb to more than $6 million, a 20 percent jump from the predisaster period.

Rochte's argument is that the head of a public company inevitably comes to look at his company as merely a financial asset. "You start laying off to make short-range financial goals, and in the process, you destroy the organization. In a private company, you're more apt to have the sense that the organization is an entity with a purpose— an organization of people with compatible skills who make a product and serve the customers. And that purpose is something worth protecting.[1]

Staying private, of course, is a viable alternative as long as the founder or founding group is alive and willing to stay in charge of the company. When the founders die or decide to move on, it is critical that the company pass on to owners capable of maintaining its original values, rooted in the founders' vision and the local community. It is, however, highly unlikely that a competent and dedicated heir will follow in the footsteps of a company's founders. A 1983 survey conducted by Chemical Bank found, for example, that of more than 1,000 small business owners who responded to the study, only 18 percent expected one of their heirs to take over the ownership and management of their firm. In contrast, 60 percent of the business owners indicated that they wanted their business to continue on independently after their death or retirement, but less than 15 percent wanted to sell out to a large corporation.[2] We believe that, among the available options, employee ownership offers the most promising alternative for ensuring the long-term survival and profitability of the firm.

EMPLOYEE OWNERSHIP: A VIABLE ALTERNATIVE

Employee ownership is not a new phenomenon in the United States. During the nineteenth century trade union leaders and political reformers looked to worker ownership as a mechanism for reversing the deleterious effects of the industrial revolution and large-scale capitalism. Employee ownership, particularly in cooperative form, was envisioned as a means to stimulate material advancement while preventing the degradation of labor. Many successful employee-owned enterprises, lasting for periods that ranged from five to thirty years, thrived during the latter half of the 1800s. The longest firm life span recorded for one of these early "cooperatives" was fifty-three years, in the case of a barrel-making company.[3] William Sylvis and the Iron Moulders Union adopted the establishment of worker-owned foundries as the union's central agenda, and the Knights of Labor, one of the first national federations of labor, maintained funds to assist in the creation of worker-owned enterprises as well as the traditional union strike fund. In fact, the concept of employee ownership as a strategy for creating an industrial partnership between capital and labor thrived well into the 1930s.

In recent years, employee ownership has again emerged as a concept of great interest in the United States, primarily, although not solely, as a result of the aggressive efforts of the inventor and promoter of the Employee Stock Ownership Plan, or ESOP, San Francisco attorney and investment banker Louis Kelso. In his book, *The Capitalist Manifesto,* and then later in *How to Turn Eight Million Workers into Capitalists on Borrowed Money,* coauthored with Patricia Hetter, Kelso argued that economic equity, labor–management peace, and continuous industrial productivity could be achieved by broadening the base of industrial ownership to include workers. Later, in 1973, now retired Senator Russell Long, the son of the notorious populist governor of Louisiana Huey Long, became Kelso's disciple and advocate, and this conversion perhaps led to the most aggressive and successful push for public policy promoting employee ownership in U.S. history. Undoubtedly, legislation drafted and promoted by Senator Long proved to be so successful because he tied Kelso's concept, the ESOP, to revisions and modifications of the tax code.

THE ESOP: AN OVERVIEW

Because of Russell Long's conversion to employee ownership and his subsequent activism in Congress, the ESOP has clearly become the best known and fastest growing form of employee ownership in the United States. Currently there are more than 10,000 partially to entirely employee-owned companies in the United States, and of these approximately 9,000 have implemented employee ownership through the establishment of an ESOP.[4] Of the firms that have opted for the ESOP route for implementing employee ownership, it is estimated that *25 percent to one-third have become employee owned as part of a strategy for enabling retiring business owners to sell their companies without liquidating assets.*[5]

In many respects an ESOP resembles any other deferred benefit, profit-sharing, or pension plan. When an ESOP is adopted, the company first establishes an Employee Stock Ownership Trust (ESOT). The company then makes annual payments into the trust which, as with pension payments, are tax deductible. Lastly, employees gradually become vested in the plan, typically during a period of five to fifteen years.

Beyond these characteristics, however, ESOPs differ dramatically from pension and other types of deferred benefit plans. The same law which was established to ensure greater pension security for employees, the *Employee Retirement and Income Security Act of 1974* (ERISA), also created a statutory framework for ESOPs with a very different and special set of conditions. Specifically, ERISA provided ESOP stock trusts, otherwise known as ESOTs, with the power and authority to legally borrow money from commercial lenders. Furthermore, ERISA established ESOPs as "qualified employee benefit programs," which meant that company contributions to ESOPs could be considered tax deductible when in accordance with allocation, vesting, and other rules established by ERISA with respect to the administration of employee benefit plans. Company donations to an ESOP are allowed to equal up to 25 percent of a firm's annual payroll and still remain 100 percent tax deductible. (Initially, after ERISA was first enacted, the upper limit was 15 percent of payroll.) ERISA also exempted ESOPs from one key aspect of the "prudent man" policy it established for employee pension and other deferred benefit plans. Not more than 10 percent of a pension plan's total assets can be invested in employer securities. Except under special circumstances, a plan that invests more than 10 percent of its assets in employer securities has made an unwise or "imprudent investment" and is guilty under the tax code of having made what is termed a "prohibited transaction." The trustees of a pension plan that has made a prohibited transaction can suffer stiff penalties and fines for having breached their fiduciary responsibility to the plan participants. In contrast, a majority of an ESOP's assets must be invested in employer stock, and it is legal, under ERISA, for an ESOP to own as much as 100 percent of an employer's stock.

Since 1974 and the implementation of ERISA, more than sixteen different laws have been passed which have directly and indirectly affected the nature and prevalence of ESOPs in the United States; and many of these laws have played a key role in further enhancing the financial attractiveness of stock ownership plans to employers.[6] Some of the most significant provisions resulted from the *Deficit Reduction Act of 1984* and are still in force today after the adoption of tax reform in 1986. Before describing these provisions, however, it will first be useful to describe how an ESOP works and how it can serve as a mechanism for reducing the cost of capital investment.

The ESOP Structure

Figure 4 illustrates how both leveraged and unleveraged ESOPs function. As Figure 4 illustrates, in the case of the unleveraged ESOP, the company in effect makes a dollar contribution to the ESOP and in turn the ESOP pays the money back to the company in return for stock. Transactions between the company and the trust do not end here, however, for, even after all of the total stock planned to be placed in the ESOP trust has been deposited, the firm must continue to make donations until the plan becomes fully funded or has

Figure 4. The Leveraged and Unleveraged ESOP

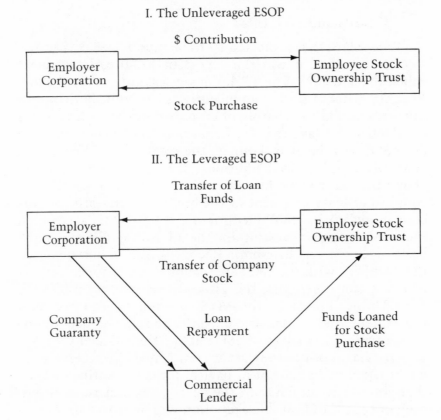

sufficient assets to buy back participant stock at full market value. In some instances, transfers of stock to an ESOP without leveraging have involved large amounts of stock. Such cases have usually involved either the creation of a payroll deduction plan, in which employees buy stock with increments out of their normal wages, or large amounts of stock have been transferred to employees in return for taking a cut in pay. In both cases the creation of a stock ownership plan and employee receipt of employer stock have been tied to an effort to save jobs and cut costs. They have been measures taken in response to crisis. More frequently, in healthy companies, stock ownership plans have been created without the use of leveraged funds through a mechanism called a PAYSOP.

PAYSOPs and TRASOPs

The *PAYSOP* was created by the *Economic Recovery Tax Act of 1981*, and it was the successor to an earlier vehicle called the TRASOP. The *TRASOP* was established by the *Tax Reduction Act of 1975* as an incentive to promote both capital investment and the sharing of employer stock with employees. Under this law, the *Tax Reduction Act Ownership Plan* (TRASOP) was created. Through the creation of a TRASOP, a company could gain an additional 1 percent credit over and above the 10 percent Investment Tax Credit if an amount equal to at least 1 percent of the qualifying investment was contributed to an ESOP meeting the rules of this act, which included immediate vesting and the allocation of stock on the basis of salary. The Economic Recovery Act of 1981 replaced the TRASOP with the PAYSOP, although companies were allowed to continue to use the TRASOP provisions up through 1984. Unlike TRASOPs, the PAYSOP is not wedded to capital investment, and it enables companies to take tax deductions for contributing stock to an ESOP at any time. Under the PAYSOP provision of the 1981 act, a company could receive a tax credit equal to ½ percent of payroll for contributing at least that amount to an ESOP in the years 1983 and 1984. Beginning in 1985 the allowable deduction was increased to .75 percent. PAYSOPs generally follow the same rules applicable to TRASOPs, but the allocation requirements are considerably stricter.[7]

Leveraged ESOPs

A leveraged ESOP, unlike a PAYSOP or unleveraged ESOP, involves the use of bank financing and provides even greater tax advantages, especially to the employer interested in using borrowed funds to finance capital improvements. As Figure 4 (II) illustrates, a leveraged ESOP borrows money from a commercial lender and uses it to purchase stock from the corporation. The corporation in turn uses the new funds to purchase new equipment, build new facilities, and so on. The ESOP's stock serves as security for the loan, along with an accompanying loan guarantee from the company. Employees vest stock in individual accounts in the ESOP; and, in the case of the leveraged ESOP, the bank loan, which was used to purchase company stock, must also, of course, be paid back. In theory, the company makes regular payments to the trust over the life of the loan, and the trust uses these payments to pay off the loan. Actually, in most cases, the company simply makes direct payments on the loan to the lender. These payments are considered to be payments on behalf of the trust, and because of this the employer is able to deduct *both principal and interest portions of the payment* from pre-tax profits. Once stock has been placed in an ESOP trust or ESOT, employees gradually vest the stock over a period that typically ranges from five to fifteen years. And even after the loan has been paid off to the lender, the company must continue to make tax deductible contributions to the plan in order to ensure that it is sufficiently funded to purchase the stock of vested employees upon quitting or retirement.

The tax advantages created to produce an incentive for the adoption of ESOPs have had a dramatic impact upon the growth of employee ownership in the United States. Although Louis Kelso implemented the first ESOP nearly thirty years ago, when he developed a plan for a West Coast newspaper in

Table 7. The Growth of ESOP, 1980–1985

	NUMBER OF ESOPs	EMPLOYEES PARTICIPATING IN ESOPs (IN MILLIONS)
1980	5,100	7.0
1981	5,500	7.4
1982	5,900	7.7
1983	6,300	8.6
1984	6,800	10.2
1985	8,000	11.5

Source: Joshua Hyatt, "Are ESOPs Feeble?," Inc. Magazine, vol. 8, no. 5, May 1986, p. 22.

1958, the number of ESOPs grew to only about 300, involving some 500,000 workers, by 1974—the year when the provisions of ERISA were first passed by Congress.[8] After this point, the number of ESOP companies increased dramatically, as the figures in Table 7 illustrate. In just five years, the number of firms with ESOPs increased to 5,100 encompassing 7 million workers, or in other words a seventeen-fold increase by 1980. From 1981 through 1984 the number of ESOP firms increased by about 400 per year; and then, in 1985, after additional tax incentives were passed by Congress, the number of ESOPs had jumped by 1200.

These most recent tax incentives created an obvious boost in interest in ESOPs, and this has been particularly true for company founders interested in getting out of the business without going public or selling out to a large corporation. Since the implementation of ERISA, it has, of course, always been possible to use the borrowed funds for a leveraged ESOP as the capital for employees to use in purchasing stock from a corporation's owner, thereby "creating a market" for the founder's interest. The *Deficit Reduction Act of 1984*, however, made this option even more attractive to both lenders and company owners. Specifically, the act includes:

a) A provision allowing an owner of an independent business to defer taxation on the gains made by a sale of stock to an ESOP... by reinvesting the gains within 12 months in the stock or stocks of other companies. When that new stock is sold, capital gains taxes would be due. At least 30% of the ownership of the firm must be held by the ESOP... after the transaction for the provision to be effective;

b) A provision allowing commercial lending institutions to deduct 50% of the interest income they receive from a loan to a company for the purpose of acquiring stock through an ESOP (the loan can be directly to the ESOP, or to the company if the company contributes an amount of stock equal to the principal portion of the loan to the ESOP);

c) A provision allowing an ESOP company to deduct dividends paid directly to ESOP participants; and

d) A provision allowing an ESOP... to assume estate tax liability of the estate of a business in return for a stock contribution from the estate worth at least as much as the tax liability.[9]

Obviously these provisions can make the adoption of an ESOP, either as a means for creating a market for an owner's stock or as a tool for financing capital investment, extremely attractive to the company, the owner, and the lenders that participate in the transaction. Today we are seeing more and more company founders becoming aware of the advantages of employee ownership as a transition strategy. The story of entrepreneur Warren Braun is an example of how this strategy can benefit the company founder, the employees, and the firm:

Warren Braun knows firsthand what it's like to be part of a financial asset. For 15 years, Braun worked happily for a Washington, D.C., television broadcaster, rising from engineer to station manager. Then in 1957, the owner retired and sold off his group of stations to the first of a succession of corporate owners. Over the next eight years, Braun worked for four different managements.

"It was terrible," Braun, now 65, recalls. "Wall Street

guys come in and load up all the debt. That creates nothing but headaches for the guys doing the work. You don't have any stability on the staff. There's chaos at the top, and it runs through everything the company does."

Frustrated, Braun decided to go out on his own, opening a television consulting business. . . . As his client base grew, he saw an opportunity for a service company providing field repair services, system design, and testing for the emerging cable-television industry. He finally incorporated ComSonics in 1972, with a clear sense of what kind of business he wanted to run.

"I felt very strongly about staying private after all that I had seen," Braun says. "I couldn't just talk about it. I had to make it happen." And so every year, Braun has been slowly selling off his interest in ComSonics to company employees, who today own 99.45% of the company. In fact, Braun who calls himself a "CEO without portfolio," is just about the only person in the company without any stock.

"I have a lot of faith in what employees can do if they are treated right and properly motivated," Braun says. "When I worked for other people, I saw colleagues work their buns off and get nothing out of it. I saw Wall Street rape employees. That confounded drive to make money quickly really does nothing for the company's performance."

Today, in an industry racked by pervasive merger mongering . . . ComSonics has developed a reputation for steadiness. . . . Annual employee turnover is less than 3%. . . . And an average 25% annual growth has been financed by reinvesting two-thirds of the company's gross profits . . .

As for Braun, he's planning to retire soon and walk away with about $1 million in cash, his proceeds from selling his interest in the company. . . . Had he gone public or sold out to another firm, he might have wound up with two or three times as much.

"I'd be the first to admit I'm not making as much as I could. . . . But I have more than enough to be comfortable.

In spiritual and moral return—well, I'd say my satisfaction
is simply far greater."[10]

GIVING U.S. COMPANIES A KICK: RAIDERS VERSUS EMPLOYEE OWNERS

Following an ownership strategy similar to Warren
Braun's, it is possible to retain the stabilizing and driving aspects of the "value-driven" corporate culture that, as we will
see later in more detail, is characteristic of an organization
under the ownership and control of its founders. If the founder's intellectual creativity and entrepreneurial skills are
passed on to the new management team, the company is
likely to be not only profitable but also socially responsible
toward its employees and the surrounding community.

Employee ownership, furthermore, may prevent the corporation from falling asleep at the helm, and force both management and employees to work hard and attune themselves
to the needs of the marketplace. This is true whether employee ownership results from the founder's sale of stock to
employees, or is implemented in a publicly traded corporation
as part of a combined employee-involvement and capital-
improvement program. Interestingly, corporate raiders like T.
Boone Pickens, Carl Icahn, Irving Jacobs, and others have argued vehemently, if not always persuasively, that their raids
on U.S. companies have helped in pressuring lazy and inefficient managers to get back to the business of managing. Thus,
the raiders argue, their activities are socially beneficial, a re-
awakening and revitalizing of corporate America. During a
panel interview conducted by Peter Jennings as part of an ABC
news series called "Wrong Way on Wall Street," corporate
raider Asher Edleman argued that

> When you begin to think of a corporation as an entity as
> opposed to its constituencies you get all kinds of aberra-
> tions . . . the entrenchment of managements, big corporate
> aircraft, lots of big perks that don't get disclosed to share-

holders, etc. I would say that corporate America needs some kick now and then to become a little bit more efficient, a little bit less entrenched, and that will probably do our economy a lot of good.[11]

The problem with this logic, of course, is that Edleman focuses on the "management of assets" and not the "management of the firm as a company." A corporate raid may well produce a reshuffling of assets and an almost instantaneous boost in the company's stock price—which means that shareholders who sell their shares make substantial profits and the raider himself makes even larger returns, often through greenmail. But the company itself is rarely improved or even left in good shape for the future. Frequently, many employees of raided companies find themselves suddenly out of work. In one of Edleman's raids, a takeover attempt against the retail conglomerate Lucky Stores, an entire subsidiary was liquidated to pay him off and purchase a sufficient number of shares to block the raid. In this case, Lucky's management and board of directors decided to shut down all of its GEMCO stores—a line of retail discount outlets similar to K-Mart—and to sell off all of this subsidiary's inventories, buildings, and real estate. All GEMCO employees were permanently terminated, leaving some 14,000 managers and workers unemployed. Reflecting on the impact of Edleman's raid, one elderly woman, who had formerly worked for GEMCO, told an NBC correspondent, "He's just padding his pocketbook. And here's grandma out on the street. He could care less about me."[12]

The social costs inflicted upon a firm's employees by a takeover attempt can be devastating, and those costs are not only in the present. In most takeover attempts, the target company incurs substantial debt to pay off the raider and support stock buybacks, and this debt in effect mortgages the company's future, usually necessitating cutbacks in long-term activities such as research and development, or the shutdown and liquidation of productive operations, as with Lucky Stores and GEMCO. Similar problems also arise when a raider is successful in taking over a company with a tender offer, since debt, high-interest junk bonds, and bank financing are generally used to finance the purchase. Thus, when the raider becomes the owner of the company, he is himself required to liquidate substantial portions of the company's assets—and therefore its jobs—in order to pay off the debt. Nicholas Brady, Chairman of Dillon, Read and Company, and another panel member in the "Wrong Way on Wall Street" series, argued that

> The contract between the U.S. corporation and this country is one of many constituencies. It has a duty to its shareholders, its employees, the community it lives in, the consumers it sells to.[13]

Obviously, Brady's perspective is much closer to our own than Edleman's. Nevertheless, we do agree that the management of many American corporations, especially the top management of America's largest firms, has become fat and lazy, concerned more with golf scores, big salaries, and corporate perks than with performance. Thus, to use Edleman's metaphor, a kick is indeed in order, but we contend that a shift to employee ownership is far more useful than corporate raiding. Employee ownership, if it includes the passing on of full voting rights to employees, can be a continuous kick directed at management—to ensure the efficient and effective use of capital—and also at workers and professional employees—to encourage them to deliver a quality product with greater efficiency.

Furthermore, employee-owned firms tend to resist mere paper manipulations of assets, or the massive destruction of large parts of the corporation simply to improve the current stock price. Employee owners are not only interested in the present value of their stock, but also in its value over the long run; and they are even more interested in their long-term job security and the employment future of their children—who may also work for the same company. Thus, when employees own a substantial block of their company's stock, it is far less likely that the company will be financially manipulated for short-term gain. Employee shareholders will obviously be more sensitive to local jobs and the needs of the local community; for, after all, the jobs are theirs, and the communities are ones in which they have ties to family, friends, and the local culture and social structure.

ECONOMIC PERFORMANCE OF EMPLOYEE-OWNED FIRMS: EMPIRICAL STUDIES

Considerable evidence supports our view that employee ownership can help to improve profitability and overall corporate performance. Probably the first comparative studies of the economic performance of employee-owned firms were conducted in the Pacific Northwest. These worker-owned enterprises produce a variety of plywood products for the construction industry. They are called "cooperative firms" because each employee shareholder owns an equal share in the business and has only one vote as an owner. In the first study of these democratically owned companies, Henry G. Dahl found during the 1950s that, on average, the cooperatives produced 115 to 120 square feet of plywood per man-hour, compared to 80 to 95 square feet in conventional companies. In other words, during this period the plywood cooperatives were found to be between 20 and 50 percent more efficient than their traditional counterparts.[14]

In the 1960s another researcher, Katrina Berman, launched her first studies of the Northwest plywood cooperatives, and found during this period that the cooperatives were averaging 170 square feet of plywood per man-hour in comparison to 120 square feet in conventional firms, or, for example, an average difference of 42 percent.[15] Later in the mid-1970s Berman acted as a consultant to a number of the plywood cooperatives who found themselves in trouble with the IRS because of the extremely high wages they were paying to their members. Wages paid to worker owners in many plywood cooperatives were on average 50 percent greater than the average union wage paid in competitor mills. The IRS argued that the cooperatives were really paying a return to capital in the form of wages and thereby avoiding corporate taxes on earnings. The worker-owned companies argued that their worker-owners received higher wages because of their greater efficiency, and they supported this argument with new research data collected by Berman which indicated that the firms ranged in efficiency from 25 to 60 percent above plywood industry averages.[16] We will discuss in greater detail how these unique companies organize themselves to ensure such economic success in chapter 7.

Although research on the plywood cooperatives of the Pacific Northwest provided the first empirical evidence of the potential economic superiority of employee-owned enterprises over traditional firms, probably the most influential research in stimulating widespread interest in employee ownership and generating public policy support for its encouragement was a study conducted by economist Michael Conte and sociologist Arnold Tannenbaum at the University of Michigan's Survey Research Center. In this 1978 study, Tannenbaum and Conte collected economic performance and ownership structure and practices information from a sample of ninety-eight companies. Of the ninety-eight, some 68 were ESOP firms. The other thirty companies had implemented employee ownership through the direct purchase of stock by employees, and some of this non-ESOP group were from the Northwest plywood cooperatives previously studied by Berman and Dahl. Of the ninety-eight employee-owned companies studied by Conte and Tannenbaum, only twenty-three provided profitability data adequate for making comparisons with conventional firms in the same industry. When profit levels for these firms were compared with average profit levels in their respective industries, the researchers found these employee-owned companies to be 1.5 times more profitable. Furthermore, the researchers also found that the only variable which seemed to significantly influence profitability was the proportion of stock owned by non-management employees. The larger the percentage of stock owned by non-managers in relation to total shares, the higher the profitability was generally found to be.[17]

A second study conducted by Thomas Marsh and Dale McAllister found that 229 employee-owned companies with ESOPs had on average twice the annual productivity growth rate of comparable conventionally owned companies.[18] In contrast, a study conducted by Brooks, Henry, and Livingston of fifty-one ESOP firms with a matched sample of conventional companies, found no significant difference in profitability.[19] A 1983 study sponsored by the National Center for Employee Ownership (NCEO) found, however, that firms which were majority owned by employees on average were generating three times more net new jobs per year than similar conventional firms. Obviously, this finding, assuming that employee-owned companies are not creating unnecessary jobs, suggests that profitability in these firms also results in very favorable conditions for local communities.[20] A 1985 NCEO study produced further evidence that employee-owned companies are both more profitable and stronger job creators than their conventional counterparts. National Center researchers found in this case that the employee-owned companies in their sample outperformed conventional competitors by 30 percent in sales growth, and again three-to-one in employment growth.[21] A 1984 NCEO study, performed for the New York Stock Exchange, also found that publicly traded companies having a minimum of 10 percent of corporate stock owned by employees on average outperform 62 to 75 percent of their competitors on a variety of measures.[22]

A study of particular interest to the issue of making the transition from founder ownership and control to an alternative ownership form was reported by Alan Cohen and Michael Quarrey in the *Journal of Small Business Management* in 1986. In this exploratory study, Cohen and Quarrey analyzed the performance of twenty-eight firms whose founder/owners had retired and transferred ownership to employees through the creation of an ESOP. The sample was small because the researchers encountered great difficulty in identifying companies on the basis of this criterion. All of the twenty-eight were small businesses with a median employment level of 150 and $13.5 million in annual sales in 1984. As their measures for evaluating the performance of these firms, the researchers used annual employment and sales growth figures. Growth in employment at each ESOP company was compared with the overall growth of employment in each firm's industry. The sales growth of the employee-owned companies was compared with that of five conventional firms in the same industry of similar size in terms of number of employees and located in approximately the same geographic region. The average annual percentage employment growth for the employee-owned companies was found to be 3.4 times greater than the average annual percentage employment growth rate at the industry level. In actual percentages it was found that, for the ESOP firms, the average annual percentage employment growth rate was 5.6 percent, compared with an industry average of 1.7 percent. From the standpoint of sales growth, Cohen and Quarrey found that the average annual percentage increase in sales was 12.7 percent for the ESOP companies, compared to 9.7 percent for matched firms in the same industry, or in other words 1.3 times greater.[23]

SUMMARY

Research findings such as those cited above have not, surprisingly, continued to fuel interest in employee ownership among business and trade union leaders who are concerned with the long-term future of American business. Similarly, in spite of the retirement of Senator Russell Long, support in Washington continues to be broad based. Among the advocates of ESOPs are Ted Kennedy—who has suggested that he would like to see legislation developed which would eventually make every major corporation in America at least 50 percent employee owned—and conservative leaders such as Orrin Hatch and even Ronald Reagan.[24] Thus, it is certainly not surprising that the book, *The 100 Best Companies in America to Work For,* cited employee ownership as one common key distinguishing factor that differentiated the 100 best firms from other U.S. companies.

In spite of all this enthusiasm, the transition to employee ownership has not been universally successful in realizing the full potential of the concept. Different companies have followed different strategies in making the shift to partial or 100 percent employee ownership, and each of these strategies has its own unique dynamics and complexities. Furthermore, some strategies are also more prone to abuse and misuse. Such issues can best be understood by examining the specific experiences of different organizations, and so it is to this task we turn in Chapter 7.

CHAPTER 6 ENDNOTES

1. Joel Kotkin. "What I Do in Private Is My Own Business." *Inc. Magazine*, vol. 8, no. 11, November 1986, p. 70.

2. Chemical Bank. *Small Business Speaks: The Chemical Bank Report* (New York: Chemical Bank, 1983).

3. Michael Conte. "Participation and Performance in U.S. Labor-Managed Firms." In Derek C. Jones and Jan Svejnar, eds., *Participatory and Self-Managed Firms: Evaluating Economic Performance* (Lexington, Mass.: Lexington Books, 1982), pp. 213–238.

4. Joshua Hyatt. "Are ESOPs Feeble?" *Inc. Magazine*, vol. 8, no. 5, May 1986, p. 22.

5. Corey M. Rosen, Katherine J. Klein, and Karen M. Young. *Employee Ownership in America: The Equity Solution* (Lexington, Mass.: Lexington Books, 1986), pp. 1, 18; Alan Cohen and Michael Quarrey. "Performance of Employee-Owned Small Companies: A Preliminary Study." *Journal of Small Business Management*, vol. 24, no. 2, April 1986, p. 59.

6. "ESOPs: Revolution or Ripoff?" *Business Week*. April 15, 1985, p. 96.

7. Rosen et al., 1986, pp. 251–252.

8. "ESOPs: Revolution or Ripoff?" *Business Week*. April 15, 1985, pp. 94–95; Rosen et al., 1986, p. 15.

9. Rosen et al., 1986, p. 253.

10. Joel Kotkin, November 1986, pp. 70, 79.

11. ABC Nightly News. "Wrong Way on Wall Street," March 5, 1987.

12. NBC News. "Wall Street: Power, Greed, Money," March 1987.

13. ABC Nightly News, March 5, 1987.

14. Henry G. Dahl. *Worker-Owned Plywood Companies in the State of Washington* (Everett, Wash.: First National Bank of Everett, 1957).

15. Katrina V. Berman. *Worker-Owned Plywood Companies: An Eco-*

nomic Analysis (Pullman, Wash.: Washington State University Press, 1967), pp. 189–190.

16. Katrina V. Berman. *Comparative Productivity in Worker-Managed Cooperative Plywood Plants and Conventionally Run Plants.* Unpublished manuscript (University of Idaho, Moscow, 1976); Paul Bernstein. *Workplace Democratization: Its Internal Dynamics* (New Brunswick, N.J.: Transaction Books, 1980), pp. 18–19; Katrina V. Berman. "Worker Management in U.S. Plywood Manufacturing Cooperatives: A Cooperative Model for Labour Management." In Frank H. Stephen, ed., *The Performance of Labour-Managed Firms* (New York: St. Martin's Press, 1982).

17. Michael Conte and Arnold Tannenbaum. *Employee Ownership* (Ann Arbor: University of Michigan Survey Research Center, 1980), p. 3; Conte, 1982, pp. 233–235.

18. Thomas Marsh and Dale McAllister. "ESOPs Tables." *Journal of Corporation Law*, vol. 8, no. 3, spring 1981, pp. 613–617.

19. L.D. Brooks, J.B. Henry, and D.T. Livingston. "How Profitable Are Employee Stock Ownership Plans?" *The Financial Executive*, May 1982, pp. 32–40.

20. Corey Rosen and Katherine Klein. "Job-Generating Performance of Employee-Owned Companies." *Monthly Labor Review*, vol. 106, no. 8, August 1983, pp. 15–19.

21. Ira Wagner and Corey Rosen. "Employee Ownership: Its Effects on Corporate Performance." *Employment Relations Today*, spring 1985, pp. 15–19.

22. Rosen et al., 1986, p. 2.

23. Alan Cohen and Michael Quarrey. "Performance of Employee-Owned Small Companies: A Preliminary Study." *Journal of Small Business Management*, vol. 24, no. 2, April 1986, pp. 58–63.

24. Telephone conversation with William Foote Whyte, Cornell University, Ithaca, N.Y., April 18, 1987.

CHAPTER 7

Six Paths to Employee Ownership

People are often surprised to learn the names of some of America's more than 10,000 employee-owned firms. Employee ownership has penetrated companies in almost every industry, high tech and low tech, and ranging from corporate giants to small family-owned firms. United Parcel Service, a company which everyone has probably used at one time or another, is employee owned, and the value of employee equity at UP is substantial. In 1982 the average employee at this more than 10,000 person firm owned stock worth approximately $160,000, in addition to normal pension benefits.[1]

Companies with employee ownership programs are also widely recognized as some of the most innovative and successful enterprises in this country. For example, Hewlett-Packard, a firm identified by Peters and Waterman in their book *In Search of Excellence* as one of America's best managed firms, has a broad base of employee ownership. HP's more than 50,000 employees own over 51 percent of its common stock.[2] Similarly, W.L. Gore and Associates, one of four "organizational gems" identified by Tom Peters in his book *Passion for Excellence*, has significant employee participation in ownership. Eighty-five percent of the company's common stock was acquired from the founding family by Gore employees through a direct purchase program, and another 10 percent of the firm's stock is owned through an ESOP.[3] At W.L. Gore, however, the stock program is called an ASOP, because anyone working for Gore is considered an "associate"—there are no managers or employees since everyone is an owner.[4] (Gore will be discussed further in chapter 9.)

Florida's largest supermarket chain, Publix Supermarkets, is 100 percent employee owned. Publix's 15,000 full-time employees acquired 84 percent of the company's stock through a direct purchase program, 10 percent through a profit sharing plan, and the final 6 percent through an ESOP.[5] Lowe's Companies, Inc., the nation's largest building supplies retailer with over $1½ billion in sales, is 30 percent owned by its employees.[6] In heavy industry, the country's largest and most profitable independent integrated steelmaker, Weirton Steel, is 100 percent employee owned. Weirton was purchased as part of an employee buyout plan from National Steel, which resulted in the saving of both 7,000 jobs and the 26,000 resident community of Weirton, West Virginia. Weirton stock is owned by its employee owners through an ESOP, and its union workers are represented on the company's nine-person board of directors by three union-selected representatives.[7] Similarly, another large industrial firm, Avondale Industries, a major U.S. shipbuilder and an employer of more than 10,000 people, is also 100 percent employee owned.[8]

Companies such as these are among the approximately 10,000 firms in the United States that have adopted `some form of employee ownership. Not all of these companies, however, have become employee owned in the same way or for the same reasons. In this chapter, we describe six different paths for becoming employee owned and the motivations that underlie them. We will also look at the consequences of each approach: consequences that have not always been entirely positive.

Whether the consequences of employee ownership are primarily positive or negative we believe is in great part a function of whether or not a "spirit of ownership" or what Rosen et al. have called in their book *Employee Ownership in America* an "ownership culture" becomes a significant feature of the way a particular organization operates and its employees look upon their relationship to the firm. It is our contention that companies that develop strong ownership cultures will be more efficient and adaptive as well as generally exude a greater spirit of cooperation and enthusiasm for organizational success than those with a weak or no ownership culture. This is so because in firms that create and sustain a strong feeling of ownership, employees not only feel motivated by the possibility of eventually reaping great rewards, but they also experience a very real feeling of responsibility for the company's future. They develop this feeling of responsibility because the firm's culture is one that encourages a high degree of employee participation in traditional management and policy-making functions, and because they gain a clear understanding of how their behavior and that of fellow employees affect company costs and profitability. This participation helps employees to see and believe that their actions can have a significant impact on the company's immediate profitability and its long-term success. Thus, in a company which develops a strong ownership culture, in which many aspects of its operations and social relations emphasize through language, policies, methods of decision making and so forth that employees are in fact owners, employees will act with the same sense of concern that is characteristic of a single entrepreneur who founds an enterprise.

Our research and personal experience, however, suggest that each of the different approaches for adopting employee ownership are not equal in their ability to facilitate the development of an ownership culture. Thus, in this chapter and the following chapter we will repeatedly examine the extent to which each of the paths has served to create what might be called an "ownership culture" or a "culture of ownership." Before examining each path in some detail, however, we will in the next section provide a brief overview of all six paths to becoming employee owned.

THE PATHS

The first and most obvious path to employee ownership, one that we strongly recommend, is as part of a specific transition strategy following the retirement, death, or withdrawal of a company's founders. Privately held companies that convert to employee ownership at this time, especially those that had been healthy under the ownership of the founding group, are the most likely to succeed. This category also represents the fastest growth area for employee ownership today. Between 25 and 35 percent of all ESOPs established since 1984 resulted from a transition strategy following the retirement of the company's original owners.

A second path toward employee ownership has emerged among the fast-growth, high-tech industries of the late 1970s and 1980s. Companies in this sector of the economy have often found it difficult to recruit and retain the kind of highly skilled workers and managers they need, given the scarcity and extreme marketability of such employees. Giving employees equity in the company has become one solution to this problem.

A third path toward employee ownership is as a start-up strategy. In many cases, particularly when a company's founders are interested in establishing a cooperative and participative management structure, a company can start with employee ownership from the beginning. Such organizations have been established by individual entrepreneurs or groups who have set out to establish companies based upon the principles and values of economic democracy. For example, many of the plywood cooperatives of the Pacific Northwest, and some of the new airlines that have emerged since industry deregulation in 1978, started out as employee-owned companies.

Employees have also become owners of a variety of private and publicly traded companies as part of ongoing programs of organizational improvement. This fourth path to employee ownership has existed since the nineteenth century, when many companies established stock purchase programs for their employees as a means for merging employee and company interests. In recent years the ESOP has become the most popular vehicle for implementing employee ownership for such purposes; and, because of its tax advantages, the ESOP has also been a tool for increasing organizational efficiency through major capital improvements. In some cases, employee stock ownership plans have made capital improvement projects, previously considered impossible, suddenly financially feasible. Some managers have even admitted that their primary motivation for adopting an ESOP was to benefit from its advantages as a financial tool. Most managers, however, do find that employee ownership also brings an improvement in employee relations, which is equally attractive.

A fifth path to employee ownership, one that recently has attracted great public interest and controversy, is the employee buyout. The buyout is a common strategy when a company faces a business crisis, when a public firm has been taken private, or when an effort has been made to avert a hostile takeover. Even more frequently, the employee buyout has been a strategy for averting an impending plant shutdown or a company closing. We have seen workers and whole communities rallying together in an effort to raise sufficient capital to purchase a company or a plant slated for closure, the victim of an absentee owner's decision to get out of the business and liquidate. Although the drama and intense publicity that typically attends these efforts have made employee buyouts the most widely recognized cases of employee ownership, they actually represent less than 2 percent of the total population of employee-owned firms in the United States.[9]

Finally, the sixth path toward employee ownership is through the process of collective bargaining itself. This is a relatively new development which emerged in the late 1970s and has continued to gather momentum during the 1980s. In response to problems of overcapacity, foreign competition, and deregulation, many companies have recently sought to reduce costs by demanding concessions from their unionized workers. In return for agreeing to cuts in wages and benefits and the relaxation of work rules, unions have demanded a share in future profits, both through profit-sharing plans and the issuance of company stock to workers. In many cases, workers and union leaders have wanted stock as a guarantee that they will share in the profits from improved company performance along with the traditional shareholders. In other cases, when workers believe the company's difficulties stem from mismanagement, they have sought to use employee stock ownership to gain some degree of influence in company decision making. The ability to vote at shareholders' meetings and elect employee representatives to the board of directors has often been seen by employees as a quid pro quo for making contract concessions, as well as an essential form of insurance against future mismanagement.

EMPLOYEE OWNERSHIP AS A TRANSITION STRATEGY

As we have mentioned, today's primary path toward employee ownership is as part of a direct transition in ownership from the founders to the employees, and we will discuss this path in more detail in the following chapter. At this point, we simply want to put the idea of a transition strategy in perspective.

Of the 1200 ESOPs created in 1985, some 300 to 400 involved an owner-to-employee transfer of stock in preparation for the owners' retirement or withdrawal from the business. The substantial number of such transfers is primarily due to the tax incentives created in the Deficit Reduction Act of 1984 and intended to encourage company owners to sell their stock to employees. These incentives make employee ownership perhaps the most financially attractive transition strategy available to the owners of private corporations contemplating retirement or seeking a way to get out of the business.

The success stories involving such a transition strategy are numerous. In 1961, for example, Lowe's Companies, the nation's largest discount retail seller of building supplies and equipment, had been in business for forty years and had seven stores and $27 million in sales. Shortly after owner Carl Buchan's death in that year, the company transferred 48 percent of its stock to the employees. By 1970, the company had seventy-five stores and $170 million in sales; by 1984, 235 stores, $2.3 billion in sales, and over 14,000 employees. The company's chairman attributes their success primarily to the positive impact of employee ownership on worker motivation and commitment to the business.[10] We will look in more detail at the specifics of Lowe's transition strategy in the next chapter.

Another successful case is Fastener Industries of Berea, Ohio, which many observers consider to be one of the best and most truly participative ESOP companies in the country. A small firm with only 115 employees, Fastener Industries makes industrial weld fasteners that are used to hold together housings for computers, metal office furniture, metal sinks and a variety of other metal containers for industrial equipment.

Fastener has been employee owned since 1980 when the firm's family-owned stock was transferred to an ESOP. Its managers credit employee ownership for the generally high level of motivation among the company's work force, and for the company's ability to stay profitable during the recession of the 1980s, when the rest of the industry was suffering losses and even plant closings. After initiating employee ownership, the company took a variety of steps to ensure the establishment of an "ownership culture" of loyalty and mutual responsibility. For example, although many ESOPs withhold full voting rights from employee stock for a period of ten to fifteen years of service, at Fastener all employees become fully vested in the ESOP and are given full voting rights after only one month. This policy instills a strong sense of ownership in each employee very early in his or her career, and probably accounts for the company's extremely low turnover rate of only 2 to 3 percent a year.

With their full voting rights, Fastener's employees are able to vote on all major corporate issues and elect all five corporate directors at the annual shareholder meetings. An ownership culture is reinforced at Fastener by a generous profit-sharing plan (in existence even before the establishment of the ESOP) which pays out an annual bonus that can equal as much as its earnings for an entire month. Fastener also maintains a no-layoff policy, so its employees feel their jobs are essentially guaranteed. Thus, there is no reason for employees to withhold ideas that may improve efficiency out of fear such actions might also eliminate their jobs. Employees at this company are truly *owners* in the full sense of the word; and, as with members of the original founding family, they do not lose their jobs when business conditions get rough.

Fastener's employee-owners also remain involved in and informed about the business through an ongoing process of shop floor participation. Supervisors meet regularly with employees after their monthly meetings with the company president, and they are required to keep workers informed on the company's performance and all important changes and decisions. Similarly, whenever a decision must be made on the purchase of new equipment or a possible change in production methods, the employees affected by the decision are consulted. Richard Biernacki, company president, holds small group meetings with different groups of workers every six months. At these meetings, Biernacki listens carefully to the concerns and ideas of each employee group, and he provides in-depth answers to their questions. All these practices have helped to ensure that Fastener employees feel a strong sense of ownership toward the company, sharing both its rewards and the responsibility for its success.

EMPLOYEE OWNERSHIP AS A RECRUITMENT AND RETENTION STRATEGY

Adopting employee ownership as a strategy for recruiting and retaining highly skilled employees is a relatively new phenomenon. This path to employee ownership stems from a combination of unusually fast business growth common to many high-tech companies over the last ten years and a certain form of professionalism among high-tech workers. Given the constantly increasing demand for their services, high-tech workers often hop from job to job in search of better compensation or more opportunity. As a middle manager at one Silicon Valley company explained to us in an interview:

> I'm really quite unusual compared to most managers and engineers in this area. I've stayed at this company for more than six years. That's not the way it is for most people,

though. They go from here to there looking for a more interesting job, a chance to get ahead or make a lot more money, and if the opportunity arises they might take off without a moment's notice.

To counter this situation, some companies have chosen to offer stock ownership to new employees, giving it to them as a benefit either through an ESOP or through a performance bonus or stock option program. In fact, throughout the industry, providing employees with equity participation has become almost a requisite condition of employment. As the president of a San José public relations firm put it, "Out here, everybody, including the janitors, expects to be an owner."[11]

Given the intense demands that can be placed upon professional employees at these firms, this type of incentive has proven particularly important to counter the effect of burnout and alienation. Jim Fruchterman, the founder and CEO of the Palantir Corporation, developers of a high-powered document scanning and word processing system, explains that the company asks its employees for "an extraordinary commitment of time and personal energy" and therefore gives them a chance to eventually own a substantial piece of the company.[12]

Employee ownership can also be a factor when attempting to recruit highly skilled people within an increasingly competitive market. Again this is particularly true in high-tech industries, where many small companies, without tremendous cash resources, have to compete for competent staff with much larger companies. At Microwave Filter Company of Syracuse, New York, for example, employee ownership has proven indispensable in the process of competing for engineering talent with industry giants such as General Electric. Microwave, a sixteen-year-old company that does about $5 million a year in sales, cannot compete on the basis of salary alone. Their top engineer earned $30,000 a year in 1985 when an experienced engineer at GE might have been making as much as 50 percent more. To counter this situation, company president Glyn Bostick decided to offer key employees lucrative stock options and allow all employees to buy public shares at 20 percent below the going market rate. Now the company's employees see themselves as having an opportunity to share substantially in the business growth they help to create.[13]

This strategy, however, is not without its problems. After all, a company is not always successful, despite the best efforts of its employees. Moreover, as with the professional managers we have criticized in earlier chapters, the new employee lured to a company by stock options may also be counting on fast short-term growth and quick wealth, instead of working toward long-term corporate stability and success. If so, then employee ownership can put the same negative pressures on a corporation as can absentee ownership. Corporate officers may find themselves focused on raising stock allocations and stock prices to appease the employee-owners, just as they might have done for ordinary absentee shareholders. Consider, for example, a recent account in the business press of something that happened at Charles River Data Systems in Framingham, Massachusetts. During a job interview with a potential new employee, the personnel manager was asked whether stock options were included in the compensation package. The personnel manager was pleased to be asked this question because the company had adopted an employee-ownership program some time before. He told the applicant that the job would indeed come with an option to purchase 1,000 shares at a specified discount price determined at the time of hiring. The applicant's response, however, was surprising:

> One thousand shares? The applicant was visibly disappointed, even annoyed. He allowed as how another company just down the road had offered him 5,000 shares. The personnel manager was speechless. Evidently the candidate hadn't a clue that 1,000 shares in one company might constitute a larger piece of the action than 5,000 shares in another—as was, indeed, the situation in this case.
>
> Taking a cue from the incident, Charles River Data subsequently announced a stock split that would multiply everyone's shares by five. The chief financial officer recalls

being bowled over by the response. "It was still the same company," he says. "Nobody's stake in the company had changed one bit. But people were stopping me in the hall and thanking me for what we did. One guy said we had done two great things for him. Not only had we split the stock, but his per-share purchase price would be one-fifth of what it had been."[14]

Obviously, situations like this do little to contribute to organizational health; in fact, they can be a detriment to long-term effectiveness and profitability. Employee ownership, to accomplish the ends we have outlined in this book and to overcome the ills of absentee ownership, must be far more than a way to get rich or a handy compensation gimmick. Employees must understand how stock ownership works, and they must have a thorough understanding and appreciation for what can make a company successful over the long haul. To accomplish these ends, a company must do far more than merely give employees stock or potentially lucrative stock options. Instead, an ownership culture must be a significant and continuous driving force for long-term organizational success.

EMPLOYEE OWNERSHIP START-UPS

Starting out employee owned is an important but infrequent approach to adopting employee ownership, at least here in the United States. Only a very small percentage of the employee-owned companies that are added to the list of employee ownership firms each year are of this variety. This is in great part because starting out employee owned is the hardest of all approaches that can be pursued, as one recent commentator explains:

Of all the ways to become an employee ownership company, starting up is the hardest. Using employee ownership in a start-up doesn't provide a market for a retiring owner; it doesn't save a firm which would otherwise close; it isn't practical as a way to raise capital; it doesn't serve to make wage concessions more equitable. Most start-up companies plow their earnings back into the company, and so have no taxable income against which they can take the deductions ESOPs offer. What employee ownership does offer new companies is a way to involve all the workers in capital ownership.[15]

Companies that decide, despite these problems, to engage in an employee ownership start-up are usually seeking one of two objectives; either they are trying to found their company upon the ideals of economic democracy or they are seeking a competitive cost advantage (because employees consider stock ownership an acceptable substitute for high fixed wage and compensation levels). We will consider the latter category first.

Cost Advantages

Companies that start out employee owned to minimize labor and overhead costs are increasing in newly deregulated industries in the transportation field. New trucking and airline firms have adopted this strategy to create new markets or to break into existing markets dominated by large firms established during the period of strict governmental control. In Chapter 8 we will examine in detail one such company and the problems it encountered, the now defunct People Express Air Lines. At People Express, applicants for employment had to purchase 100 shares of company common stock before being hired. Lately, several other new low-fare air carriers have adopted a similar strategy. One, which is still operating profitably and which has grown substantially since the passing of the 1978 Air Line Deregulation Act, is the Phoenix-based America West Airlines.

Like People Express, America West also required a purchase of company stock as an initial condition of employment. However, rather than all buying the same number of shares of stock, America West workers and managers must purchase a number of shares that is equal to 20 percent of their first year's base pay. In addition, they adopted a variety of participative management practices, such as work teams and shared job roles within teams. In this way, the company has sought to achieve maximum flexibility, low fixed wage and salary costs, and high levels of employee motivation, none of which exist at the large unionized air carriers. Company president and co-founder Mike Conway, a former Continental Air Lines vice-president and controller, explained that this policy, ". . . is predicated on the simple idea that if we're successful, there's enough for everybody. And if we're not successful and don't have profits, the whole thing comes apart like a cheap watch. . . . Those who frown on the complexity of doing things that make people enthusiastic are missing a bet."[16] The concept seems to have worked. America West has grown substantially since it was first organized, taking a large share of the Western market away from major airlines which service the Southwest and the West Coast. Costs are low and productivity high at America West, in large part because of the attitude of motivated owners like twenty-seven-year-old customer service representative Mike Ehl, who said, "Every time I go out to the airport, I feel excited about what I'm part of . . . [equity participation] creates a bond that joins people and makes us think and work harder together."[17]

Worker Cooperatives

Although the success of a company like America West is impressive, most companies that pursue employee ownership as part of a start-up strategy are not of this type. The typical employee ownership start-up is usually comprised of a group of workers who want to implement economic democracy in the workplace through establishing a cooperative enterprise. Cooperative firms, commonly referred to as producer or worker cooperatives, are relatively rare in the United States, apart from the plywood cooperatives of the Pacific Northwest and some firms that have been formed by various counterculture groups since the antiwar era of the late 1960s and early 1970s. In a number of other countries, however, cooperatives have become a significant sector of the economy. In Europe, several nations have decided to encourage the formation of worker cooperatives, as we have encouraged the creation of ESOPs, to counter unemployment and revitalize industry.

In 1984 Italy led the world in the number of worker cooperatives with 11,203 firms employing 428,000 workers. Although the cooperative movement has existed in Italy since the 1800s, more than half of these firms were started during the ten-year period from 1971 to 1981. In 1983 France claimed some 1,269 worker cooperatives employing 40,423 worker-owners; 66 percent of these firms had been established after 1978. The United Kingdom has also begun to experiment with this form of employee ownership as a way to deal with Britain's sagging economy. In 1984 the United Kingdom could count 911 worker cooperatives with an employment level of 20,000 workers. Half of this number had been established during the preceding five years.[18] The most successful attempt to build an economic base on a system of worker cooperatives took place in the Basque Region of Northern Spain where people of Basque descent have established a network of approximately 178 cooperative firms with more than 20,000 worker owners.[19] This system was not supported by the government; rather, it was initiated through the efforts of a Catholic priest, Father Don José Maria Arizmendiarrieta, and a group of young men who had studied under him at a village vocational school which he founded.

Worker cooperatives are not all formed for precisely the same reasons, nor are the motives of all members of any given cooperative exactly the same. Nonetheless, it is safe to say that all worker cooperatives are created with a structure of ownership and a method of management intended to make the workplace a democratic institution. Worker cooperatives are intentionally founded upon principles of economic democracy. To be a cooperative, and therefore a democratically operated enterprise, a firm must adhere at least loosely to the following six basic criteria, which, as Paul Bernstein has suggested, are necessary conditions for workplace democracy:

1. Employee participation in decision making, through both direct and representative forms of participation.

2. Frequent feedback of economic results to all employees, both in the form of money paid out and as information shared by word-of-mouth and formal reports.

3. Full disclosure of information, especially financial data, which in a traditional firm would only be available to members of top management.

4. The guarantee of specific individual rights similar to those guaranteed in the political world as individual liberties.

5. An independent board of appeal through which workers can seek redress on matters of dispute without fear of reprisal and with a guarantee of fairness and objectivity.

6. A culture or specific set of attitudes, which include a sense of self-determination, a willingness to take political action, and a sense of ownership and responsibility.[20]

The Plywood Cooperatives

The ways in which Bernstein's six criteria come into play in a worker cooperative are well illustrated by the plywood cooperatives of the Pacific Northwest. As mentioned in the preceding chapter the worker-owners of these companies participate in the functioning of their businesses in a very complete and democratic fashion, and this all begins with the concept of being a member and owner and not just an employee. When an individual wishes to join a plywood cooperative, there must first be an opening for a new owner and, if so, the individual must contribute an initial amount of capital, thereby buying out the interest of a departing worker-owner. Some observers have referred to this requirement as "buying a job," but members of a worker cooperative look at this payment quite differently. Leamon J. Bennett, who in 1979 was president and CEO of Puget Sound Plywood, explained to David Ewing, former editor of the *Harvard Business Review*:

No member has bought a job. . . . He has joined an association in which people band together to manufacture a
commodity that none of them could produce alone. The
results of their efforts belong to all. Even though he can't
look at the plant, the machinery, and the inventory and
say, "I see my 1/240th interest," he does own such an interest and is in a sense in business for himself.[21]

This requirement of making an initial capital investment
before becoming a member of a cooperative plays a significant
function in terms of ensuring that no one is granted admit-
tance to a cooperative firm without first making a financial
sacrifice symbolizing their commitment. Historically, this
has been a practice common to all of the Northwest plywood
cooperatives. For example, in the case of the first plywood cooperative, the Olympia Plywood Company of Olympia, Washington, all of the firm's initial founding group of 125
carpenters, mechanics, and lumbermen were required to contribute $1,000 of their own money to the venture. By making
this contribution, each employee-owner received under contract one share of company stock, which entitled them to an
equal vote with all other members in company affairs, an
equal share of any profits, and a job in the company. Some of
these workmen drew on personal savings, or cashed in savings
bonds. Others agreed to take a deduction from their wages, or
took mortgages out on their personal property. Thus, when
the company started manufacturing in August, 1921, it had
an adequate capital base; and since plywood was at that time
a relatively new industry, Olympia Plywood prospered.[22]
Olympia was the only cooperative plywood company in
the Pacific Northwest for over fifteen years. Just before the
beginning of World War II, three more cooperatives were
started in Washington following the same pattern. These
three firms were Anacortes Veneer, Inc., Peninsula Plywood
Corporation, and Puget Sound Plywood. Together they, along
with the first company, Olympia Plywood, accounted for the
production of six plants operating during the Second World
War. These six plants produced 20 to 25 percent of total in-

dustry output.[23] By the mid-1950s, when the last of plywood cooperatives was being formed, the number reached a peak of between twenty-six and thirty-five firms.

At this point enthusiasm for creating plywood cooperatives ceased. Part of the reason was market saturation. There was also, however, considerable unfavorable publicity, resulting from lawsuits filed against an unusual class of business promoters which had emerged as a spin-off of the cooperative movement. These promoters marketed themselves as sales agents for the firms and brokers for raising capital by selling cooperative shares of newly forming companies. The selling of shares actually became a speculative activity, and some promoters sold workers phony shares or shares at inflated prices. Eventually, criminal charges and several civil suits were brought against some of these middlemen. These events threw a negative light on any plan to start a new cooperative firm, plywood or otherwise, and so interest in building new companies disappeared.[24]

Today there are only eleven plywood cooperatives still in operation as cooperatives (some have become private firms or subsidiaries of other companies). These eleven firms, however, still account for approximately 25 percent of plywood production in the United States.[25] We will return to the reasons for the decline later in this section. For now we will focus upon the democratic management practices of the cooperative firm.

Although each of the plywood cooperatives have certain practices that are uniquely their own, their basic characteristics are similar and consistent with Bernstein's six criteria of workplace democracy. They are not perfect in realizing these objectives, however, and we will discuss their key weak points as we move through the discussion.

As noted above, an individual cannot become an owner and member of a cooperative without first paying an initial fee which entitles him or her to one share of company stock. In most cases, it is not possible to join a cooperative until someone who is already a member retires and wants to sell their share. Upon retirement, members are required to sell their shares and cannot keep them—since to do so would make them absentee owners. The shares are transferable, but the retiring employee-owner must first offer to sell to the cooperative itself. Even if a cooperative chooses not to buy the share, the cooperative's board of directors must approve the person to whom the share is sold. As one plywood company president explained, "After all, . . . we're not just hiring; we're taking on a new member."[26]

Democratic Management in the Plywood Coops. Once a cooperative member owns a share, he or she is entitled to a say in company affairs equal to that of other cooperative members. This means that the member has the right to elect the company's board of directors and its top corporate officers. All members of the board of directors must be working members of the cooperative, and during the working day they perform normal duties such as operating machinery, moving material, grading lumber, and so forth. The board of directors in turn elects the board chairperson or CEO, and they select and appoint the company's top management team, which in the typical plywood firm includes a general manager who oversees daily operations, a plant supervisor, a sales manager, a logs purchaser, an accountant, a shipping expediter, and their respective assistants. All of the individuals in these positions are usually cooperative members, except the general manager who is a hired hand. The reason this is the case is that, in order to hire a competent general manager, most cooperatives must pay far more money than would be paid to a member.

The board of directors of a plywood cooperative is quite different from the board of directors of a traditional capitalist firm. The members of a cooperative's board receive no extra compensation for their work on the board, and they meet frequently, at least twice each month and sometimes once a week, to discuss a wide range of issues. Areas of board responsibility include such matters as reviewing questions and complaints received in the shop, interviewing new job applicants, hearing disciplinary cases, deciding on contracts with customers and suppliers, creating and reviewing plans for capital improvements, and determining the firm's marketing strategy. The general manager sits in on the board meetings in which these issues are discussed in a respected but purely advisory capacity with no vote.

Plywood cooperatives operate with, in addition to the board of directors, a number of standing committees, which perform functions normally done by an administrative staff or through the collective bargaining process in a unionized setting. The representatives on these committees are either selected by the board of directors or elected by the membership at large. Committees selected by the board of directors are usually responsible for monitoring, coordinating, and coming up with ideas for change in areas such as safety, company audits, production control, machinery, plant operations, and insurance. Committees that are elected by the members at large tend to deal with delicate issues such as job descriptions and job bidding, grievances, and the equalization of all members' working hours. The board of directors and these various committees therefore help to fulfill Bernstein's second criterion for workplace democracy by providing workers with broad decision-making powers through the representatives they elect to these positions. The grievance, job bidding, and equalization committees also fulfill Bernstein's requirement that an independent board of appeal exist apart from the traditional management structure.

While this representative system of democracy covers most matters, issues having to do with the spending of money or the allocation of resources require a vote by the entire membership of most cooperatives. Thus, the bylaws of most cooperatives set limits on how much money can be spent by the board of directors for new equipment without the vote of the general membership. At some cooperatives the limit is as low as $20,000 to $25,000. The board may also be required to take such matters as major contracts to the full membership, and certainly any decision to raise or lower base wages. Such issues are discussed at the annual shareholders' meeting or, if pressing, at a special general meeting of all coop members. Leamon Bennett describes the way the annual meeting as well as any special meetings function in the following interview excerpt:

> We begin them generally at 8 a.m. in a hall uptown. They're held on workdays, usually on Saturdays. We pay straight-time pay for attendance, which is time-and-a-half on Saturdays. The mill operates six days a week. We follow Robert's Rules of Order. Presentations are made and inquiries from the floor responded to. Then there's usually a motion to accept a plan of action and a vote.
>
> If there's a problem, we hold a special meeting. Special meetings are limited to the subjects that are mentioned in the letters sent out to each shareholder. Occasionally, we'll have a meeting on an issue like whether to buy a piece of equipment—expensive equipment. We'll have that right here in the mill. It's just a matter of getting together and setting up a PA system in the shop. The meeting'll last perhaps 30 minutes, depending on the amount of discussion.[27]

Keeping Coop Members Informed. Measured against Bernstein's second and third requirements for workplace democracy, the performance of the plywood cooperatives is exceptional. Most plywood cooperatives go to great lengths to provide the membership with all financial information they want or need as Paul Bernstein explains below:

> To supplement the informal communication network where worker-directors talk with their friends back on the production line, company issues are presented to shareowners in more formal ways. In the most concerned companies, monthly reports are sent to each worker's home. These reports give the company's profit-and-loss statement, its output, inventory, sales situation and other crucial economic transactions usually reserved for top executives in the standard corporation. In less diligent worker-owned firms, a shorter statement is prepared quarterly and left in a stack on a table for interested work-

ers to pick up. Reports from the twice-monthly board meetings are posted in most companies. At year's end the company financial statement is circulated to all worker-owners, and in at least one firm, a complete audit is mailed to each member, revealing exactly what has been paid to every other member of the firm.[28]

The pay system for cooperative members and the bonuses paid from profits are also a very powerful source of feedback to cooperative members. Bonuses are paid as often as quarterly. All members, whether they are janitors or accountants, are paid the same hourly rate, a rate determined by the economic health of the company. For example, when the plywood market was very strong during the construction boom of 1979 to early 1981, many of the cooperatives were paying a base wage rate of about $12 per hour, plus providing worker-members with many hours of overtime at time-and-a-half pay. Thus, at the healthiest firms during this period, many employee-owners were earning in excess of $40,000 a year before profit sharing. When the recession began to hit in 1982 with a slump in construction resulting from high interest rates, the base rate for cooperative members was dropped by between 10 and 25 percent in unadjusted dollars and as much as 50 percent in adjusted dollars.[29] Because each member receives an equal share of company profits, he or she must also share in the firm's losses. In good times, therefore, pay and profit bonuses are typically better than at traditional capitalist companies, but in bad times the reverse may be true. Credited profits may be used to absorb losses and the base wage rate dropped to keep costs low and thereby ensure the cooperative's survival.

In bad times the fringe benefits provided for cooperative workers may also be reduced, but even then they are still quite good compared to other companies. Fringe benefits at the plywood cooperatives often include free lunches in the company cafeteria, full medical care coverage for all family members including dental and eye care, and life insurance.

Workers are even able to purchase gasoline at wholesale prices through the cooperative.

All of these factors help to create a system of organizational rewards and governance that is highly democratic but still very efficient and profitable. There are, however, several important flaws in the cooperative system as implemented by the plywood cooperatives of the Pacific Northwest. Perhaps the most notable is the way in which membership has been tied to the concept of purchasing equity or attached to property rights. In other cooperatives, such as those in Mondragon of the Basque Region of northern Spain, these two aspects are separated. When a person joins one of the Basque cooperatives, he or she puts up an initial capital payment to become a member, approximately $3,000 to $5,000, and by paying in that initial investment immediately becomes a member with all the rights of membership. The money invested is entered in a company capital account for the individual, and the funds in the capital account grow each year if the firm is profitable. The actual rights of membership, however, are treated separately from the capital investment so that there is no monetary value attached to a member share as there is in the plywood cooperatives. Consequently, in cooperative firms such as those established in the Northern Region of Spain, the actual price of membership stays at a reasonable level over the years, rather than growing in price due to capital accumulation. In contrast, at most plywood cooperatives, the value of cooperative member shares has grown in value over the years to amounts as large as $100,000. This situation has led to an undermining of some of the equalitarian principles upon which the firms were founded, and even forced some cooperatives to go out of business or sell out to outside interests in order to allow the members to take out the full value of their invested capital.

In addition, the ownership structure of the plywood cooperative has also tended to produce a significant inconsistency in policy that degrades the overall concept—the hiring of nonowner employees. Plywood cooperatives have for many years been known to hire on additional employees who are not members. A 1982 survey of the eleven existing cooperatives showed, for example, that the average cooperative firm maintained a nonmember work force of approximately 15 percent of total employment, with one firm at a low of 3 percent and another at a high of 63 percent.[30] In many cases, these employees, like the general manager, are highly skilled individuals such as electricians and mechanics who are unwilling to work on the equalized pay basis that is required of the membership. In other instances, many of these "hired hands" are simply temporary help who are the children of the cooperative members there to earn some extra money for school during summer or winter vacations. In cases where a cooperative hires from 30 to over 60 percent of the total work force as nonmember employees, it is obvious that the practice is more permanent and thus creates a constant group of "second class" citizens. This situation is in great part created by the plywood cooperatives' ownership structure, which attaches property rights to membership rights rather than charging a standard membership fee.

Under the plywoods' system of cooperative ownership, there is tremendous incentive to not create new shares, because that simply reduces the dollar value of the existing shares, which cannot be allocated on the basis of any more than one to each person in order to maintain a cooperative one-person-one-vote control structure. As one cooperative member explained when asked why his firm did not create new shares and let new members into the system, "You'd be cutting the melon into thinner slices."[31] As a result, a permanent underclass is created which has little chance of obtaining full membership rights because of both stock price and a limited number of shares and who, like hired hands in any private firm, do the work that the owners cannot or will not do.

As we have seen, there are now only eleven plywood cooperations in existence today, compared to twenty-seven or more in the late 1950s. Of the sixteen that have disappeared, only nine (33 percent) did so as a result of business failure. This figure is even more impressive when compared to the performance of the plywood industry as a whole. In 1963, the total number of plywood mills in the Western United States reached a high of one hundred forty-one, but by 1982 there were only thirty-five such firms operating in the region, which include the cooperatives.[32] The seven other plywood cooperatives that disappeared during this same period were not failures; rather they were sold to wealthy private investors or conglomerates interested in getting into the high quality lines of plywood which are the cooperatives' specialties.

Thus, some of these small, successful cooperatives, typically ranging in size from 80 to 450 workers and from $3 million to $15 million in sales, were gobbled up by corporate giants like ITT and the Times-Mirror Corporation. This happened, ironically, because they were more successful in terms of profitability and sales growth than their ownership structure could handle. Potential new members could not afford to pay $100,000 for a share, or even to make the $20,000 to $40,000 down payment on a share of cooperative stock. Many cooperatives' owners were left with no choice other than to sell out to outside interests. Obviously, this was not a failure in traditional business terms, but it is a failure from our perspective. You can't get much more absentee-owned than being bought out by ITT. Subsequent research at firms that were acquired has revealed the characteristic impact of absentee ownership. For example, at one firm that was acquired by a large conglomerate, the number of production supervisors had to be increased by eight, even though the number of employees dropped to 100. As one worker at this former cooperative put it, "Before, a guy took real pride in his work. Now we come just for the money."[32]

In spite of these potential problems, it is clear that the plywood cooperatives are a powerful example of an ownership culture in action. And it is clear from the experience of cooperative firms in other countries that the problems presented by the American Plywood cooperative model can be solved with minimal structural adjustments. We hope that such alterations may in fact be considered by new groups attempting to start up cooperative firms here in this country. In fact, there is some indication that the stigma surrounding organizing new cooperative firms in the Pacific Northwest may have finally lifted; for recently a cooperative sawmill was established in Anacortes, Washington. Perhaps in the future we will see more such cases, and maybe this time they will avoid the problems of the past.

EMPLOYEE OWNERSHIP FOR ORGANIZATIONAL IMPROVEMENT

Many companies, both private and publicly traded, have adopted employee ownership in recent years as part of an overall strategy for stimulating organizational improvement. Indeed, during the five years immediately following the creation of major tax incentives for establishing an ESOP, many companies saw the ESOP as primarily a financing tool for making major capital improvements. This use of ESOPs did in fact strengthen many companies by allowing them to expand or become more efficient by upgrading plants and equipment, but it completely ignored the fact that ESOPs were created as "employee benefits." Indeed, many managers and corporate officers gave little if any thought to the possibility that a sharing of equity might also facilitate better employee–management relations and increase employee motivation. This is evidenced by the fact that as many as 85 percent of the ESOPs created during this period gave employees no voting rights whatsoever, even after they had completed the full period of vesting.[34] Once this situation became apparent, and many critics complained that this practice was prostituting the original intended purpose of ESOPs, Congress expanded on ESOP law in the *ESOP Improvements Act of 1980*. This act required that publicly traded companies with ESOPs give employee participants full pass-through voting rights on their allocated shares and that privately held firms provide voting rights on certain defined major issues which would affect the value of the stock or the job security of the employee stockholders.

Unfortunately, only a relatively small number of companies have chosen to adopt an ESOP primarily for its benefits as a device for increased employee motivation. In fact, a National Center for Employee Ownership study conducted in 1983 found that only 7 percent of the companies that had established ESOPs up to that point believed in the value of employee ownership enough that they would have adopted it without the tax incentives.[35]

One firm which saw the larger value of employee ownership early in the history of ESOPs is American Recreation Centers, a firm which owns and operates twenty-three bowling centers in Northern California and employs 800 people (450 full-time employees). American Recreation was founded in 1961 when its first bowling center was opened in Sacramento, California. From the outset the company had a progressive philosophy regarding the relationship of employee compensation to company performance. Thus, American Recreation instituted a variety of bonus programs and sales commissions as part of the employee compensation package early in the firm's history as well as a generous profit-sharing plan in which all employees participated.

In 1974, American Recreation Centers created one of the first ESOPs in the country and used it as a replacement for the profit-sharing program. Management chose the ESOP over the profit-sharing plan because they felt it would help employees to become more involved with their work. Because the company could make larger contributions to an ESOP, management also felt it would have a greater impact on employee interest and motivation. To augment the stock ownership plan as well as the firm's other bonus and commission programs, the company initiated a practice of holding regular monthly meetings at each bowling center where all employees could meet with management to discuss concerns, solve problems, and re-group to meet goals. In addition to monthly meetings, the company also introduced a number of practices to keep employees in touch with the firm's performance and attitudinally in tune with an ownership culture. A few of these practices are listed below:

1. Treating employee owners like all shareholders, including the distribution of all quarterly and annual reports as well as the annual proxy solicitation.

2. Paying regular dividends on stock.

3. Incorporating a discussion of the ESOP and significance of employee ownership in the new employee orientation program.

4. Providing a full description of the employee ownership plan in the company employee handbook.

5. Focusing on employee ownership in the company newsletter.

6. Holding small group meetings on employee ownership.[36]

Because top management believes in the value of employee ownership and has incorporated it into their overall business strategy as a central component, they support the concept with great enthusiasm which spreads to everyone. Company president Robert Feuchter said, for example, "I'm a great believer in people owning stock in the companies they work for. I used to work for [another company] and it was clear that you were a hired hand. I always wanted to own something."[37] Feuchter believes that his employees have similar interests and that by fulfilling this desire, productivity, employee relations, and overall profitability have improved dramatically, and that this is evident in the firm's economic performance in recent years. Total sales increased annually by $1 million between 1979 and 1984, and profits increased by $800,000 during this same period.[38]

Another enlightened company, which adopted an ESOP early on in 1974 for the purpose of bringing employee and employer interests more in line, is Quad Graphics of Pewaukee, Wisconsin. Quad Graphics adopted employee ownership as a natural complement to a management philosophy that emphasizes high levels of employee involvement in operational decision making and substantial employee responsibility for

company success. In fact, Quad's unusually participative system of management, as well as its substantial financial success, resulted in an *Inc. Magazine* cover story in October of
1983 entitled "Management by Walking Away." This title refers to the rather unusual company practice of having all managers leave the plant for an entire day each year, leaving the
running of the company to the employees alone. This tradition is reflective of an innovative approach to company management in general, and it is symbolic of the event that led
the firm's chief founder, Harry Quadracci, to create Quad
Graphics.

In 1970 Quadracci walked away from a major printing
firm in which he had worked his way up from corporate counsel to vice-president and general manager of the Wisconsin
division. When he left he set out to start his own printing
business. It was not until 1972 that the new company had its
first full operating year, and in that year it started out with
eleven other partners, 20,000 feet of plant space, and only one
printing press. By 1983 the firm had grown to 2,000 employees, one million feet of floor space, and two more plants—one
in Wisconsin and one on the East Coast. Quad Graphics has
maintained a compound sales growth of between 30 and 40
percent annually since it was founded.[39]

One reason that Quad Graphics has been so successful is
because Quadracci is farsighted and also a risk taker. Thus,
when he started the firm, a color press was purchased which
at the time was quite unusual, given the limited number of
publications printed in color. Quadracci's choice was right,
though, and today Quad Graphics prints such high-volume
publications as *U.S. News and World Report, Harper's, Newsweek, Mother Jones,* and *Playboy.*[40]

Although technological superiority and farsightedness
have played a significant role in the company's success, even
more important has been Quad's ownership culture. From the
outset, when Quadracci and his co-founders started the company, they wanted to create a system free of class divisions
with great flexibility and high levels of employee skill and
motivation. In short, they wanted everyone to feel like an

owner. A good starting point was to call everyone a "partner"—which, after 1974, and the creation of an ESOP which today holds approximately 37 percent of the company's stock, they were. To reinforce this ownership culture, every new employee has a mentor to work with them throughout their first year at Quad Graphics. During the first two years new employees go through a rigorous technical and social training program which prepares them to work in Quad's unusual work atmosphere in which employees are expected to make the system work without being given orders. Managers are there to help, but not to tell people what to do or to force them to do their jobs. Such behavior is antithetical to the idea that everyone is a partner.

Thus, employees at Quad Graphics are expected to perform their duties, and share other people's duties, with a great degree of self-management. When they work they work very hard, but plenty of time is left for other interests in life. At Quad Graphics the work week lasts only three days of twelve hours each; for the rest of the week Quad partners are off. During their days off, though, they do not necessarily leave their relationships from work behind. The company emphasizes the idea that Quad is a "family" in many ways. The company newsletter is called *Family*, and Quad supports a variety of activities and facilities which exist to provide recreation and to encourage personal improvement, not only for "partners" but also for their families. Company perks for all employees include a company sports center, a 40-acre campground and recreation park, a summer camp for kids, on-site college course offerings, and even a company sports car race.

All of these practices at Quad Graphics seem to have combined to create a true ownership culture in which all employees—or partners, rather—feel personal responsibility for the future of the company. An example of this spirit is exemplified by the behavior of a group of senior pressmen who were concerned about the ability of the junior pressmen to do their job in meeting the high standards of quality expected from Quad Graphics. Because of this concern they initiated a training program for the junior pressmen on their own, including the development of the program's curriculum. They did not seek management approval or advice; they simply took the job upon themselves because they saw a need. Quadracci did not even know about the program until after it had already taken place.[41]

On another occasion, Quadracci's "walking away" style of management led to a unique and very cost effective approach to managing transportation. For several years the company's truck drivers had been hauling loads to customers but returning with empty trucks, making the cost of transportation very high. Concerned about this waste of resources and loss of revenue, Quadracci decided to ask the truck drivers if they thought they could haul something back in their empty trucks. They returned his inquiry by asking him what he thought they should haul back. Quadracci merely shrugged and said, "How should I know? I don't know anything about driving an 18-wheeler. . . . I'm not going to find your loads."[42] After saying this he just walked away. The truck drivers then realized that they really were partners, and they went to work on creating a transportation system that would generate revenue. Today this group has turned itself into a semi-autonomous division of the corporation which operates as a profit center run by groups of employees. They maintain their own records, track their performance, and independently compete on contracts.

EMPLOYEE BUYOUTS AND CONCESSION BARGAINING

We will discuss the last two paths toward employee ownership together because their dynamics and problems are similar. Indeed, in many cases, the two are difficult to distinguish. Most employee buyouts include some concessions by the employees—usually a reduction in wages and benefits and some relaxation of work rules and job restrictions. Similarly, both employee buyouts and deals in which employees accept stock in exchange for concessions are usually responses to a present or imminent financial crisis.

There are essentially two varieties of employee buyout—

the leveraged buyout (LBO) initiated to take a public company private and avoid a hostile takeover, and the buyout initiated in response to the imminent closing of a plant or company. (Note that we are are not suggesting that all LBOs are employee buyouts; what we are concerned with here are cases where employee ownership, and specifically an ESOP, has been used as a vehicle to help the management team take a company private.) Both types of buyout are a response to a perceived crisis in which many jobs or a whole company may be lost. Both also commonly share the same problem: an inability of the participants to work together in harmony once the period of crisis is over.

Taking a Company Private with an ESOP LBO

The motivating crisis behind an employee LBO is the threat of a hostile takeover by another corporation or a professional corporate raider. As we noted in Chapter 5, corporate raiders mount takeovers of companies whose stock price is undervalued in relation to the actual or liquidation value of company assets. If a corporate raider succeeds in taking over a corporation, then it is very likely that the company will be taken apart and its assets sold off in pieces in order to pay off the bank loan and the debt incurred through selling junk bonds to finance the takeover. It is the fear of becoming one of the liquidated parts that moves union leaders and workers to wholeheartedly support a management-initiated LBO. Thus, in these cases, an ESOP in effect becomes the financing vehicle for fighting off the takeover attempt—by buying back the shares of public stockholders and the raider. It was through just such a process that the textile firm, Dan River, Inc., of Danville, Virginia, became an employee-owned company.

The workers at Dan River, however, are not quite as enthusiastic about employee ownership as employees at some of the other companies we have reviewed in this chapter. In fact, many Dan River employees are downright angry at management for having gotten them involved with employee ownership.

At Dan River, the motivating force for becoming employee owned was a takeover threat by corporate raider Carl Icahn. To avoid an Icahn takeover, Dan River employees joined together with management in support of a LBO financed by an ESOP. The entire work force was highly motivated to avoid a takeover, and 58 percent voted in favor of terminating their pension plan and replacing it with the ESOP. Management convinced the workers that terminating their pension plan was necessary because the company could not afford to retire the debt generated by the ESOP and also make pension payments.

Thus, Dan River's work force supported the LBO because they believed that they were preventing the wholesale elimination of their jobs. Today they have come to wonder if they might not have done better under Carl Icahn. Since the buyout was implemented in early 1983, for example, management has shut down four Dan River plants and sold a fifth plant. As a result of these actions, as well as severe layoffs in existing operations, Dan River's work force declined from 12,000 employees at the time of the buyout to only 8,000 by April of 1985. Management has claimed that these actions would have been necessary even without the buyout because of increased foreign competition and a drop in demand in major markets. However, the workers believe that, to a great extent, the cutbacks were necessary as well to provide the cash needed to repay the company's horrendous debt load; or, as UTW Local 248 president Kim Meeks put it, "Paying back that $100-odd million loan wasn't going to come out of the air. It had to come out of the workers' sweat."[43]

Dan River workers are also angry because they feel that, while they are working harder with fewer coworkers, they are enriching management far more than themselves. The following description of the stock program helps to clarify why employees have such feelings:

> In setting up the ESOP, Kelso & Co. created two classes of common stock. ESOP acquired 70% of the company with a $110 million investment in Class A common stock priced at $22.50 per share. A group of 26 managers, along

with a Kelso investment fund, put up $4.3 million to buy 30% of the company mostly in Class B common stock at $2.06 per share. The Class A common stock will always be worth about $22 more per share than management's Class B. But if the company grows, management's stock will get a disproportionate share of the upside. The value of the stock is reviewed once a year by an independent appraiser. If Class A climbs to $26, for example, Class B stock will have a value of about $4—a 100% gain compared with a 16% rise for the ESOP stock.[44]

This arrangement has caused Dan River workers to feel they were manipulated and used. As one salaried employee explained, "A lot of us feel that we got took."[45] This feeling is further reinforced by the fact that management set up the ESOP using only the minimal requirements for employee participation required by the law. Ironically, if Dan River had at least remained partially publicly owned, and not taken on so much debt, the company would have been required to give employees full pass-through voting rights. Instead, as a private firm, Dan River only needs to provide employees with the right to vote on major issues, such as sale of the firm, a merger, or a liquidation, and that is precisely all the say workers have in company affairs.

Corporate managers and officers set up the ESOP so that United Virginia Bank serves as the ESOP trustee; the trustee votes employee stock according to management instructions. Although the company provides quarterly reports on the firm's financial performance to the ESOP trustee, the reports are not shared with employees, and so they have no idea what the company's actual sales or earnings have been or how the valuation of their shares compares with management's B shares. This situation, not surprisingly, has led employees to believe that management is trying to hide their own inflated gains from employee eyes. Consequently, union officials advise other workers and union leaders to think twice about getting into the kind of employee ownership scheme they have experienced; or, as UTW General Counsel D. Bruce Shine said, "If you are going to get into an ESOP, you sure as hell don't want one like Dan River's."[46]

The Dan River case is typical of many ESOP leveraged LBOs which often seem to be structured so as to minimize any possibility of an ownership culture. In an earlier case, the Okonite Company of Ramsey, New Jersey, a high-performance marine and nuclear power plant cable manufacturer, employee-owners have gone on strike four times since the firm was first taken private through an ESOP in 1976. Since the ESOP was created, management has tried to downplay the significance of ownership as much as possible, and employees have no say in company affairs as stockholders. In fact, at Okonite, "employees are not called owners but referred to as beneficiaries, and management has made a conscious effort to avoid creating any expectations whatsoever that an ESOP should confer upon workers any of the traditional rights of ownership." In fact, the concept of having employees get more involved in the company as a result of ownership participation is considered such an anathema by top management that the firm's CEO, when asked by *Fortune* if there had been any improvement in productivity since the buyout, said "Why should there be?"[47]

Comments such as that made by the CEO of Okonite seem almost incredible in light of the positive impact which employee ownership and an "ownership culture" have had on so many organizations. However, simply trying to ignore the existence of employee ownership, hoping that employees will forget that it is there, is highly unrealistic. Instead, the consequence of becoming employee owned and then trying to deal with the situation in this manner has precisely the opposite effect and brings great tension to the labor–management relationship. Workers at another employee LBO company, Raymond International, for example, dubbed management's potentially lucrative B shares "Killer Bees"; and the U.S. Department of Labor had to step in and recommend that management adjust its proposed equity share downward from 33 percent to 20 percent. Nevertheless, the results of the deal were still perceived as highly inequitable by the work force, with management gaining a 20-percent stake in the company for $5.4 million at a price of $1.09 per share, while employees paid $10 per share price for Class A stock purchased with a $100 million loan.[48]

Buyouts to Prevent Plant Closings and Concession Bargaining

Employee buyouts to avert a plant or company closure have also been plagued with some of the same problems as the "anti-takeover LBOs" discussed above. Early buyouts suffered from these problems during the 1970s, when employee buyouts were a relatively new and unknown phenomenon on the American industrial scene. In these early cases, as well as in more recent ones, concession bargaining has usually been inextricably linked to employee acquisition of employer stock. In some cases concessions have been made, and employees have also paid money out of their own pockets to purchase stock. An employee buyout of the now defunct Rath Packing Company, a pork-slaughtering and meat-processing firm headquartered in Waterloo, Iowa, required that employees make a number of wage, benefit, and work rule concessions as well as pay $2.00 per share for Rath stock. For over a year, Rath employees had a sum of $20.00 deducted from their weekly paychecks until they had collectively bought a 60 percent share in the company, which was placed in an ESOP trust.

In other cases, such as the South Bend Lathe Company, employees actually put up no money, nor are their wage concessions considered to be payment for employer stock. Instead, a bank loan provides the financing to purchase employer stock, and employees become vested in their stock, and therefore their voting rights, following a traditional vesting schedule. In these cases the ultimate consequences of the institution of employee ownership are often just as negative as the "anti-takeover buyouts."

Indeed, employee buyouts which save jobs but deny workers participation in the company as owners create, in effect, a "time-bomb"; this is because, in most cases, the workers made a tremendous sacrifice to make the buyout possible. Once the bloom of having saved their jobs wears off, however, disillusionment often sets in. In the final stage, this disillusionment eventually leads to employee strikes and demonstrations. Often conflict becomes particularly acute in such cases, because the process of saving a plant or company has involved a communitywide rally for support in which both labor and management appealed to community leaders and the federal government for help in saving the business. During this period of mobilization, everyone involved thinks that once the buyout is consummated, a spirit of harmony and cooperation will prevail. Unfortunately, in real terms, this means that labor anticipates that management will start listening to them, and management anticipates that owning stock, with or without a vote, will result in workers suddenly understanding the superior wisdom of management.

Not surprisingly, at least in retrospect, neither management's or labor's unarticulated expectations will be realized, and when employees discover that they can't force a change by exercising their rights as shareholders, they turn to traditional economic action by striking. At South Bend Lathe, for example, workers went on strike against their company in 1980 after five years of employee ownership without voting rights. During the strike some workers carried placards with statements like "ESOP's Fables" and "Owners On Strike." A young machinist who had been an activist during the buyout effort told reporters:

> What we have had there for the last five years is ownership without control. We've bent over backwards since 1975 to make a good product and keep it selling . . . we've kept our mouths shut—covered up our differences with management to avoid publicity . . .
>
> But all we got was the same treatment we had before the ESOP, maybe even worse. We make no decisions. We have no voice; we're owners in name only.[49]

Incidents such as this were common to employee buyout efforts initiated from the mid- to late 1970s. Repeatedly, companies or plants were saved from destruction through a cooperative effort by labor, management, and the community, only to be torn apart later because of the failure of most of these plans to provide workers with meaningful participation and channels of communication within the business. Consequently, beginning in the early 1980s, after labor leaders learned of the experiences of others, workers and their union officials began to demand substantial involvement in the corporations they became involved in saving. At first this started quietly and somewhat tentatively, beginning with such limited interventions as the UAW's demand to have Douglas Fraser sit on Chrysler's board of directors. As time progressed, such demands became far more radical and militant. Thus, at Rath Packing Company, leaders of Local P–46 of the United Food and Commercial Workers not only demanded full voting rights, but actually required that workers obtain controlling interest with 60 percent of the corporation's stock, the majority of board seats, and a comprehensive system of labor–management consultation. At a ball bearing company, Hyatt Clark of Clark, New Jersey, now also closed, UAW officers and their members were unable to secure voting rights until a $100 million loan was paid off, but they forced the company to give them three union seats on the firm's board of directors. Unions at Western and Eastern Air Lines also secured board positions in return for taking stock in exchange for concessions. At Eastern Air Lines, an impressive and immense system of both cooperation and codetermination in company decision making was created, with workers participating in problem-solving teams at the rank and file level and union officials being involved in the determination of corporate strategy and the approval of financial expenditures.

Many observers were deeply impressed by these far-reaching attempts to drastically alter the traditional order of corporate governance. And initial results at such firms as Rath, Hyatt Clark, and Eastern Air Lines were extremely impressive. The response from employees was enthusiastic, and company bottom lines showed dramatic improvement. Unfortunately, these positive results were short-lived, and, like the earlier buyout cases, this second stage in employee buyouts and concession bargaining also began to deteriorate into open warfare between labor and management. In part, this process of deterioration was the result of the extremely turbulent market environments in which these companies were trying to survive. Intense competition and generally industry-wide overcapacity hardly created a milieu for the slow and careful evolution of employee-ownership cultures.

Stress was also heightened by underlying conflicts created by labor's success at getting their way. That is, the management of these firms, especially top management and the company's corporate attorneys and bankers, felt that it was they who had been cheated. Resentment ran deep against the success that unions such as the Machinists, UAW, and Food and Commercial Workers had at strong-arming their way into the world of corporate finance and policy making. Consequently, in these cases, a climate of manipulation by management and sometimes rather arrogant pressuring from the unions began to wear away at the public face of cooperation and harmony.

Today we are beginning to see a new phase in concession bargaining and employee buyouts, starting with a realization from both sides of the table that an employee-ownership culture cannot be created either by trying to "run the business like it has always been run" or by workers and union leaders attempting to strong-arm management. Both of these approaches eventually deteriorate into open warfare. Thus, at Weirton Steel in Weirton, West Virginia, management and the union worked together in cooperation in trying to reach a buyout, and afterward in trying to make the company profitable. Weirton's CEO did not try to block labor participation on the board of directors, and he actively supported and pushed the development of a system of labor-management cooperative problem-solving teams throughout the organization. In another, smaller case, the management and workers of Seymour Brass in Seymour, Connecticut, work hand in hand to transform their company from a beleaguered absentee-owned operation to a successful worker cooperative based upon a system of one-person-one-vote, just like the plywood cooperatives in Oregon and the state of Washington. Similar developments have also occurred in a number of instances, including the buyout of stores formerly owned by A&P in Philadelphia, Pennsylvania, and some smaller enterprises in Burlington, Vermont.

With this new phase in the development of worker buyouts and concession bargaining, perhaps we will now see the development of a sensible and productive path to employee ownership that has potential over the long run. Without a supportive and cooperative attitude from both labor and management, it is unlikely that this approach to employee ownership can ever succeed. A profitable enterprise, especially in a highly competitive and turbulent marketplace, can never be created on the basis of either management or labor forcing the other into submission. This is especially true in industries where labor–management conflict has been a way of life for years and both sides have plenty of experience in how to fight.

SUMMARY

As we have seen in this chapter, there are many paths a company can follow to employee ownership. Not all of these paths are equally positive in their impact on organizational performance and employee–management relations. Adopting employee ownership as a transition strategy for moving from founder control and ownership to a new ownership structure is perhaps the most promising of all the paths. Employee ownership can also have problems as a transition strategy, however, if certain conditions are not met, or if the transition is made only partially. We will discuss the nature of these problems and illustrate them through several case studies in the following chapter.

Using employee ownership as a strategy for recruiting and retaining employees, our second path, is not as positive an approach as path number one. As we saw from the case examples, this strategy for introducing employee ownership is often unconnected to any broader organizational strategy for creating an ownership culture. In these cases ownership is often reduced to nothing more than a compensation gimmick, and as such it can easily be manipulated, causing strange organizational contortions and fostering greed and excessive self-interest more than long-term commitment. As such, we would suggest that deciding to offer employees stock or stock options on which to speculate is not a useful approach to countering the problems of absentee ownership and creating an employee-ownership culture. In fact, this use of employee ownership may in fact draw everyone into behaving in ways that are ultimately harmful to the long-term future of the company.

Starting out employee owned is probably the most fascinating of the different paths; and it is clear that this path can, in many cases, lead to some amazing results, in terms of creating both very intense employee-ownership cultures and impressive economic performance. Employee ownership should be considered more often as a viable strategy for starting a business capable of exceptional dynamism, and this is true whether the goal is to create a competitive maverick in a mature industry or a business based upon principles of economic democracy. Whether led by a single entrepreneur or by a group of blue-collar entrepreneurs wanting to start a cooperative such start-ups can succeed.

In the latter case, it is important that cooperative groups embarking upon these ventures be careful that they are sufficiently capitalized, and that they have done the necessary homework and business planning to discern if the venture can in fact succeed on a basic financial level. Given the success of the Northwest plywood cooperatives, as well as that of the several thousand cooperative firms now operating in other countries, these do not seem to be insurmountable obstacles. Indeed, cooperative start-ups, if they are not short on capital or business expertise, may actually have a far easier time developing a dynamic employee-ownership culture than those employee ownership start-ups that are organized and led by an individual entrepreneur. It can be extremely difficult for a company founder—or even a group of entrepreneur founders—

to make a successful transfer of responsibility and power to their employees who may see them both as visionaries and as benefactors.

Obviously, we support the concept of adopting employee ownership as a strategy for organizational improvement. This, of course, assumes that company managers and officers are interested in something more than merely taking advantage of the tax incentives available. This use of an ESOP may make a few lawyers, accountants, and valuation firms wealthy, but it is really an abuse of the intended purpose of the ESOP which was granted its special privileges because it is first and foremost an employee benefit. As an employee benefit, the ESOP can have a tremendous positive impact upon a firm and employee motivation and morale. The extent of this impact depends primarily on the commitment of management to combine equity participation with other forms of participative decision making so as to create an all-encompassing culture of employee-ownership.

The last two paths to employee ownership are somewhat more equivocal and complicated cases. LBOs that are structured and used to entrench incumbent managers and provide them with great financial benefits at limited personal cost are clearly a perversion of the ESOP. Experience at companies like Dan River and Raymond International have hardly helped to promote employee ownership, and any employee or union official should be wary of a similar proposition put forward to them by a top management team. It may, indeed, make sense to join together to fend off a hostile takeover, but if such actions require that a firm incur massive debts, then the sacrifice and future gains must be borne equally by manager and worker alike. The creation of huge disparities between the work force and the managers who talked them into going along with an LBO may create an "anti-employee ownership culture." This cannot be good for anyone.

Employee buyouts where workers, community leaders, union officials, and managers join together to save a company or plant, and concession bargaining in which stock is traded for contract changes may also result in disaster. Here again, the structure of the reformed organization and contract relations must reflect a fair and even sharing of the burden of responsibility for saving or revitalizing a business. A feeling of shared sacrifice brings people together in solidarity against even the most difficult of odds. Feelings of inequity make solidarity impossible.

A thorough and far-reaching process of culture change must be initiated from the beginning of any such effort; or, as we have seen, the old problems will eventually arise, and the organization may be unable to survive the turmoil. Everyone must change their approach to going about the business of doing their jobs and making the organization succeed. Managers cannot assume that they have always been right and that the employees will agree with them once they, too, have become capitalists. Union representatives and employees cannot assume that management has always been wrong and now they will do the changing. Both sides must work wholeheartedly toward necessary and shared goals, and the effort must not be so undercapitalized that it will fail, regardless of the infinite capacities of the human mind and body.

CHAPTER 7 ENDNOTES

1. William Baldwin. "The Myths of Employee Ownership." *Forbes*, vol. 133, no. 9, April 23, 1984, p. 110.

2. John Simmons and William Mares. *Working Together* (New York: Alfred A. Knopf, 1983), pp. 209–210.

3. Corey M. Rosen, Katherine J. Klein, and Karen M. Young. *Employee Ownership in America: The Equity Solution* (Lexington, Mass.: Lexington Books, 1986), p. 220.

4. Michael Pacanowsky. Communication in the Empowering Organization. Forthcoming in J.A. Anderson, ed., *ICA Yearbook II*. Beverly Hills, Calif.: Sage Publications, 1987.

5. Rosen et al., 1986, p. 233–234.

6. Rosen et al., 1986, p. 225.

7. Ibid., pp. 242–244.

8. Michael Quarrey, Joseph Blasi, and Corey Rosen. *Taking Stock:*

Employee Ownership at Work (Cambridge, Mass.: Ballinger Publishing Company, 1986), p. 1; James Cook. "The Ownership Culture." *Forbes*, vol. 138, no. 7, October 6, 1985, p. 72.

    9. Rosen et al., 1986, p. 16.

    10. Quarrey et al., 1986, p. 129; Rosen et al., 1986, pp. 156–157.

    11. Bruce G. Posner. "In Search of Equity." *Inc. Magazine*, vol. 7, no. 4, April 1985, p. 51.

    12. Ibid., p. 55.

    13. Ibid.

    14. Ibid., pp. 55–57.

    15. Rosen et al., 1986, p. 160.

    16. Posner, 1985, p. 53.

    17. Ibid.

    18. William Foote Whyte. *Statement to the Special Commission on Employee Involvement and Ownership, Commonwealth of Massachusetts* (Ithaca, N.Y.: Cornell University, March 10, 1987), p. 7.

    19. Gary Hansen. Speech given at Brigham Young University, School of Management, Provo, Utah, February 1987.

    20. Paul Bernstein. *Workplace Democratization—Its Internal Dynamics* (New Brunswick, N.J.: Transaction Books, 1983), p. 9.

    21. David W. Ewing. "When Employees Run the Business." *Harvard Business Review*, vol. 57, no. 1, January-February 1979, p. 75.

    22. Katrina Berman. *Worker-Owned Plywood Companies* (Pullman, Wash.: Washington State University Press, 1967), pp. 85–92.

    23. Bernstein, 1983, p. 14; Christopher E. Gunn. *Workers' Self-Management in the United States* (Ithaca, N.Y.: Cornell University Press, 1984), p. 100.

    24. Katrina Berman. "The Worker-Owned Plywood Cooperatives." In Frank Lindenfield and Joyce Rothschild-Whitt, eds., *Workplace Democracy and Social Change* (Boston: Porter Sargent, 1982), p. 163.

    25. Gunn, 1984, pp. 101–102.

    26. Bernstein, 1983, p. 24.

    27. Ewing, 1979, p. 81.

    28. Bernstein, 1983, p. 17.

    29. Gunn, 1984, p. 115.

    30. Gunn, 1984, pp. 101–102.

    31. Bernstein, 1983, p. 21.

    32. Gunn, 1984, p. 102; American Plywood Association. *Management Bulletin*, no. FA-215 (Tacoma, Washington, March 12, 1982); American Plywood Association. *Plywood Statistics* (Tacoma, Washington, July 10, 1982).

    33. Bernstein, 1983, p. 19.

    34. "ESOPs: Revolution or Ripoff?" *Business Week*, April 15, 1985, p. 95.

    35. Rosen et al., 1986, p. 26.

36. Ibid., p. 147.

37. Ibid.

38. Ibid., p. 146.

39. Ellen Wojahn. "Management by Walking Away." *Inc. Magazine,* vol. 5, no. 10, October 1983, pp. 68–72.

40. Rosen et al., 1986, p. 166.

41. Wojahn, 1983, p. 70.

42. Ibid.

43. "ESOPs: Revolution or Ripoff?" *Business Week,* April 15, 1985, p. 97.

44. Ibid.

45. Ibid.

46. Ibid.

47. "What Happens When Employees Buy the Company." *Fortune,* June 3, 1980, pp. 108–111.

48. "ESOPs: Revolution or Ripoff?," p. 102.

49. William F. Whyte, Tove H. Hammer, Christopher B. Meek, Reed Nelson and Robert N. Stearn et al. *Worker Participation and Ownership.* (Ithaca, N.Y.: ILR Press, 1983), p. 92.

CHAPTER 8 ═══════════════════

Beyond the Founder's Vision

There have been some remarkable success stories of company founders who incorporated employee ownership into the structure and culture of their companies. It should be clear from our discussion so far that we encourage all founders to seriously consider employee ownership as an integral part of their withdrawal from the business. Not all founders, however, realize the full positive effects of employee ownership. In fact, some, as it turns out, have proven to be the most significant obstacle to making an effective transition in ownership.

In recent years, some 25 percent to over one-third of all companies adopting employee ownership have done so as part of a strategy for enabling their founders to withdraw from the business. This growing trend makes it particularly important today to learn from the problems and successes of earlier cases.[1] The case studies provided in this chapter and the next will, we hope, help other entrepreneurs and managers develop alternative ownership structures and transition strategies that work.

MOTIVATIONS FOR ADOPTING EMPLOYEE OWNERSHIP

When we examined several different cases in which a founder decided to create a new firm on a foundation of employee ownership, or to institute employee ownership at an existing firm, we found that their respective motivations for making such a commitment were varied and mixed. In some cases, an owner is motivated by little more than a desire to create a market for his or her stock. More often, though, a founder's decision to institute employee ownership is motivated by a number of other significant considerations.

Some business owners see employee ownership as a way to achieve a certain personal immortality. It was partly for this reason, for example, that British industrialist Ernest Bader converted his successful chemical company in Wollaston, England, into what he called the Scott-Bader Commonwealth. After twenty years as the company's owner, Bader, along with his son Godric, transferred 90 percent of the company's stock to employees by placing it in a commonly held trust. Bader and his son retained the additional 10 percent, along with the right to assume emergency takeover powers in the event of financial crisis. Finally, in 1963, the last 10 percent of Scott-Bader stock was transferred to a trust governed by seven trustees: Ernest, Godric, and five others elected by employees.[2] A complex system of boards and councils was also created to govern the organization so that, as long as it was profitable, it would be a uniquely democratic enterprise self-managed by its worker-owners.

Bader knew that, by creating such a system, he would be long remembered by the work force as their benefactor. As a religious Quaker, however, he also hoped that the rest of the world would look to the firm as a model for a more democratic and humane industrial order. In fact, he intended the Commonwealth to be a microcosm of a more just society. As with many other entrepreneurs, Bader saw employee ownership as a means to realize a social, political, and religious ideal that was of great significance in his life.

Jerry Gorde, founder of the Richmond, Virginia-based Virginia Textiles, a very successful advertising specialties and clothing firm, chose similarly to incorporate employee ownership into the start-up of his business out of political and social ideals. Before becoming an entrepreneur, Gorde had spent four years traveling around the U.S., a life inspired by Jack Kerouac's *On the Road*. He also worked as a political activist on the National Council of the Youth International

Party, or, as they were better known, the "Yippies." Obviously enough, running a business in the traditional way was unacceptable to Gorde. So when he founded Virginia Textiles in 1977 with some of his friends from his Yippie days, they introduced employee ownership and participative decision making as a conscious strategy. For Gorde, the sharing of ownership was "the best way to satisfy individual economic necessities and preserve personal freedom while maximizing profits."[3] The concept worked. The business, which was only a tiny printed T-shirt operation when he bought if for $3,000, grew to a $12-million enterprise, and Gorde was recognized in 1983 as Small Business Person of the Year by the State of Virginia.[4] Virginia Textiles even made the *Inc. Magazine* list of the 500 fastest-growing U.S. companies three years in a row.

Most entrepreneurs, however, do not have such expansive and ideological reasons for instituting employee ownership. In many cases, employee ownership is simply a means to pay back loyal employees to whom a founder feels responsible after many years of working together in building up the business. A classic example of this motivation is provided by Joseph Nederlander, the founder and chairman of Ticket World Inc. Nederlander provided ownership participation for his key employees because of his concern for their future and as a gesture of appreciation. As an *Inc. Magazine* article explained, Nederlander's sensitivity to these issues had actually started some thirty-five years earlier when he first saw Arthur Miller's play, *Death of a Salesman*.

> "Do you remember that scene toward the end of the play?" Nederlander asks, meaning the one in which Willy Loman gets fired by the son of the man he has been working for all those years ("There were promises made across this desk!" Willy says, "You can't eat the orange and throw the peel away—a man is not a piece of fruit!")
>
> With his four brothers, Nederlander has spent his life in the theater business, managing a family empire that includes no fewer than ten theaters on and around Broadway. Nederlander was already in his fifties when he founded the

fully computerized ticket company in 1979. The six young men he hired have made the business what it is today. So he has given them equity. "If I have a stroke and die," says Nederlander, "I don't want to have one of these guys coming in here and finding he doesn't have a job. How do you reward a young guy for loyalty? They get so good they can go other places. I hear them calling their wives at 9 o'clock to say they're missing dinner. They're giving their leisure time. . . . How do you say thanks to people like that?"[5]

Lastly, many founders have introduced employee ownership out of a belief that doing so would more closely align the interests of the company and its employees. They believe that the introduction of ownership participation will build a highly motivated team of workers and managers who are willing to put forth their best to build a profitable enterprise. In this case, employee ownership is viewed as a significant incentive for ensuring maximum growth and profitability. Working together in cooperation is held up as an ideal; or as Larry Ellison, the president and CEO of Oracle Corporation, a ten-year-old software development and marketing corporation, said: "It's a matter of personal preference. . . . I would just rather be a member of the winning Super Bowl team than a singles champion at Wimbledon. I mean suppose you win the singles tournament, who do you embrace at the end of the final match . . . your racket?"[6]

EMPLOYEE OWNERSHIP: FOUNDER-CENTERED OR EMPLOYEE-CENTERED?

Although a founder's decision to introduce employee ownership into his or her firm can involve all of the motives cited above, and often several of them in combination, the way in which employee ownership is implemented usually falls under one of two categories or types—founder centered or employee centered. Efforts to introduce employee ownership that fall under the founder-centered category are dominated by the founder's needs and expectations. In such cases the founder is the chief sponsor and promoter of the new form of ownership; and, in addition, he or she also dominates and controls the way the new ownership structure is realized.

By contrast, in employee-centered cases, the founder eventually moves from a directive to a facilitative role and seeks to institutionalize the key values and behaviors of a value-driven culture into the organization itself. In such cases, ownership is used to reinforce a culture which will live with or without the presence of the founder.

We believe that an employee-centered approach to employee ownership is far more likely to produce an effective and lasting start-up or conversion. In Chapter 9 we provide some specific guidelines and examples of how such a strategy can be implemented through a thoughtful and comprehensive transformation of corporate culture. In the rest of this chapter, we will illustrate the difference between founder- and employee-centered approaches by examining the history of several employee ownership cases.

THE ENTREPRENEURIAL PERSONALITY

As we have seen, a conversion to employee ownership can be used to institutionalize the values and beliefs that previously made a company successful. Ironically enough, however, the founder's own personality can sometimes be an obstacle to the successful completion of this process. In fact, the same personality traits that are essential to building a successful company may also tend to prevent employee ownership from taking root. Not many people have the ability to take risks, nor do they have the other mental and emotional qualities required to be a successful entrepreneur. But then, not many entrepreneurs are willing to invest their time and effort to create a company in which they must share power and profits with their employees.

Entrepreneurs seem, by nature, to be "take-charge" personalities who are willing to jump into unknown territory and seize profit-making opportunities. Such individuals like working for themselves and typically avoid occupations where they are required to work for other people. Entrepreneurs are seldom known for their humility, but it is their arrogance that propels them to take the risks necessary to start and build an enterprise. They are frequently charismatic and strong-willed people who like following their own instincts, and who may stick stubbornly to a strategy long after the average person would quit.

Such characteristics do not match easily with the conditions required for creating a self-sufficient system in which employees share the ownership and the decision-making power. It can be difficult for even the most idealistic of entrepreneurs to control their own instincts in a way that ensures organizational success. Whatever their motivations, it can also be difficult for entrepreneurs to restrain themselves from intervening whenever employee-owners make decisions other than the ones they, personally, would have made. Employees can easily be overwhelmed by the power and force of an entrepreneur's personality, remaining dependent upon his or her judgment. In some cases, this dependency can lead to the downfall of a once-profitable and dynamic organization, as the following case illustrates.

PEOPLE EXPRESS—OWNERSHIP, PROFITS, AND PARTICIPATION

People Express, a firm that had a relatively short but influential and tumultuous life span, provides an excellent example of a founder-centered employee ownership start-up. From the outset, Donald Burr, the principal founder of People Express, adopted employee ownership and employee participation as central components of the firm's strategy. For Don Burr, employee ownership and a participative approach to management were necessary conditions for enabling People Express to carve out and maintain a new and profitable niche in the marketplace.

In the late 1970s, Don Burr, a thirty-nine-year-old Harvard MBA with fourteen years of work experience on Wall Street and as a top executive at Texas International, decided to leave TI and start a new air carrier of his own, along with fifteen other former TI managers. On April 7, 1980, they organized the new company, which they named People Express. The Airline Deregulation Act of 1978 provided the window of opportunity for this innovative venture—breaking into a marketplace which until then had been controlled by the government and dominated by a group of large companies.

A Unique Strategy

Burr's strategy went straight to the core values underlying airline deregulation—competition and efficiency. He believed that air travel could become a commodity affordable by nearly everyone. He insisted that it was possible to provide air travel at a cost equal to or even less than that of traveling by car or bus, and definitely at a substantially lower price than that offered by major air carriers. Thus People Express targeted a market that had been ignored by traditional air carriers—the working class traveler, students and other members of what executives in the industry call "the backpack crowd." Burr referred to his customers as either the people with little money or those with plenty of money who wanted to keep it.[7]

To offer air travel at a commodity price, People Express had to emphasize volume. For years other air carriers had maintained profitability by passing on increased costs to the customer. In contrast, People Express created a system capable of generating a profit with a small yield per customer, because its pricing strategy ensured that its flights would be filled with many more passengers than other airlines. A few statistics help to clarify just how People Express did business.

In 1983, the company's most profitable year, People Express generated a yield of only about 5.5 cents per available seat mile (ASM), compared to 11 cents for American Air Lines, 13 cents for Delta, and over 14 cents for Republic.[8] On the other hand, in 1983, People Express flew with an average of 75 percent of its seats filled on every flight, compared to under 65 percent at American Air Lines, 54 percent at Delta, and approximately 55 percent at Republic.[9] And People needed to keep its planes this full because it had to fill an average of 72 percent of its seats just to break even. By contrast, in 1983 the breakeven point for United and American Air Lines was 60 percent; for Delta it was 54 percent and at Republic, 57 percent.[10]

To make this strategy work, People Express consistently had to attract lots of passengers. This they accomplished with their low prices. But to ensure that these prices would yield a profit, People also had to find a way to keep its operating and overhead costs far below those of other carriers. Their success in this area is illustrated by the data in Table 8. Where industrywide operating expenses averaged out to about 8 cents per ASM during the four and one-half years from January 1, 1981, through June 30, 1985, they were not quite 5½ cents per ASM for People Express during this same period. However, even with low costs, the company also had to be careful that none of the major carriers perceived it as a serious threat. In a head-to-head fare war it was clear that People could never win against the cash "war chests" of companies like Delta and United. Thus, Burr and his management team decided to initially focus on air routes that were "over priced and under ser-

Table 8. Operating Expenses: People Express Versus Industry Average, January 1, 1981–June 30, 1985

	PEOPLE EXPRESS	INDUSTRY AVERAGE
1981	6.4 cents*	8.1 cents
1982	5.0	7.9
1983	5.5	7.8
1984	5.4	7.7
1985	5.0	7.9
Average	5.46	7.88

Per available seat mile

viced."[11] Evidently this strategy worked. For example, Frank Borman, former CEO of Eastern Air Lines, said during an interview in early 1986:

> We didn't really take them seriously. We couldn't imagine that they could ever be a significant factor in the marketplace. People Express was catering to a whole different market, you know the guys that have long hair and beards and carry knapsacks and packs where our customers are business executives and relatively well-to-do air travelers.[12]

By carefully choosing its routes, People Express quietly entered the industry without becoming a target for extermination by its competitors. Maintaining a low cost structure, however, required a radically different approach to the concept of service. The key to this concept was the elimination of any unnecessary "frills." Instead of allowing passengers to check in bags at no cost, for example, all bags not carried on board required a minimum $3 service charge. Similarly, lavish meals were eliminated, and customers were required to pay extra for beverages or a cold snack. Aircraft were also used more efficiently by flying them ten to eleven hours a day (compared to a seven-hour industry average), and modifying them to reduce fuel costs by as much as 50 percent. The company even increased the number of seats in each Boeing 737 from 90 to 118. All of these changes helped to keep People's costs low by industry standards.

Ownership and Participation

These innovations, however, were relatively unimaginative compared to those adopted in the areas of management and employee relations. People Express had little trouble recruiting new employees. The glamour and adventure associated with the airline industry ensured a steady supply of new recruits, and on average more than 100 people would apply for any job advertised. However, since part of the industry's attractiveness is also a function of its high wages and excellent benefits, it was necessary for People to create incentives that would reward employees for performance rather than through high fixed-wage levels. It was also necessary to have a more flexible work force than other airlines with their union work rules and strict job classification systems. The higher costs imposed by such inflexibility would have made the company's pricing strategy impossible.

People's strategy for maintaining low costs and high flexibility was a participative system of management wedded to a structure of employee ownership. During his years at Texas International, Burr had come to the conclusion that bureaucracy and strict specialization led to great inefficiency and rigidity. His vision was to create an alternative corporate structure which would eliminate these rigidities and maximize the use of human resources, or, as he said himself: "... there was a better way of doing things within the American system of democracy, in which people are free to produce. If you give people freedom, they will produce better on balance."[13]

In effect, Burr promised his employees interesting jobs and future wealth by joining in a partnership to create a new concept, and the cost figures in Table 8 show that the partnership did work. How well it worked, in fact, is witnessed by the firm's meteoric rise during its first few years and the substantial financial commitment made by each People Express employee upon joining the company.

Every full-time employee at People Express was required to purchase a minimum of 100 shares of company common stock as an initial condition of employment. To help new employees to meet this requirement, the company sold them the 100 shares at a price 60 percent below the market rate and offered low interest loans to finance the purchase which could be paid back through payroll deductions. To ensure that employees remained active and concerned shareholders, company policy also required that they hold on to their stock for several years. People Express encouraged its employees to continue to buy more stock by offering them the right to buy additional shares at the discounted rate after finishing one year of employment. Many employees took advantage of this offer, and some even invested their entire life savings in the company.

By the end of 1982, People Express employees had bought 4.5 million shares of common stock, or approximately one-third of the company. Thus, the airline's performance was a matter of considerable significance to them. This was true, not only because they had paid for the stock with money out of their own pockets, but also because a significant portion of their actual earnings were contingent upon growth in the value of their shares as well as bonuses paid out from two profit-sharing programs. Participation in the profit-sharing plans began after the first year of full employment. One plan, the *First-Dollar Plan*, was paid out quarterly as a percent of each quarter's profit performance. The second plan, the *Sustained-Profit-Sharing Plan*, rewarded employees for yearly profits regardless of quarterly performance.[14] These profit-sharing bonuses amounted to as much as 50 percent of an employee's annual compensation, and this kept employee attention fixed sharply on People's performance. This was especially true because their earnings from normal salaries and wages were significantly below industry standards, in some cases by more than 50 percent. Benefits, however, were competitive and included 100 percent coverage on medical and dental expenses, $50,000 in life insurance, and a promise of lifetime employment.[15]

People Express pilots were paid a base salary of $30,000 compared to the $60,000 average for members of the Airline Pilots Association (ALPA).[16] People's customer service employees, who performed both ticket agent and flight attendant functions, started out at $17,500, which was well above starting rates for ticket agents at other carriers but substantially below the $25,000 to over $35,000 paid to union flight attendants. Donald Burr even drew a surprisingly low salary of $48,000 per year. These lower compensation costs were, of course, exactly what the airline needed to pursue its strategy of offering super low fares which averaged 40 percent below the competition during peak hours and as much as 60 percent lower at off-peak times.

People's low compensation costs also helped to reinforce a unique system of management and work organization in which employees were expected to share work responsibilities at all organizational levels. This strategy enabled People Express to achieve a maximum utilization of human resources. This concept was operationalized by designating all employees "managers" and by organizing their jobs in terms of a grouping of functions that would have normally been isolated from each other at other companies. People was therefore able to operate with a very "lean" and "flat" organization that could perform most of the same functions as other carriers but with far fewer people.

Essentially, at People Express, there were only six full-time job classifications, compared to literally hundreds at other airlines. These six classifications included: Managing Officers (responsible for developing corporate policy); General Managers (daily direction of operations); Team Managers (responsible for facilitating coordination and communication between work teams); Maintenance Managers (monitored and directed maintenance of buildings, aircraft, and ground equipment performed by subcontractors); Customer Service Managers (employees responsible for coordinating vendor handled reservations with ticketing, selling tickets in-flight, gate keeping, and flight attending); and Flight Managers (responsible for piloting aircraft).

In terms of the daily functioning of the airline, this policy meant that no one was exempt from pitching in and helping out in any area where their services were needed. Flight Managers (FMs), Customer Service Managers (CSMs), and Maintenance Managers (MMs) were organized into permanent teams which worked together by rotating and sharing duties on a daily basis. These work teams did not have supervisors imposed upon them by top management, but rather elected their own team leaders to coordinate work and communication between team members. Team leaders were not, however, responsible for supervising or directing the teams because these groups were intended to be self-managed and responsible for controlling, monitoring, and evaluating their own performance on a group basis.

After its first full year of operations, the team concept had worked out well, but with more than 1,000 employees coordination and communication between teams became strained. Therefore, an additional level of middle management, called Team Managers (TMs) was created to provide this coordination. The role of Team Managers was not, however, full-time. TMs were limited to spending 50 percent of their time in this function, with the other 50 percent dedicated to performing core activities such as customer service, flight management, or maintenance management.

In addition to the sharing of work roles within established work teams, People Express employees were also expected to spend at least four days each month working with members of top management on staff committees which were assigned responsibility for handling traditional staff functions such as personnel, finance, advertising, and so forth. This strategy, although unorthodox, helped to keep the cost of overhead down, encouraged cooperation, and gave employees tremendous variety in their jobs. One recent commentator described just how the system worked for a typical Customer Service Manager (CSM):

> While working in their line activities, a team of CSMs will divide up duties, selling tickets on board the plane, manning the check-in desk at the terminal, and looking after passengers aloft. If any problems arise the team system gives them the power and flexibility to rearrange their jobs to cope with the problem. Upon switching to staff work CSMs may take reservations, keep the books, or visit travel agencies to advertise the airline.[17]

People's six Managing Officers (MOs) and General Managers (GMs) were also expected to share functions by serving on the company's thirteen staff committees. Further sharing was promoted through a lottery system which rotated managers through the staff committees on a monthly basis. These thirteen committees were in turn directed by four management Advisory Councils which monitored the company's four major functional areas and handled problems beyond the scope of day-to-day operations. The four Advisory Councils were designated as the Operations, People (employees), Marketing, and Finance/Administration Advisory Councils.[18] People's MOs and GMs served on the Advisory Councils and staff committees with other People employees who had been elected by their peers. The four Advisory Councils met weekly to keep MOs and GMs informed on organizational needs and to solve various technical problems. Two members of each Advisory Council were in turn elected to serve on a systemwide Coordinating Council which met bimonthly to coordinate the activities of all Councils and staff committees and to provide top management with an overview of their efforts. All these committees, although cumbersome, encouraged a tremendous cross-utilization of resources. And the sharing did not stop there; for top and middle management were also expected to help out at the level of basic operations. Thus, it was not unusual to find members of top management and even Don Burr himself helping out by filling in at the gate or even during a flight. This spirit of sharing likewise encouraged front-line employee/managers to share duties as well so that it was commonplace for pilots, for example, to help out with pre-flight ticketing at the gate. Tickets were also sold in-flight by flight attendants, thereby minimizing the cost of maintaining an extensive network of separate ticket agents and customer service people on the ground.

Economic Performance

Measured in traditional business terms, the company's unorthodox management practices seemed to work. When flight service started on April 30, 1980, People Express owned only three Boeing 737 aircraft and offered service between just three cities—Buffalo, New York; Newark, New Jersey (the company's main base of operations); and Norfolk, Virginia. After the first full year of operation in 1982, the company's fleet of aircraft had grown to seventeen Boeing 737s and a work force of 1,208 people, including 478 part-time employees.[19] In April of 1982, after only a year in operation, People Express turned its first operating profit, and by the end of that year it had made a net profit of $1 million from an operating profit of $10.5 million. At this point the value of People Express stock had more than tripled from an original price of 4⅛ to 12⅞. By the end of 1983, the company had grown to 2,596 full-time employees and a fleet of forty-nine aircraft. Sales had grown to $287 million, with a year-end net profit of $10.4 million. More than 6 million passengers had flown on People Express by the end of 1983, and the stock price had climbed to as high as $38.00.

At this point, People employees were high on both the company and employee ownership. Some employees had amassed small fortunes over a period of less than three years. Shares that had been purchased in the first year had grown nearly 1,000 percent in value, and for some People Express employees their stockholdings were valued at between $100,000 and $200,000. For the average employee, personal holdings of company stock had reached a value of approximately $55,000.[20]

The Founder Destroys His Dream

The euphoria did not last long, however, for by the close of 1984 the company was beginning to deteriorate just as rapidly as it had risen to success. Don Burr's "take-charge" hard-driving personality and entrepreneurial desire to build an empire came in direct conflict with those precious principles of freedom, ownership, and participation which he had so fervently advocated as the cornerstones of the People Express culture.

Of course, the growth which was a natural outcome of

People's success in exploiting a new market strained the company in and of itself, but Don Burr pushed for growth far beyond the bounds of natural development. His optimism and sense of invulnerability led him to believe he could do so without risk, or as he said in a magazine interview:

> ". . . we just bought planes, hired people, and put them in the air. Grow, grow, grow. . . . We went around telling everybody that we're going to be great and conquer the world."[21]

This growth created tremendous management problems. New employees and new managers were recruited at a far faster rate than it was possible to socialize them into the "People Express Way"—or even to make a reasonable decision as to whether they would fit into the organization. The company's personnel group found themselves spending literally twelve hours a day and six days a week recruiting new people, and the corporation's entire top management team became overwhelmed by the task of conducting orientation training sessions for new employees, which took from four to eight hours every week. As these demands mounted, it became increasingly difficult for managers to engage in the sharing of functions so central to People's corporate strategy. As work became more chaotic and the situation more difficult, Don Burr pushed harder and became domineering and directive.

Company president H. Pareti reported, for example, that Burr began to expect everyone to work twelve to fourteen hours a day, and even started scheduling Pareti's work day. Such actions were hardly consistent with a philosophy of participation, and Pareti claimed that when he tried to explain his need to spend time with his family, Burr simply could not understand. Pareti finally gave up and resigned from the presidency in early 1985.[22]

Unfortunately, as members of his management team began to complain or leave, Burr only hardened in his position. He felt that he knew what was right for the company, and no one was going to prevent it from reaching its full potential.

As a result, he began to espouse a different view of participation, as he explained in 1985:

> Leadership is not pandering to what people say they need. It's defining what the hell people need. . . . That's not what builds empires. . . . It's not "Don Burr says it, and I'll do it." It's "Don Burr says it, by God, and that's what I want to do."

Burr's concept of participatory management had shifted from building consensus from the bottom up to demanding consensus for Don Burr's demands and Don Burr's ideas. Anyone that chose to disagree with him found themselves quickly ejected from the organization. Lori Dubose, the company's original human resource officer, who had been earlier held up by Burr as a model employee because of her hard-working spirit and lack of fear when it came to speaking her mind, found herself fired for disagreeing with him one too many times. She explained, ". . . I challenged him and asked questions. Now I think it was a mistake. He didn't want to hear it anymore." Another corporate officer complained that "He's a total absolute dictator. The guy doesn't want anyone around who will challenge him."[23]

Thus Burr chose to ignore the advice of his colleagues and even attacked them for giving it. He pressed hard for faster and faster growth, pushing the company into a head-to-head battle with the nation's largest air carriers. The major airlines fought back by cutting their fares, and the impact was devastating to People's cash flow. The company's profits and cash flow were further ravaged by Burr's decision that growing from within was not fast enough to realize his dream, and so he went out on a binge of acquisitions that eventually proved to be the company's downfall. He purchased Britt Airways and Provincetown-Boston Airline, but the final nail in the People Express coffin was his decision to pay $300 million for the troubled Frontier Airlines.

Burr envisioned this last acquisition as the route to making People Express a major airline with routes covering the entire United States. This was certainly not a match made in heaven. Frontier's old-line, unionized, and highly adversarial culture did not fit well with the People Express concept of a flexible work organization, and Frontier employees were less than enthusiastic about negotiating their wages down to levels as low as those of their new parent. Burr even attempted to introduce his company's no-frills service to Frontier passengers, but they left the airline in droves, and the company's reservations dried up overnight. He gave up on this idea quickly, and in fact decided not only that Frontier would return to its status as a full-service carrier, but that People Express would follow suit by introducing a first-class section on many of its flights.

All of these actions had a devastating impact on People Express. By the close of 1985, the company was spending more than $1 million a day in cash to keep the ailing Frontier afloat, and long-term debt had increased to $540 million, which was a 65.9 percent increase over the previous year and ten times greater than when the company was first organized.[24] People had incurred a net loss of $27.5 million, and interest expense had climbed to $61.8 million, or nearly six times the company's highest net profit earned in 1983. Perhaps most devastating of all, the company's stock price dropped to only $9 per share, and this had a devastating effect on the work force. As Vincent Pantano, one of People's first customer service managers, explained, "When the stock price was high, it was great. But when it's low, it's demoralizing."[25]

The stress under these conditions was tremendous. Reminiscent of the mass suicide tragedy that occurred at Jonestown in Guyana, employees began referring to Burr as the Reverend Jim Jones, and when he tried to encourage them with pep talks they called his speeches "Kool-Aid." A comment frequently exchanged by angry employees was, "Have you had your Kool-Aid today?"[26] Burr had changed from a far-sighted visionary to a suicidal maniac in the eyes of the work force, and reinforcing this perception was the resignation of some sixty-five pilots during the first quarter of 1985 alone.

Eventually, Burr gave up hope of saving Frontier and tried to sell it to United Air Lines, but the company could not reach an agreement with the unions and eventually backed out. Therefore, to halt the $1 million a day drain on People's cash flow, Burr finally decided to take Frontier into Chapter 11 bankruptcy in 1986, and after considerable negotiating sold it to Texas Air at a substantial loss. A short time later, People Express also flew its last flight in February of 1987, just before Burr sold it to Texas Air for only $125 million. When he announced the sale to People's employees, many cried while some sat stunned in shock and disbelief. Some employees lost their entire life savings, and what had once been hailed as a revolutionary concept in air travel was now condemned as a failure.

THE LINCOLN ELECTRIC CASE

The story of the Lincoln Electric Company of Cleveland, Ohio, provides an interesting and valuable contrast to the People Express experience. Employee ownership, although not introduced as part of a start-up strategy at Lincoln Electric, was introduced early on in the life of the firm, and as at People Express, ownership was combined with a variety of other incentives and participatory mechanisms intended to support the company's successful business strategy. Unlike People Express, though, Lincoln Electric's founders held true to their original philosophy of ownership, participation, and cooperation, and allowed the company to grow gradually, slowly institutionalizing the central values and practices of the "value-driven culture" they had started. As a result of this decisively "employee-centered" approach, Lincoln Electric, after more than ninety years, is still the country's most successful manufacturer of electric welding equipment and supplies.

Lincoln Electric was founded by John C. Lincoln in 1895; in 1907 he was joined by his brother James F. Lincoln, who brought new and complementary skills to the firm. John was an engineering and technical genius, and during his life he was awarded over fifty patents for a wide array of inventions ranging from an electric drill to meat-curing equipment. James, on the other hand, was a very astute and competent manager. Thus, John's creativity provided the company with an important leading edge in product technology, and the organizational skills of James helped to ensure success in the marketplace and the creation of an innovative and highly efficient workplace.

Lincoln Electric initially started out as a manufacturer of electric motors, a product which they had dropped for many years but returned to in 1955. In 1911, though, Lincoln began to produce and sell arc welding machines, a product for which Lincoln has since gained fame throughout the world. Of particular significance in the firm's development was John Lincoln's invention of a portable welding machine. The machine made welding possible in almost any situation, and gave the company a technological edge over two giants in the field, Westinghouse and General Electric. Eventually Lincoln ran General Electric out of the arc welding business altogether, and today Westinghouse has only a very small corner of this market.[27] This edge helped the firm to grow from sales of approximately $30 million and a net profit of $200 thousand in 1935 to $333 million in sales and a net profit of nearly $21 million some fifty years later in 1985.[28] Technological advancement and creativity are not the only factors that have contributed to Lincoln Electric's superiority in the marketplace. Perhaps the most significant contribution to its economic success was made by a unique system of incentives and a spirit of ownership which pervade all aspects of this organization's culture.

The Lincoln Electric Philosophy

This sense of ownership and a strong feeling of personal responsibility for Lincoln Electric's destiny is shared by all employees, and it is in great part an outgrowth of the philosophy and values of James Lincoln. Central to Lincoln's philosophy was an emphasis on maintaining a balance among the interests of owners, customers, and employees. The extent to which this philosophy has become embedded in the ongoing culture of Lincoln Electric as an accepted and enduring way of life is well illustrated by the following two statements. The first was made by James F. Lincoln in an interview with a Harvard case writer, and the second was made by Lincoln Electric's third chairman, William Irrang.

> It is the job of the Lincoln Electric Company to give its customers more and more of a better product at a lower and lower price. This will also make it possible for the company to give to the worker and the stockholder a higher and higher return.[29]
>
> James F. Lincoln, 1947

> The success of the Lincoln Electric Company has been built on two basic ideas. One is producing more and more of a progressively better product at a lower and lower price for a larger and larger group of customers. The other is that an employee's earnings and promotion are in direct proportion to his individual contribution toward the company's success.[30]
>
> William Irrang, 1975

James Lincoln's philosophy derived from his religious beliefs, which emphasized hard work and a high level of respect for the talents and abilities and responsibilities of all humankind. Lincoln believed that, "Development in many directions is latent in every person."[31] He observed that most American companies failed to make full use of their workers because they could not recognize their talents, or, worse, were afraid to face the challenge that unleashing those talents in the workplace would represent. Lincoln was not at all afraid of the task of managing a diverse, talented, and highly motivated work force, and he viewed his role as one of helping to create a climate where all employees were respected and considered potentially equal in the value of their respective contributions to the enterprise. He explained:

> It becomes perfectly true to anyone who will think this thing through that there is no such thing in an industrial

activity as Management and Men having different functions or being two different kinds of people. Why can't we
think and why don't we think that all people are Management? Can you imagine any president of any factory or
machine shop who can go down and manage a turret lathe
as well as the machinist can? Can you imagine any manager of any organization who can go down and manage a
broom—let us get down to that—who can manage a broom
as well as a sweeper can? Can you imagine any secretary
of any company who can go down and fire a furnace and
manage that boiler as well as the man who does the job?
Obviously, all are Management.[32]

Thus, for Lincoln, the challenge of managing the corporation was twofold: first, to develop and institutionalize a system of organization which would forge a spirit of cooperation
and mutual respect between all employees, worker and manager alike; and second, to provide individual incentives and
bring the organization's collective talents to bear in creating
an efficient and profitable operation. His success in building
such a system and making it work is clearly evident when
Lincoln Electric's performance is compared with that of U.S.
industry as a whole. Over the period from 1934 through 1974,
for example, the productivity for all manufacturing industries
in the United States increased by approximately 200 percent,
whereas Lincoln Electric's productivity improved by over 600
percent for the same period. Certainly, this represents a very
significant record in terms of efficiency improvement, and it
enabled Lincoln to actually reduce its prices for many years.
Even with the effect of significant inflation by the mid-1970s,
the company was still selling most of its products at a price
only 40 percent higher than in 1934, compared to an average
price increase of more than 250 percent for all U.S. industry.[33]
Even today, some Lincoln Electric products are being sold for
a price that is less in absolute dollars than during the early
years of the company. For example, in 1915 the company was
selling one of its first arc welders for $1,550. A comparable
welder sold for only $950 in 1982.[34]

MECHANISMS FOR CREATING
AN OWNERSHIP CULTURE

The Lincolns built a business that produced these kind of results by creating an organizational culture that fulfilled James Lincoln's ideal of "every employee a manager." The culture has been institutionalized through the combined forces of stock ownership and a comprehensive system of performance rewards and worker participation that have instilled an intense sense of ownership and responsibility from the chairman of the board to the sweeper on the shop floor. Today, approximately 50 percent of Lincoln's stock is held broadly by its employees. The shares that comprise this 50 percent are called "blue stock" and can only be held by "working" employees. Blue stock shares must be sold back to the company whenever an employee leaves Lincoln Electric, and this prevents the firm from shifting from internal to absentee control. The firm buys back the shares at a price based upon a fair valuation of book value.

As shareholders, Lincoln employees participate like any stockholders with the power to elect the firm's board of directors and decide company policy through voting at the firm's annual meetings. Furthermore, with 50 percent interest, they are the company's largest stockholder group. The Lincoln family still holds roughly 30 percent of company stock, and the remaining 20 percent is comprised of shares held in trust for corporate officers and a very small number of shares of public stock, called "gold stock," which can be traded over the counter. However, the majority of "gold stock" shares are also owned by Lincoln employees.[35] The economic value, as well as the influence afforded by Lincoln's employee stock ownership, has been substantial. During the four decades that transpired between 1934 and 1974, an average after-tax return on equity of between 10 and 15 percent was consistently sustained. A strong sense of employee ownership and economic incentive has not, however, been solely limited to the ownership of company stock. A comprehensive system of bonuses and participative mechanisms have been complementary and equally important in this respect. These include:

1. Wages based solely upon a piece-rate incentive system.

2. A year-end bonus which can equal and even exceed an employee's regular yearly pay.

3. Guaranteed employment of at least 75 percent of the normal forty-hour work week for all Lincoln workers.

4. An emphasis on equality of treatment—no special executive privileges such as dining rooms and private parking spaces.

5. A worker-elected twelve-member advisory board responsible for raising issues of employee concern with management and getting action on such concerns.

All manufacturing jobs at Lincoln Electric are compensated on a piece-rate incentive basis. Standards, following the values of James F. Lincoln, are set by time study, and they "... can only be changed when management has made a change in method of doing that particular job and under no other conditions."[36] Employees also have the right to appeal rates they feel are unfair, and management goes to great lengths to ensure that fairness is maintained. Consequently, the restriction of output, or what Frederick Taylor once called "systematic soldiering," is unheard of, and it is not uncommon for Lincoln employees to exceed two to three times their standard base rate. Under Lincoln Electric's incentive system, workers are also not tempted to boost production at the expense of quality; for an employee makes no earnings whatsoever for rework, and must repair bad parts on his or her own time without compensation.

Beyond the possibility of making higher earnings through exceeding established piece-rate standards, Lincoln Electric's employees also share substantially in company profits through a year-end bonus, which has been paid consistently since it was first instituted in 1934. Thus in 1985, for example, Lincoln's 2,405 employees were paid substantial bonuses in some instances in excess of their actual normal wage for the year.

The size of each employee's bonus is determined by a merit rating system which is administered by his or her immediate supervisor in collaboration with other departments that possess relevant information (the Production Control Department, Inspection/Quality Control, Time Study, Engineering, etc.). Each employee is rated semiannually on the following dimensions.[37]

- Dependability
- Quality
- Output
- Ideas and cooperation

The average rating for all employees at Lincoln Electric must equal 100 percent, but individual merit ratings can vary widely. Thus merit scores at Lincoln have ranged from as low as 40 percent to as high as 160 percent. To determine the actual individual bonus payment, these scores are in turn multiplied by an overall bonus percentage which is determined each year by the company, depending on Lincoln Electric's profitability. Thus, if the bonus level decided upon for a given year was 50 percent, the actual payment to an employee with a 160-percent merit rating would be computed by multiplying 0.5 by 1.6, resulting in a bonus equal to 80 percent of the employee's regular take-home pay. Between 1945 and 1975 the average bonus ranged from 78 to 129 percent of employees' normal earnings.[38] Thus, many Lincoln employees have more than doubled their earnings as a result of the bonus program, and, as the data in Table 9 make clear, the average employee bonus between 1979 and 1985 ranged from a high of $20,753 in 1981 to a low of $8,551 in 1983.

Obviously, the opportunity to earn such considerable financial rewards by contributing to the successful performance of the company is a significant source of motivation for Lincoln employees. At some companies, however, any increase in efficiency leads to the loss of some jobs; and one might

Table 9. Year-End Bonus System: Lincoln Electric Company, 1979–1985

	NUMBER OF EMPLOYEES	TOTAL BONUSES (IN MILLIONS)	AVERAGE BONUS PER EMPLOYEE
1979	2,611	$44.1	$16,890
1980	2,637	43.3	15,420
1981	2,684	55.7	20,753
1982	2,634	36.9	14,009
1983	2,561	21.9	8,551
1984	2,469	32.7	13,244
1985	2,405	38.1	15,842

Source: Lincoln Electric Company, Condensed Comparative Statement of Financial Condition: 1979–1985, *Lincoln Electric Company, Cleveland, Ohio.*

imagine that fears about job security would discourage employees at Lincoln from making the effort necessary to keep this kind of performance system working. At other companies, such fears are real and legitimate, but at Lincoln they do not exist.

In 1951 the company first began to experiment with the concept of guaranteed employment security, and in 1958 the policy was adopted formally as the *Guaranteed Continuous Employment Plan*. Since 1958, Lincoln workers have been guaranteed a minimum of 75 percent of the normal 40-hour work week regardless of economic conditions faced by the company. Thus, during a recent one-and-a-half-year period of reduced sales and considerable economic distress, which began in 1983, all employees took a reduced thirty-hour work week. However, because of such collective sacrifice, which is surely representative of the kind of dedication that might be expected from serious owners, Lincoln still made a profit of $16 million in 1983, and a 53 percent bonus pool was in fact paid out.[39]

Lastly, in addition to the ability to influence company policy through voting at annual meetings and the election of company directors, Lincoln employees also participate directly in the day-to-day decision making of the company. The bonus system, of course, encourages all employees to develop and submit ideas that save the company money and improve its products. Lincoln Electric employees are also able to air their concerns and seek rectification of problems through a twelve-member worker Advisory Board which is composed of and elected by workers. The board meets twice a month to hear employee complaints and concerns and works through solutions with the company president and the chairman of the board. Most issues are acted upon immediately, and those that require further investigation and research are assigned to the executive responsible and must be addressed within two weeks or by the next Advisory Board meeting. The Advisory Board and this process are a company tradition at Lincoln Electric, and have been since this practice was first initiated in 1914.[40] Mechanisms such as this help to ensure that the interests of Lincoln's employee-owners are addressed and responded to on a timely basis. Unlike absentee owners, and very much like company founders, employee-owners have a close and intimate interest in company operations because they are involved in company affairs daily. Thus, mechanisms like Lincoln's Advisory Board, as well as the substantial economic incentives provided through stock ownership, piece rates and merit bonuses, are a vital and necessary component of a successful strategy for maintaining an "ownership culture" through employee ownership. The Lincoln Electric Company is a classic and impressive example of such a successful transition strategy.

ALLIED PLYWOOD CORPORATION

Lincoln Electric is an extraordinary example of a sophisticated and all-encompassing strategy for institutionalizing an ownership culture and for preventing future domination by absentee owners. At other firms, ESOPs have provided company founders with an attractive mechanism for facilitating a careful and well-planned withdrawal from their business. An excellent example of just such a use of an ESOP in a small but profitable company is provided by the story of Allied Plywood Corporation of Alexandria, Virginia.

The Allied Plywood Corporation was founded by Ed and Phyllis Sanders in 1951 with an initial investment of $10,000. By the mid-1970s, this wholesale plywood and construction supply firm had grown to include over twenty full-time employees and several million dollars in sales, and the founders were beginning to think about retirement. However, with no immediate heirs, the couple was forced to seriously consider several options for withdrawing from the business: selling their interest back to the corporation, selling Allied to a larger company, or financing an employee purchase of their company through the creation of an ESOP.[41]

From a financial perspective, the idea of simply selling their stock to the company was hardly attractive. Their initial investment had grown considerably over time, and the gains they would realize as a result of the sale would be taxed at a rate of 70 percent (today the figure would be 50 percent). Selling out to a large corporation was by far more acceptable: If Ed and Phyllis Sanders sold their company for cash to an outside group they would be taxed at only the capital gains rate of 28 percent (20 percent today); and if they chose to accept instead of cash the acquiring corporation's stock as payment, they would not be taxed at all on the transaction.[42] In spite of the financial advantages, they were not enthusiastic about this option either; for they had maintained a close relationship with their work force throughout the years and had even instituted a generous profit-sharing plan to enable employees to benefit from the growth of the business. The founders felt that by selling out to another corporation they would be selling out their friends and loyal employees as well. Ed Sanders, in describing the dilemma, told researchers:

> Well, it's mainly from my obligation to the people that have been here for so long. [I] couldn't see it. We have a bonus setup, and I could see that going down the drain in a hurry . . .

If another company merged or bought it, well, all they'd do is sit back and look at the balance sheets and the profits [and] losses. And that's all they care about. And they hire somebody with a whip from someplace to come in . . . and straighten it out. And then all they do is look at profit, top and bottom. That's the way they work. They even advertise it.

Some of these big conglomerates have thirty different divisions. And they're going to buy and sell here . . . and sell the ones that are losing money and buy five that are in a sympathetic industry. I know the way they are.[43]

Because of these concerns, the founders of Allied Plywood chose employee ownership through the adoption of an ESOP as the strategy for preparing for retirement and bringing about a shift in ownership. Initially, the ESOP was not leveraged when it was first implemented in 1976. The company simply made cash contributions of approximately 24 percent of payroll to the plan trust each year, and the trust, in turn, gradually began to purchase the Sanders's stock. In 1982, the year that Ed and Phyllis decided to complete their retirement, the plan purchased a final 40 percent block of stock. Under the plan, all employees would participate in the ESOP after one year, with complete vesting taking place after ten years. In 1986, Allied's twenty-five-person work force became fully vested with employees owning 100 percent of Allied's stock. In order to keep the firm employee owned and controlled, all workers were required upon leaving the company to sell their shares back to the ESOP. No one was allowed to retain their shares when their employment at Allied ended.

Since the institution of the ESOP, Allied's performance has been excellent. Sales have grown steadily and profits have been consistent, despite a lengthy period of depression in the housing industry. Only one employee had left the firm by the end of 1984, and the combination of the ESOP, wages, and Allied's profit-sharing plan has resulted in an average annual employee compensation of between $30,000 and $50,000.[44] Allied Plywood's stock has also continued to grow in value at an average annual rate of 14 percent since the ESOP was first established.[45]

Even today, however, after the company had become 100 percent employee owned, Allied Plywood still has some distance to go in setting up formal mechanisms of participative decision making. Since 1980, federal law has required that employee participants in an ESOP at a publicly traded company be provided with full pass-through voting rights like all holders of common stock. This is not the case for private companies, which are only required to provide employees with the power to vote their shares on major decisions such as mergers and liquidations that can significantly affect the value of their shares and job security. Like many company founders, Ed Sanders was hesitant about immediately providing Allied workers with a significant vote over the assets he had spent so many years building up. He explained to researchers:

> If we were to have the vote pass through on all that stock that they have, here I'd be with half my life's work invested, with minority say in what I'd had full control of. I think a vote pass through is fine once my interest had worked down to be somewhat like theirs.[46]

Once Ed and Phyllis Sanders finally retired in 1982, employee involvement in decision making began to increase substantially. Thus, today, employees now elect three representatives from their own ranks to the company's seven-member board of directors—one person from the office and sales staff and two from the warehouse. The firm's new president and vice-president, Robert Shaw and Gene Scales, are board members, and so are two nonemployees, the company's accountant and attorney. In addition to electing three directors, Allied employees also now vote on major capital expenditures. They have also reinstituted a practice of periodically holding employee-owner meetings after work to discuss and solve company problems. The meetings were initiated by Ed Sanders to complement the ESOP, but he eventually decided they were not worthwhile and discontinued them. Apparently, Allied's employee-owners felt differently and decided to restore the after-work sessions. Allied's employees have not yet pressed for the implementation of full pass-through voting rights.

LOWE'S COMPANIES

Large companies also make effective use of employee ownership as a transition strategy. One of the most impressive success stories is that of Lowe's Companies—the nation's largest discount seller of home building supplies and an employer of more than 14,000 and annual sales of over $2.3 billion. Lowe's has been extraordinarily successful under employee ownership. Louis Kelso once said that it was "the most successful example of what employee ownership might achieve."[47]

An employee ownership transition strategy was actually first conceived of at Lowe's Companies more than twenty-five years ago after one of the company's founders, Carl Buchan, bought out the interest of the other partners in the business. Shortly after, Buchan began to consider ways in which he might be able to eventually pass the company on to his employees. To accomplish this end, he created a company profit-sharing plan on June 1, 1956.[48] His intention was to periodically sell substantial blocks of stock to the plan, and then have his estate contribute the balance to the trust upon his death. Describing this concept in 1960, he wrote, "I desire to build this business into the largest and most successful in the world, owned and controlled by those who did it."[49] Making the transition came far more quickly than either Buchan or Lowe's management and employees had ever anticipated; for Carl Buchan died only a short time later that same year at the age of forty-four. Fortunately, Lowe's top management teams took Buchan's idea quite seriously. They then put it into effect in the following way:

> The management team that Buchan had assembled worked feverishly to salvage the plan for employee ownership. The profit-sharing trust, only three years old, had

very limited funds and could not afford to buy the company from Buchan's estate. Early in 1961, however, the managers found a solution. Of the one million extant shares of Lowe's common stock, employees and business associates of Buchan's owned 110,000 shares. The profit-sharing trust bought the remaining 890,000 shares from the Buchan estate for about $6 per share. The trust obtained the cash for this purchase from a short-term loan and then repaid the loan with the proceeds of a public offering of 410,000 shares at $12.25 per share. Using this strategy employees captured 480,000 shares, or 48 percent, of Lowe's stock.[50]

After this dramatic shift to employee ownership, growth which had been steady under Buchan's leadership took off at an accelerated rate following the basic strategy he had developed. Buchan's innovation was the creation of "one-stop" centers where contractors and "do-it-yourselfers" could purchase all materials, tools, and instructional materials for home improvement projects at a single location and at a reasonable price. He established the first such center in 1949 in North Wilkesboro, North Carolina, and purchased his stock direct from manufacturers, thereby effectively eliminating wholesaler mark-up. The concept was a success, and the business grew from $4 million in 1953 to $27 million and seven home center stores with a total of fifty employees in 1961.

After Buchan's death and the shift to employee ownership, company growth was phenomenal; and by 1970 Lowe's had opened seventy-five stores and was grossing $170 million. Lowe's managers credited much of this success to employee ownership.[51] Robert Strickland, the chairman of Lowe's Companies, explained:

> How do I know it works? How do I know that Lowe's growth wasn't influenced more by geography, or the business we're in, or management skill, etc.? In the late '50s and early '60s there were at least five companies like ours in the Sunbelt—one in Virginia, one in South Carolina, one in Florida, and two in North Carolina. Same geog-

raphy, same business, different management, of course, but not bad management. Three of the companies didn't make it on their own and sold out. The fourth company is about one-fourth our size, and they have just adopted an employee stock ownership plan. Survival of the motivated and the productive.[52]

However, Lowe's success with employee ownership almost created its own self-destruction. Company growth and profitability caused the value of Lowe's stock to soar, and employees who retired were leaving the company wealthy. One employee, Charles Valentine, a company truck driver who was earning $125 a week, became an instant celebrity when a *Newsweek* article reported that he had retired in 1975 after seventeen years at Lowe's with $666,000 worth of stock.[53] Unfortunately, retirement benefits like this created a tremendous incentive for employees to leave the company early. In 1971 alone some thirteen store managers, salespeople, warehouse employees, and office workers left the company, taking with them $17.5 million in company stock and, by 1975, more than fifty Lowe's employees had retired with equity in the six figures.[54] This mass exodus of wealthy retirees rapidly eroded the company's human resources as well as the proportion of total equity owned by working employees. Employee stockholdings also began to decline during the period, as the company was forced to comply with the "prudent man ruling" which limits the amount of employer securities a pension or profit-sharing plan can legally hold. Consequently, by 1977, employee stockholdings had dropped from a high of 50 percent in 1968 to a low of 17 percent. In 1968, the average Lowe's employee had owned some 5,000 shares, and by 1977 this number had dropped to around 1,000 shares. This was a discouraging state of affairs for Lowe's remaining employees; and, in a very real sense, the company had become a victim of its own success.

Fortunately, ERISA, the same law that forced the company to drastically diversify its profit-sharing plan assets, provided an alternative for revitalizing the spirit of ownership at

Lowe's Companies through the creation of an ESOP. In 1977, after reading about the legislation that had established ESOPs as qualified employee benefit plans, Lowe's management realized that here was a vehicle through which they could reinstitute the policy they had carried out through the profit-sharing plan and at the same time remain in full compliance with federal law. They therefore decided to freeze the profit-sharing plan in 1978 and adopt an ESOP.

After freezing the profit-sharing plan, the company vested all employees fully, regardless of their years of service, and gave them ten options for determining what to do with the value of their plan accounts. They were told that they could choose to take any combination of Lowe's stock and cash they desired based upon increments of 10 percent. Thus, employees could choose to take 100 percent stock and no cash, 90 percent stock and 10 percent cash, 80 percent stock and 20 percent cash, and so forth, all the way to no stock and 100 percent cash. When the actual decision was made, the response of Lowe's workers and managers was clearly an affirmation of their support for employee ownership; for 79 percent chose the 90 percent stock option and another 11 percent chose the 80 percent option.[55]

Today, between the stock that was frozen in employee profit-sharing accounts and the new ESOP, Lowe's Companies' employees now own approximately 30 percent of the firm's stock. Lowe's employees enjoy full pass-through voting rights because the rest of the company's stock is publicly traded. The company has also instituted a number of mechanisms for employee participation. Employees at every Lowe's Home Center meet weekly with local management to discuss and solve problems, as well as receive information from management. Employees at each Center also elect a representative to sit on a companywide Advisory Committee which receives reports from top management and makes recommendations. Lowe's also has a budget and financial control committee and employee-management committees to investigate and develop new products and company services. A great deal of attention is given to employee ownership through posters, a company newsletter that keeps employees informed on Lowe's performance, and even a videotape which describes the ESOP in detail. All of these activities help to contribute to a spirit of cooperation and ownership, but Lowe's nonmanagement employees do not participate on the firm's Board of Directors. Three of the company's directors are employees, but they are all from the ranks of management. This may have some bearing on the fact that when the National Center for Employee Ownership collected survey data at Lowe's they found that the work force still felt that they had relatively little influence over company decision making.[56]

Notwithstanding the desire of Lowe's Companies' employees for greater participation in company decision making, it is clear that they are wholehearted supporters of employee ownership. As long as the company is successful and continues to grow it is unlikely that this support will disappear; for there is periodically the reminder that when a Lowe's employee retires he or she is likely to be far better off than the average retiree who leaves American industry. Charlie Valentine, the $125-a-week truck driver who left Lowe's in 1975 with better than a half million dollars, is today a successful independent businessman. He is currently operating two cattle ranches and a dairy farm which he purchased with his retirement money. Ferrell Bryan, another Lowe's employee who retired in 1975, left the firm after twenty years at the relatively young age of forty-seven. When he retired he took half his retirement of $500,000 in cash and the other half in Lowe's stock. Only six months after leaving the company his $250,000 in stock had climbed to a value exceeding $350,000.[57] A third employee, Cecil Murray, who retired in 1975 at age 50, after many years as Lowe's personnel manager, left Lowe's with the hefty sum of $3.5 million.[58]

SUMMARY

The cases we have reviewed in this chapter illustrate how the founders of four different companies incorporated employee ownership as a transition strategy, Allied's founders were able to protect the job security of their employees and the long-term survival of the firm they had worked so hard to build.

The Allied Plywood case provides an excellent example of how employee ownership can help the owners of a small but very profitable privately owned enterprise make a financially intelligent transition into retirement. By using employee ownership as a transition strategy, Allied's founders were able to protect the job security of their employees and the long-term survival of the firm they had worked so hard to build.

Employee ownership fit well into the existing culture and practices of Allied Plywood Company. Allied's lucrative profit-sharing plan had already created an attitude of ownership among the company's employees; therefore, the addition of actual stock ownership was a natural extension of the profit-sharing concept. The transition process was also implemented intelligently by carrying it out gradually over a relatively long period of time. This gave both the founders and their employees a chance to adjust to the change. The adjustment, however, might have been made somewhat more complete, and an "ownership culture" more firmly embedded into the fabric of company life, if Ed Sanders had passed on the reins of control and the full rights of ownership to all employees at some point during the eight to ten years he and his wife spent phasing themselves out of the business.

Although Ed Sanders's control of the process of shifting to employee ownership, was "founder-centered," it was not extreme. However, it is clear that moving to employee participation was still a difficult change for him to make. Unilaterally discontinuing employee meetings, as well as failing to build in a target date for passing on full voting rights to all Allied employees, significantly restricted the extent to which the company fully institutionalized an ownership culture. Employee meetings in particular could have served as an important vehicle for upgrading employee knowledge and skills so that Allied's work force could comfortably and responsibly assume control of the company. Now that their benefactors have left, it is inevitable that employees will eventually feel that they are entitled to exercise these rights, but if they have to fight to receive them the organization could be destroyed in the process.

The Lowe's Companies case is an example of how employee ownership can work effectively as a strategy for both ownership transition and organizational improvement in a relatively large enterprise. As its top management attested, employee ownership was the key factor that enabled Lowe's to become the largest and most profitable company in its particular industry, with "... profits per employee two to three times better than those at a smoothly-run pair of retailing giants, Sears and J.C. Penney."[59] In the Lowe's case, however, due to the founder's sudden death, the transition to employee ownership was also rather sudden, and with little time to prepare. Nevertheless, the ownership change that took place was substantial, because Buchan's management team had been well schooled in his ideas, facilitating a viable approach to the transition. Thus, ownership was transferred, with a profound motivating effect upon Lowe's workers and managers. The absence of a well-worked-out plan and structure of ownership, however, did present the company with problems later on; for though the employees were in fact highly motivated, they were not necessarily motivated to stick with the company over the entire span of their career life. Thus, the success of the firm actually encouraged a gutting of the organization's employee ownership base, and it caused a heavy drain on the firm's cash flow as enriched employees and managers became anxious to cash in on their fortunes through early retirement. This experience reminds us that the adoption of employee ownership requires careful planning and implementation; for without the proper mechanisms to control the in-flow and out-flow of employees into an ownership plan, a successful program may result in its own cannibalization.

The Lincoln Electric and People Express cases present an intriguing contrast. Both companies chose to incorporate an intense spirit of ownership into their strategies for doing business, and did so in a much more far-reaching sense than the majority of companies that adopt employee ownership. The difference in the success and survival of these two firms is especially interesting to many advocates of employee ownership, who argue emotionally and often persuasively that a change in ownership must be accompanied by major changes in the way companies are governed and run. This is not merely an argument that employee owners must have precisely the same rights as any other stockholder, but rather a call for radical reformation of the traditional corporate structure, a more democratic and participative approach to management, and a broader sharing of earned surplus.

Although neither People Express nor Lincoln Electric represent as highly a democratic approach to corporate governance and management as, for example, the Northwestern plywood cooperatives or other cooperatively owned businesses, it is clear that the degree of employee involvement and participation implemented in both cases far exceeded that of the majority of capitalist firms in existence today. Their contrasting experiences, however, point to the fact that mechanisms are merely that; they are no substitute for serious commitment and gradual development. Certainly no mechanism of ownership will be sufficient in the absence of rigorous financial management and carefully planned organizational growth. In fact, it is apparent from both the Lowe's and the Allied Plywood cases that sophisticated and far-reaching reforms in management and work organization are less likely to ensure the survival of an employee-owned company than sincere commitment and cautious adjustment to employee ownership.

In the case of People Express, there is some indication that commitment to the organization's espoused ideals was not entirely sincere or complete. From the outset the company planned to keep costs down not only through its unique reward system and approach to management but also by maintaining a relatively large part-time work force to cover overload and less attractive duties. The part-time work force received no benefits, stock ownership, or participation in profit sharing; and, because of their lowly status, they became known within the organization as the "Non-People People." Thus, participation was not afforded to everyone at People Express, and those who were left out were by definition second-class citizens of the organization, a group that it was permissible to exploit. Indeed, everyone at the company, except Don Burr himself, was a kind of second-class citizen, because Burr retained a certain proprietary right in the organization as its sole enlightened leader. Burr's ill-conceived acquisition of Frontier Air Lines, and the fleet of planes he built so quickly he couldn't train pilots to fly them, suggest that he was building an empire, not an ownership culture. But whatever Burr's own motives, it is clear that, at People Express, the implementation of employee ownership and its mechanisms were blunted by Burr's founder-centered approach.

Lincoln Electric was (and is), obviously, a dramatically different case. There, a commitment to shared ownership, equity in the distribution of rewards, and employee participation in decision making are, collectively, the foundation of the business. The founders perceived themselves to be fulfilling their religious beliefs through a unique system of ownership, management, and organization, and they sought to develop and guard that system by maintaining an all-important balance among the interests of employees, owners, and customers. They adopted a strategy that worked, and they did not abandon it for the thrill of fast growth or the personal rewards of empire-building. They supported the company's steady growth almost entirely with self-generated funds, and did not mortgage its future with heavy borrowing.

The contrasting cases of People Express and Lincoln Electric clearly reveal the fundamental differences between the founder-centered and employee-centered approaches to implementing employee ownership. The former gives employees a stake in the organization, but almost no say about its future. The latter creates a culture of ownership where every employee has a fair share of the rewards and the full responsibility to sacrifice for the future good of the organization. Such a culture of ownership requires more than the mere financial ownership of stock or a few innovative management schemes.

We will consider how to create such a culture in the following chapter.

CHAPTER 8 ENDNOTES

1. Alan Cohen and Michael Quarrey. Performance of Employee-Owned Small Companies: A Preliminary Study. *Journal of Small Business Management*, vol. 24, no. 2, April 1986, p. 59.

2. Paul Bernstein. *Workplace Democratization—Its Internal Dynamics* (New Brunswick, N.J.: Transaction Books, 1983), p. 39.

3. Corey M. Rosen, Katherine J. Klein, and Karen M. Young. *Employee Ownership in America: The Equity Solution* (Lexington, Mass.: Lexington Books, 1986), p. 161.

4. "Will Success Spoil Jerry Gorde?" *Inc. Magazine*, vol. 8, no. 2, February 1984.

5. Bruce G. Posner. "In Search of Equity." *Inc. Magazine*, vol. 7, no. 4, April 1985, p. 55.

6. Ibid.

7. Peter Nulty. "A Champ of Cheap Airlines." *Fortune*, March 22, 1982, vol. 105, no. 6, pp. 127–134.

8. Eastern Air Lines. *Industry Comparison Chart Book: 1979–June, 1985* (Miami, Fl., October 1985), p. III-1.

9. George Russell. "Air Pocket in the Revolution." *Time Magazine*, July 7, 1986, pp. 36–37; Eastern Air Lines, October 1985, p. III-2.

10. Eastern Air Lines, October 1985, p. III-3.

11. G. Alberto Zarate. *The Rise and Fall of People Express Airline.* Unpublished working paper, Brigham Young University, Provo, Utah, April 17, 1987, p. 6.

12. Interview with Frank Borman, Miami, Florida, January 1986.

13. Zarate, 1987, p. 20.

14. "People Express Airline: The Organizational Structure." *Employee Ownership*, vol. III, no. 3, September 1983, p. 1.

15. Zarate, 1987, p. 12.

16. Nulty, 1982, pp. 127–134.

17. *Employee Ownership*, September 1983, p. 5.

18. Harvard Business School. *People Express, Part I: Policy Formulation* (Cambridge, Mass.: Harvard Business School Press, 1983).

19. Zarate, 1987, p. 1.

20. *Employee Ownership*, September 1983, p. 1; Rosen et al., 1986, p. 232.

21. George Gendron. "Bitter Victories." *Inc. Magazine*, vol. 7, no. 8, August 1985, pp. 25–34.

22. Stratford Sherman. "An Airline Rebel Takes Off Again." *Fortune*, vol. 112, no. 12, November 25, 1985, pp. 129–136.

23. John Byrne. "Up, Up and Away? Expansion Is Threatening the 'Humane' Culture at People Express." *Business Week*, November 25, 1985, pp. 80–90.

24. Penelope Wang. "A Last Frontier for People Express." *Newsweek*, September 8, 1986, p. 40.

25. Byrne, 1985, pp. 80–90.

26. Zarate, 1987, p. 26.

27. Raymond Moley. *The American Century of John C. Lincoln* (New York: Duell, Sloan and Pearce, 1962), p. 71; William Baldwin. "This Is the Answer." *Forbes*, vol. 130, no. 1, July 5, 1982, p. 50.

28. Harvard Business School. *The Lincoln Electric Company* (Cambridge, Mass.: Harvard Business School Press, 1975), pp. 2, 16; Telephone interview with Betty Misley, Lincoln Electric Company, May 5, 1987.

29. Harvard Business School. *The Lincoln Electric Company*, 1975, p. 3.

30. Lincoln Electric Company. *Employee's Handbook* (Cleveland, Ohio, 1975).

31. James F. Lincoln. *Incentive Management* (Cleveland, Ohio: The Lincoln Electric Company, 1951), p. 7.

32. James F. Lincoln. *What Makes Workers Work* (Cleveland, Ohio: Lincoln Electric Company, 1951), pp. 3–4.

33. Harvard Business School, *The Lincoln Electric Company*, 1975, pp. 17–18.

34. William Baldwin. "*This Is the Answer.*" *Forbes*, vol. 130, no. 1, July 5, 1982, p. 50.

35. Telephone interview with Betty Misley, May 5, 1987.

36. William Irrang. *The Lincoln Incentive Management Program*. Lincoln Lecture Series. (Tempe: Arizona State University, 1972), p. 13.

37. Telephone interview with Betty Misley, May 5, 1987.

38. Harvard Business School, *The Lincoln Electric Company*, 1975, p. 5.

39. Telephone interview with Betty Misley, May 5, 1987.

40. Harvard Business School, *The Lincoln Electric Company*, 1975, pp. 7–8.

41. Patrick M. Rooney. "Worker Control: Greater Efficiency and Job Satisfaction." In *Proceedings of the National Employee Ownership and Participation Conference*, p. 128. Guilford College, Greensboro, N.C., October 12–14, 1984.

42. Michael Quarrey, Joseph Blasi, and Corey Rosen. *Taking Stock: Employee Ownership at Work*. Cambridge, Mass.: Ballinger Publishing Co., 1986, pp. 80–81. Rosen et al., 1986, pp. 206–207; Quarrey et al., 1986, pp. 81–82.

43. Quarrey, et al., 1986, pp. 81–82.

44. Ibid., pp. 84–86; "Employee Ownership and Productivity." Report from *Congressional Record*, vol. 127, no. 187, Tuesday, December 15, 1981, U.S. Senate (Legislative day of Monday, November 30, 1981).

45. Rooney, 1984, p. 128.

46. Quarrey et al., 1986, p. 86.

47. Rosen et al., 1986, p. 160.

48. Ibid., p. 225.

49. Ibid., p. 157; "Profit-Sharing: Lowe's Largesse." *Newsweek*, March 31, 1975, p. 61.

50. Quarrey et al., 1986, pp. 131–132.

51. Ibid., p. 132.

52. Rosen et al., 1986, pp. 156–157.

53. "Profit-Sharing: Lowe's Largesse." *Newsweek*, March 31, 1975, p. 61.

54. Ibid., p. 61.

55. Quarrey et al., 1986, p. 134.

56. Rosen et al., 1986, p. 160.

57. Robert L. Strickland. Remarks made at the Second Annual ESOP Symposium, Georgetown University Law Center, Washington, D.C., September 25, 1980.

58. "Buchan's Million Dollar Prophesy Comes True." *Building Supply News*, December 17, 1984. "Profit-Sharing: Lowe's Largesse. *Newsweek*, March 31, 1975, p. 61.

59. "Profit-Sharing: Lowe's Largesse." *Newsweek*, March 31, 1975, p. 61.

CHAPTER 9

Creating a Value-Driven Corporate Culture

In the previous three chapters, we outlined the need for alternative ownership structures that can reduce or reverse some of the negative consequences of absentee ownership and professional management. In this chapter, we will look at the connections between ownership structure and corporate culture, arguing that both must be changed to create a truly productive organization that *adds value* to its customers, its employees, and its environment. Many well-known books—including Peters and Waterman's *In Search of Excellence*, Ouchi's *Theory Z*, and Deal and Kennedy's *Corporate Cultures*—have argued that an organization's culture does indeed contribute to its success and survival. Our own studies support this view, as far as it goes. These writers, however, suggest that culture can be changed simply by "reorienting" employees to a new set of values. Corporations are urged to devise new slogans, espouse new corporate philosophies, and create new symbols. Our own observations suggest, to the contrary, that this approach usually fails in the long run. In practice, the effects of absentee ownership tend to overpower any efforts to create a culture inconsistent with the owner's demands for short-term returns. However, by allowing employees to become owners of the companies they work for, an ownership culture—where employees are committed to the firm's long-term development—can be created.

As we have noted, even a change in ownership may not lead to the desired results, because managers and employees who have become accustomed to focusing on short-term profits often find it difficult to change their habits. For example, in a number of employee buy-out cases, many observers assumed that workers would take more interest in making decisions and improving productivity. In fact, however, workers and managers simply could not understand how to relate to each other in a nonadversarial way. In Yugoslavia, as another example, workers who have a long history of worker ownership and control over decision making in their factories often reward themselves with fat raises while failing to make needed capital investment. Thus, even when workers have ownership, they may support values and make decisions that are counterproductive. This is why we believe that a fundamental shift in American business practices must involve simultaneous changes in *both* ownership structure and corporate culture.

WHAT IS CULTURE?

Before discussing corporate culture, we must first define it. There has been much debate and controversy over what constitutes a corporate culture. We have found it useful to think of culture as a pattern of artifacts, perspectives, values, and assumptions that are shared by a group or organization.

Artifacts are the more overt aspects of a group's culture, such as its language, stories, rituals, behavior patterns, and dress. These are "tangible" aspects of the culture that can be heard, seen, smelled, or touched. Anyone who has visited different companies can recognize that each somehow "feels" different—different dress, different jargon, different physical layout, different atmosphere. These artifacts have deeper meanings, however, which lead us to deeper levels of culture.

Perspectives are rules that members of the group use to act appropriately in a given situation. A "situation" may be anything from a specific encounter—such as greeting the boss in the morning—to ongoing issues of organizational politics—such as "how one gets ahead in this company." In some cases, perspectives are formalized in standard operating procedures. In others, they are informal in nature and communicated through organizational stories or myths. Members of an organization use these perspectives to navigate through the various situations they encounter each day.

Values are broadly applicable rules or standards that can be consistently applied in a wide variety of general situations. Organizational values can often be defined in simple statements such as "be honest," "the customer comes first," "never kill a new idea," "be creative," and so forth. Often corporations attempt to articulate their values in formal statements of the corporate goals or philosophy. Of course, the organizations may not always live up to these announced values, so one must distinguish between an organization's "ideal" and "real" values.

At the deepest level of culture are what we call *assumptions*—the basic premises or foundation of the other levels. Assumptions are basic beliefs about time and space or good and evil, about how members of the group relate to one another, survive as a group, discover truth, and make the "right" decisions. The categories of common assumptions found in organizations along with the possible orientations within each category are listed below.[1]

1. *The Nature of Relationships*—Are relationships between members of the organization assumed to be primarily lineal (i.e., hierarchical), collateral (i.e., group oriented), or individualistic in nature?

2. *Human Nature*—Are humans considered to be basically good, basically evil, or neither good nor evil?

3. *The Nature of Truth*—Is "truth" (i.e., correct decisions) discovered from external authority figures, or is it determined by a process of personal investigation and testing?

4. *The Environment*—Is there a basic belief that humans can master the environment; or must be subjugated by the environment; or should attempt to harmonize with the environment?

5. *Time*—Are members of the organization primarily oriented to the past, the present, or the future?

6. *The Nature of Human Activity*—Assumptions about the nature of human activity can be divided into three approaches:

A. A "Doing" orientation—Are humans basically active?

B. A "Being" orientation—Are humans passive and unable to alter existing circumstances?

C. A "Being in Becoming" orientation—Is a person's primary goal the development of self as an integrated whole?

To illustrate how even one category of assumptions can influence an entire culture, suppose that members of a group assume that other members of the group are not to be trusted. Such a belief would greatly affect the group's artifacts, perspectives, and values. If, however, the group assumed that people are basically good and can be trusted, a whole different culture would be created. Thus, when attempting to decipher the culture of an organization, it is important to uncover the set of tacit assumptions that underpin the more overt levels of culture.

THE ASSUMPTIONS OF THE "ABSENTEE" CORPORATE CULTURE

Throughout this book, we have looked at many specific aspects of absentee ownership and professional management that constitute, in effect, a form of negative, or an unsuccessful, corporate culture. Now we are in a position to analyze the deeper assumptions that underlie this "absentee" culture. Our studies suggest that the cultures of absentee-owned, professionally managed companies are generally founded on six specific assumptions.

The Nature of the Environment

Managers of absentee-owned firms often take more of a reactive than a proactive stance toward their environment.

Rather than spending time creating new markets or developing new products, they frequently must fight takeover attempts and struggle to remain profitable while servicing a tremendous amount of debt. Success is deemed to be a function of opportunistic takeovers of other companies, and long-term planning and development for the parent business is generally given only lip service. Furthermore, general management and financial skills that can be applied to all organizations and industries are seen as being the key to effective performance in the marketplace. Given this orientation, corporate strategies are formulated based on short-term, financial criteria.

Human Nature

As we have seen, professional managers and absentee owners tend to take a rather neutral or distrustful stance toward company employees. Employees are seen as assets to be used in the production process, and are generally not viewed as friends or colleagues. In fact, many professional managers make it a point not to get close to their employees, since they may have to make decisions that are not in the employees' best interests. Employee security or emotional health is not usually considered an appropriate criterion for decision making. Moreover, employees are often assumed to be the cause of many of the organization's troubles. They are a problem to be managed, not a resource to be developed.

The Nature of Relationships

In absentee-owned companies, relationships are usually assumed to be "individualistic" in nature; that is, employees are supposed to look out for their own self-interest. Individual rewards, power, status, and career advancement are deemed to be paramount, and this focus on the individual tends to create competition and conflict in the organization. While individuals will serve on a team, they will do so only if it benefits their own interests. Loyalty to the firm is usually marginal at best. If a better job opportunity comes along, the employee will take it.

The Nature of Truth

In absentee-owned companies, whatever is best for the bottom line is assumed to be "right." Economic gain is the primary consideration. Managers follow the rules and decision models of professional and "scientific" management to maximize returns, usually without consulting employees.

Time

In the absentee-owned firm, there is often little emphasis on developing a long-term strategy. Professional managers tend to be opportunists who focus their efforts on the present. Given such a "present" orientation, the absentee-owned company tends to drift with the prevailing wind, never setting a straight course for an ultimate objective.

The Nature of Human Activity

As we have seen, employees in an absentee-owned company are assumed to be assets of the corporation who carry out the wishes of management without question. Given such an assumption, there is little reason to emphasize employee development and training, and little time or effort will be spent to improve the lot of the average employee. Those who fail to perform will be reprimanded or replaced.

THE ASSUMPTIONS OF THE "EFFECTIVE" CORPORATE CULTURE

A number of recent writers have looked at the relationship of organizational culture to business effectiveness.[2] All of them posit a set of specific values and assumptions that they believe constitute an effective corporate culture. While we do not believe that any single type of culture will necessarily correlate with success in an organization, there do appear to be some striking similarities among the kinds of cultures that, according to these writers, are linked to long-term success. Furthermore, these assumptions underpinning these "effective" cultures appear to be the antithesis of the assumptions that form the foundation of the absentee-owned, professionally managed firm. A comparison of these assumptions can be found in Table 10.

As the table illustrates, there is a marked contrast between the assumptions of the absentee-owned and the effective corporate culture. Each of the assumptions about human nature, relationships, and human action that we have discussed in the context of the absentee culture finds a corresponding positive manifestation in the effective culture. The effective culture instills a sense of pride in employees, who are thus motivated to add value to the customer. By developing a distinctive competence in a particular market, the effective company is able to gain a competitive advantage through superior quality, lower prices, or better service. Such companies avoid diversification into areas they know little about, and avoid focusing corporate energies on finding acquisitions or avoiding a takeover.

People are seen as the key to success. Worker involvement and the idea of productivity through people is a common theme, and training and development for employees is a high management priority.

The metaphor of the family tends to characterize relationships in the effective organization. Employees remain committed to the company and its ideals, teamwork and cooperation are accepted values, and competition between employees manifests itself in a healthy way as conflict of ideas, not of status or position, in which individuals struggle to push their way to the top at the expense of others.

Such firms solve problems in the present, but they are also future oriented, emphasizing careful planning to achieve shared goals. New products and ideas are encouraged. Employees attempt, not only to adapt to circumstances, but also to shape their environment in a positive way.

Table 10. Assumptions of "Absentee" and "Effective" Corporate Cultures

CATEGORY OF ASSUMPTIONS	ABSENTEE-OWNED, PROFESSIONALLY MANAGED FIRMS	EFFECTIVE FIRMS
Nature of the environment	Success through financial dealings and "general competence" (reactive stance)	Success by adding value to the customer and developing a "distinctive competence" (proactive stance)
Human nature	Neutral or distrusting	High trust
Nature of relationships	Individualistic	Group oriented and egalitarian
Nature of truth	Found in the "bottomline" and in professional rules and models; individual decision making	Found through debate and conflict; group decision making
Time	Present oriented	Future oriented, while honoring the past
Nature of human action	Humans are a means to an end—they are to be used/exploited	Humans are ends in and of themselves and should be developed

Perhaps we have idealized slightly the assumptions that underlie effective corporate cultures and organizations. Granted, no real organization is likely to make all the "right" assumptions as described above; and even if they did, there is still no absolute guarantee of success (despite what Peters and

Waterman and other writers may say). But any observation of real companies does reveal this striking contrast between the assumptions of "absentee" and "effective" cultures. To survive in the marketplace in the long term, any company must add value to its customers and add value to its employees. Absentee-owned firms, in general, do neither. A significant shift over to this sort of value-driven culture may be the key to achieving long-term business success.

CREATING AND CHANGING CORPORATE CULTURES

To develop strategies for changing a corporation's culture, we must understand how organizational cultures in general are created and sustained. There are four primary sources of organizational culture. The first source, ownership, we have discussed in detail throughout this book. Ownership structures imply a certain distribution of power and wealth in the organization and determine its behavior. Thus, different ownership patterns support different artifacts, perspectives, values, and assumptions. In the previous chapters, we have already discussed how some alternative forms of ownership can be used to bring about organizational change.

The leaders of the organization are a second key source of its cultural assumptions. As we mentioned, the core values and assumptions of a company's founders often become that company's culture, for they have the power to determine what is right and wrong or good and bad for their employees—and reward them accordingly. Thus an organization's founders and leaders are often, in effect, the creators of its culture.

Often foundations of culture are laid as members of an organization attempt to solve two basic problems.[3] First, as members of an organization attempt to adapt to a potentially hostile environment, they also adopt certain artifacts, perspectives, values, and assumptions deemed necessary to "succeed" in that environment. Second, as the organization attempts to integrate all its different members to work together cooperatively, it also develops interpersonal and intergroup behaviors that are added to the cultural mosaic.

This set of determinants—ownership, leadership, environmental adaptation, and group integration—gives us clues to how we might change a given culture. Since we have already discussed some alternative forms of ownership, we will turn our attention to the other three.

Before doing so, however, we should note that cultures of organizations often change by going through major crisis and "revolution." Dyer has noted, in studies of companies such as General Motors and National Cash Register, that cultural change is precipitated when an organization faces a crisis that its leaders are unable to solve.[4] Such a crisis undermines the power of the leader until new leaders emerge with new ideas. A power struggle ensues, with the winners demonstrating how their set of beliefs and values is the most appropriate one for the organization. When this kind of revolutionary change occurs, the organization may be in turmoil for some time, and its energies may be directed away from running the business. Valued employees may leave or become casualties of the conflict. In any event, such changes can leave permanent scars and even call the organization's survival into question. The changes that we are advocating will require drastic measures, and are, in many ways, revolutionary in nature. We believe, however, that there are ways to minimize or avoid some of the potential negative consequences of revolutionary change.

CREATING THE VALUE-DRIVEN CULTURE

To change an organization's culture so that it will begin to respond to the demands of the market and the needs of employees requires new strategies in many of the traditional areas of management. The following list represents the activities that we see as crucial in shaping a new corporate culture:

1. Developing a strategic focus

2. Creating new leadership patterns

3. Selecting and socializing employees

4. Emphasizing long-term rewards

5. Creating an effective organization design

We will discuss each of these in turn.

Developing a Strategic Focus

As we have seen, an organization's culture is partially created as its members attempt to solve the basic problem of adapting the organization to its environment. In absentee-owned, professionally managed companies, the characteristic strategy for "success" is to acquire other companies, to be acquired, or to buy and sell assets. The implementation of such a strategy requires primarily financial or legal skills. This reliance on what are widely seen to be the "general competencies" of management leads to many of the problems addressed in this book.

We believe, by contrast, that managers need to develop a distinctive competence, a set of unique skills, for adding value to the customer in terms of higher quality, better prices, or better service. We find that those organizations that have been able to create a niche in the market and provide distinctive products or services are best able to survive in the long run.

This distinctive kind of managerial competence requires an understanding of the customer's needs and the technologies required to deliver the product or service to the customer. By fostering such skills among its employees, an organization develops its strategic focus; and the clear articulation of this strategic focus allows employees, in turn, to understand how their work adds value to the organization's customers. Some of the companies we have discussed that have been able to do this well are Lincoln Electric, Quad Graphics, and Lowe's Companies.

Creating New Leadership Patterns

Because leaders have great power to shape a group's basic assumptions, and often are called upon to sanction or condemn behaviors considered appropriate or inappropriate, they are frequently the key to changing the corporate culture. An organization's leaders must articulate the strategic focus, and provide a general sense of direction. They must have a tangible and specific understanding of the corporation's markets, products, and customers. Without such understanding, leaders often find themselves making poor decisions. In one organization, for example, top management decided to buy a firm that made household appliances in order to acquire new products for their European market. Unfortunately, the decision makers didn't understand that the voltage and other features of their newly acquired product line were not compatible with the needs of Europeans. The mistake proved to be very costly. Such blunders, incredible as they seem, are not uncommon when the leadership does not have the requisite knowledge and skills.

We observe, in many of the absentee-owned companies we have studied, that the focus on rewards and perquisites detracted from developing a competitive advantage. When owners and managers are concerned primarily with their own prestige and positions, the customer is often neglected. In the Digital Equipment Corporation (DEC), to take a contrasting example, the founder, Ken Olsen, attempts to downplay all the conventional status symbols of organizational life. There are no private parking spaces. The corporate offices have a spartan appearance. The traditional and often costly trappings of corporate power are nowhere to be seen. Preferring to devote the company's energies to remaining competitive, Olsen works with employees at all levels to understand and solve problems. As one DEC employee describes:

> In this plant there is a crew of women who have had a very close relationship with Ken Olsen over the years. He will periodically sit down and have tea with them just to find out how they are doing. He may also spend three or four days working with a very low level designer on improving the aesthetics of some packaging. He'll roll up his shirtsleeves and get involved himself. Ken never adopted the

symbols of power, and never lost a very simple appreciation of people.

At DEC, Ken Olsen's actions demonstrate his chief interest:
helping his employees better serve their customers.

In addition to their knowledge, their skill, and their focus
on the customers, business leaders need to develop a long-
term "vision" for their employees so that employees can organize their activities to achieve long-term objectives. In
many cases, employees in absentee-owned firms have little
idea where the company is going or even who will own them
tomorrow. At best, this causes employees to focus on short-
term results; at worst, it paralyzes them. Without a sense of
direction—a sense of *values*—employees feel cast adrift, and
are unable to devote their full energies to adding value to the
customer.

Selection and Socialization

Once a strategic focus is selected and the organization's
leadership has developed a set of long-term objectives, employees must be selected and trained to meet those objectives.
In absentee-owned firms, financial and legal skills are seen as
paramount; but in successful, effective organizations, such
skills are valued insofar as they support the engineering, manufacturing, or other work that the organization really exists
to do. Thus, without neglecting financial and legal skills, organizations should focus their hiring efforts on finding individuals with skills that add value to the customer. Employees
with a combination of technical and financial skills are perhaps best of all, since they will have the ability to understand
both the complexities of the organization's business and the
bottom line. Above all, organizations must find employees
who can add value, not just add up numbers.

Beyond specific skills, furthermore, employees also need
to understand the nature of the business and the core values
of the company. New employees sometimes flounder because
they fail to obtain this critical knowledge. To avoid this prob-

lem, DEC conducts what are called "boot camps" for employees who have been with the company less than one year. The boot camps are run by company "old-timers" who take two to three days to spend time with the new recruits. They tell stories, answer questions, and generally help the neophyte understand the nuances of the business. The boot camps have been highly successful. They have broken down barriers between older and newer employees and created a broad support system for the new recruit. The distinctive competence necessary to run today's corporations itself requires distinctive knowledge and skills which must be transmitted to new employees if the company is to survive.

Reward Systems

Developing a reward system that encourages adding value to the customer is often very difficult. In the absentee-owned company, employees are usually rewarded for individual contributions in the short run. Competition for high monetary rewards is encouraged. While such competition may be quite exciting, it creates a winner-loser syndrome whereby many employees feel like failures and only a few reap large rewards. In most cases, employees must act in concert with one another to add value to the customer. Thus, reward systems should encourage cooperation and focus on the ultimate goal of serving the customer. Moreover, the reward system should not be driven by quarterly numbers and quotas. We studied one rapidly growing high-tech firm, whose survival is contingent upon developing new markets. However, the company has a reward system that *is* designed to reward those who meet quarterly quotas. This focus on short-term results was encouraged by the venture capital group that initially funded the venture. Moreover, they promised the CEO a $1 million bonus if he doubled sales each year in order to encourage a quick return on their investment. Given these incentives, the sales representatives, who should be spending a considerable amount of their time learning about new potential markets and developing new business, neglect this aspect of their jobs because they want the immediate rewards. This organization continues to have difficulty developing new products and markets because employees feel compelled to meet these quotas. Nevertheless, the corporation's absentee-owners are unwilling to allow the management to miss short-run targets—even at the expense of long-term growth and stability. Recently one-half of the company's 1,200 employees were laid off because sales have lagged and new product development has been stymied.

As we have suggested throughout, employees and managers of absentee-owned companies are usually more concerned about their own careers than they are about their clients and co-workers, and more interested in serving themselves than in serving the customers. Up to a point, of course, all people are concerned with themselves, but this extreme pursuit of self-interest at the expense of the organization is clearly detrimental to business performance. In many large Japanese companies, by contrast, employees are not given their first promotion for seven years! During that extended period, employees concern themselves less with career advancement and more with learning the business. While we do not advocate so long a waiting period for American workers, we do believe that employees should invest their competitive energies in their organization rather than against their co-workers.

Reward systems should encourage employees to use initiative. At DEC, the company rewards employees who are innovative, rather than stifling their creativity with organizational barriers. A story often told by DEC managers illustrates this point:

> There's a phrase at DEC: "Do what's right." There was once a manager who wanted to do something and made a proposal to his boss. His boss said, "No, you can't do that, that's crazy." And so he pushed back, he did what was right. He went to the next guy up—and was told that the idea was crazy. So he went to the vice-president level and they told him it was crazy, but that he should "do what's

right." Finally he wound up in Ken Olsen's office, and Ken told him it was crazy but "do what's right." That kind of thing is a piece of the culture that says if it's right, you do it, but it better be right if you've gone all the way. And if you make it work you'll get rewarded for it.

To encourage this kind of risk-taking and creativity and to focus on long-term results will require fundamental changes in the corporate reward systems that we see in American firms today.

Creating an Effective Organization Design

In most organizations, the various subunits—engineering, manufacturing, sales, and so forth—must coordinate their activities to effectively deliver the organization's products. In practice, however, these subunits tend to develop their own interests, and to see other subunits as competitors or adversaries. This is particularly true in absentee-owned firms where individual initiative is valued more highly than cooperation. Moreover, when people are being treated as assets, and see themselves as vulnerable to being laid off, dismissed, or believe the company will be sold to outside interests, they tend to build walls around themselves and their departments for self-protection. In such a climate, the various departments can become little islands, isolated from the other parts of the organization as well as from the customer.

To avoid these problems, organizations should be designed to encourage collaboration between subunits. Cross-functional teams, quality circles, and workers' committees can be used successfully to facilitate communication and cooperation across functions. When individuals are assigned to work with others outside their department to solve interdepartmental problems, mutual understanding and commitment to the organization can be generated. In one highly successful company, each department and division treats each other according to what they call a "customer/vendor" relationship. Other departments are seen as key "customers" whose support is needed if the company is to succeed. By treating other divisions and departments as customers, teamwork and collaboration across functional and divisional boundaries are encouraged.

We do not believe that teams, quality circles, and other similar devices are a panacea for all organizational problems. But it is clear that the lack of team spirit and cooperation so evident in absentee-owned firms works against the organization's overall effectiveness; and, by extension, cross-functional coordination and communication will be essential for future success.

A VALUE-DRIVEN ORGANIZATION

One company that appears to have many of the qualities of an effective corporate culture is W.L. Gore and Associates, which we briefly discussed in an earlier chapter. This company has been described as one of the best companies to work for in the United States[5] and has been cited for its achievements in the popular press. Founded in the late 1950s by Bill Gore, a scientist who had worked at Du Pont on new applications for Teflon, the company has grown rapidly by emphasizing many of the "effective" values discussed in this chapter.

Michael Pacanowsky, a professor of communications at the University of Utah, spent a year working at Gore, attempting to understand its unique culture. Pacanowsky describes Gore as a "lattice organization," meaning that lines of communication are open to all levels of the organization.[6] Employees at Gore are supposed to talk to those individuals whose help is needed to get the job done. Authority is not fixed or assigned, but based on what is needed to complete a particular task. Work is accomplished through personal commitments to excellence, not through formal rules or job descriptions.

At the heart of the Gore culture are four basic values:

"Fairness," "Freedom," "Commitment," and what is called "Waterline"—a notion that others need to be consulted if a decision is made that could seriously damage the company. Those at Gore use the analogy that the company is like a ship that will sink if holes are bored in it below the waterline. If one is doing something "below the waterline," something that might sink the ship, then participative decision making is crucial. Boring holes "above the waterline," as it were, can be done with little or no consultation. These four values instill in Gore employees a sense of direction, of loyalty, and a commitment to serving the customer and helping each other.

To create a more egalitarian atmosphere in the company, all 4,000 employees become owners after one year of service. Thus, they are called "associates" rather than employees. Terms like "boss," "manager," and "supervisor" are replaced with "leader" or "sponsor" in an attempt to deemphasize difference of status and position and foster collaboration. One associate, Sarah Clifton, wanted to know how to word her title on her business cards which she would give to friends and business associates. Her supervisor told her that since titles didn't matter in dealing with people on the outside she could select any title she wished. He suggested "Supreme Commander" and had business cards made up that identified her as such.

The company knows what it does well: developing new applications of Teflon. Its Gore-Tex fabric, used in a variety of garments because it insulates and "breathes" simultaneously, was a significant innovation. To carry out the company's mission, associates are asked to develop what is called "credibility"—the development of technical competence, good judgment, and a history of meeting commitments. The company's ownership structure, management style, and corporate culture combine to instill in its employees a sense of long-term commitment to the company, a focus on customer service and employee development, and an overall atmosphere of freedom and responsibility seldom found in American corporations.

As Pacanowsky has pointed out, the Gore culture "empowers" the employees to accomplish both personal and organizational goals. This is done by

- Distributing power and opportunity widely

- Maintaining open, decentralized communication

- Encouraging group and intergroup problem solving

- Challenging people in an environment of trust

- Rewarding and recognizing people to encourage high performance and personal responsibility

- Becoming wise by living through and learning from organizational ambiguity, inconsistency, contradiction, and paradox

As Pacanowsky concludes,

> Most organizations make you aware of the limitations placed on people by the organization, but at Gore, I felt that what limitations there were were the limitations *of* people placed on people. . . . the organization makes it possible for people to do their utmost.[7]

SUMMARY

In this chapter we have attempted to differentiate between the kinds of assumptions underpinning the absentee corporate cultures and the cultures of more effective organizations. As we have seen, the absentee cultures are based on assumptions that encourage short run results, treat people as assets, focus on individual rather than group achievement, and prize generic management skills. In contrast, the assumptions underlying the behavior of effective firms promote a long-term, developmental perspective regarding their employees and their external markets. Such assumptions are created by the type of ownership structure employed as well the orientation of top management.

To change from an absentee culture to one that adds value to customers and employees is not likely to be easy. Changing the ownership structure to include broader participation by members of the organization is often the key to creating a new culture. Our studies of culture change in many organizations indicate that without a change in ownership structure, it is difficult to change an organization's basic assumptions. Changing ownership structure, however, is not sufficient to guarantee change to a cultural pattern that facilitates long-term growth and development.

To create a new cultural pattern, enlightened leaders are needed to select a strategic direction for the firm that will focus the employee's efforts to develop a distinctive competence. Along with this strategic focus, the organization must select the "right" people and teach them the needed social and technical skills that will enable them to add value to the company. Long-term rewards, cooperation and teamwork, and a sense of ownership and commitment are needed to create the value-added culture. This process of changing the absentee corporate culture to a more effective one is not likely to be easy, but must be undertaken by many American corporations who are currently managing their way into oblivion.

CHAPTER 9 ENDNOTES

1. For a fuller discussion of these six categories of assumptions, see Edgar Schein. *Organizational Culture and Leadership* (San Francisco: Jossey-Bass, 1985).

2. See, for example, Thomas J. Peters and Robert H. Waterman. *In Search of Excellence* (New York: Harper & Row, 1982); William Ouchi. *Theory Z* (Reading, Mass.: Addison-Wesley, 1981); Donald K. Clifford and Richard E. Cavanaugh. *The Winning Performance* (New York: Bantam, 1985); Alan J. Wilkins and Kerry J. Patterson. "You Can't Get There from Here: What Will Make Culture-Change Projects Fail." In Ralph H. Kilmann, Mary J. Saxton, Roy Serpa and Associates, eds., *Gaining Control of the Corporate Culture* (San Francisco: Jossey-Bass, 1985).

3. See Schein, 1985.

4. Dyer, W. Gibb, Jr. "The Cycle of Cultural Evolution in Organiza-

tions." R. Kilmann, M. J. Saxton, R. Serpa and Associates, eds., *Gaining Control of the Corporate Culture* (San Francisco: Jossey-Bass, 1985).

5. Robert Levering, Milton Moscowitz, and Michael Katz. *The 100 Best Companies to Work for in America* (Reading, Mass.: Addison-Wesley, 1985), pp. 128–130.

6. Michael Pacanowsky. "Communication in the Empowering Organization." In J.A. Anderson, ed., *ICA Yearbook 11* (Beverly Hills, Calif.: Sage Publications, 1987).

7. *Ibid.*

CHAPTER 10 ═══════════════════

Policy Implications for the Future

Throughout this book we have been questioning the value and effectiveness of absentee ownership and professional management. Moving beyond our initial critique, the last few chapters of this volume have suggested alternative stock ownership structures and approaches to building an effective organizational culture.

We now address questions of a more macro nature: What can be done to confront the adverse effects of management education? How might cooperative efforts between management and labor aid an entire industry in the struggle for survival? Are there creative state-level strategies that might be developed to facilitate local ownership and economic growth? Finally, we explore issues of national policy in order to examine what might be done at the federal level.

Our criticism of professional management implies as well a criticism of the process of professionalization itself. We have argued that today's managers are self-obsessed, driven primarily by a concern for their own power and their own career paths. Despising the reality of the shop floor and its blue-collar workers, today's managers have lost a degree of real humanity. These technocrats of the modern corporation lack even a sense of *noblesse oblige* as they manage by the numbers, work their deals, and focus on short-term results.

The professionalizing of management starts with MBA programs, but what, we ask, can be done to improve such programs? In our view, the quantity of MBAs now outstrips the quality of the education they receive. We question whether there is really any need for the recent, dramatic growth in the number of graduate programs in business. There are now well over 600 MBA programs in the country, the majority unaccredited. Many schools are simply going through the motions of academic ritual without much substance. We think that some important first steps toward reversing the unhappy trends we have been discussing in this book would be to reduce the flood of generic young professionals coming into the job market, and to overhaul the educational programs of business schools.

Indeed, if our critique of professional management is correct, the American system of business education, with its emphasis on short-term, bottom-line results, is a major cause of American industrial decline. What can be done to improve this system? Here are some suggestions:

- The MBA curriculum must move away from its narrow obsession with economic criteria and computer skills toward a broader sensitivity to what Douglas McGregor, years ago, called "the human side of enterprise." A curriculum that focused on basic organizational concepts, verbal and written communication, and general interpersonal skills would tend to produce more well-rounded managers who can be team players.

- Business schools would also be strengthened by creating new courses on business and society, allowing students to analyze and discuss the complex interconnections between corporations and the communities that surround them. Too few of today's MBAs ask themselves what they can do to contribute to society. The recent rush of scandals on Wall Street, and many other similar developments, suggest a crucial need for courses on ethics and corporate morality to supplement those on investment banking.

- We also recommend that more attention be paid to the selection of students for MBA programs. In the view of Curtis Tarr, Dean of Cornell's School of Management, students ought to be admitted who have potential as leaders, not just winners. Society does not need tens of thousands of new degree-based technocrats every year; rather, it needs leaders with character, integrity, and a vision of the future.

- Preparation of MBA professionals needs to move beyond the current emphasis on finance to more practical, hands-on training in manufacturing and work methods. Programs should be created which combine engineering with management courses, characterized by product expertise and quality control systems. Business faculty need to generate practical, shop-floor experiences for students, as interns and/or consultants, in which MBAs would learn to roll up their sleeves, get down into the bowels of the factory, and learn about technologies and people in the "real world."

- Finally, we believe that MBA programs must move away from their current, almost totally ethnocentric curriculums, which center on American textbooks and business cases involving the Fortune 500 companies. The emergence of a global market has revealed American business's profound ignorance of other cultures and values. We believe that cross-cultural research, foreign languages, and in-depth study of international business ought to be the core of a business education. To think that a superficial exposure to international issues is sufficient is to ignore fundamental shifts in today's managerial world. The U.S. has not lost its competitive position because the business environment suddenly internationalized, but because American managers did not (and do not) understand what was going on in other national economies.

Industry-wide Innovation

What can be done at the level of an entire industry to turn around economic decline? First, America needs to recreate a climate of experimentation in which managers actively try out new strategies instead of hoping conditions will change by themselves.

More specifically, the struggle to revitalize troubled industries requires new forms of labor-management cooperation. It seems a curious anomaly that in America, when economic problems hit an industry, relationships between unions and managers take a turn for the worse. At the very time when working together is most critical, the two parties begin to argue. The recent impasse between U.S. Steel (USX) Corporation and the United Steel Workers is a particularly vivid illustration. Beset by encroaching foreign producers, plagued by excess capacity, troubled by massive losses, what do the two groups do? They decide to fight, each pointing a finger at the other.

Such tactics defy all logic. Social scientists theorize that two parties facing a common crisis tend to unite to achieve a common goal. But here, when basic survival should be an obvious goal to both sides, the evidence suggests instead a program of mutual suicide.

To face the external threats confronting American industry, we need reconciliation and collective efforts on the part of labor and management alike. The recent salvaging of the shipping industry in Scandinavia is a successful illustration of such cooperation on an industrywide level. The major industries in the United States will have to attempt similar coalitions between labor and company interests if they are to regain their competitive position.

Another intriguing solution to some industrywide problems is the unconventional idea that, instead of growing increasingly larger, companies ought to become smaller, leaner, and more effective. Here, the case of steel provides a more positive illustration.

In sharp contrast to the sluggish management culture of the traditional steel industry is what has come to be known as the mini-mill enterprise. Mini-mills are relatively small, low-cost steel plants using state-of-the-art technology and, in most cases, nonunion labor, to fashion small, specialized steel products. They began in the 1950s when the big steel companies made a technological change from open hearth to basic oxygen furnaces, which required 30 percent less scrap metal.

This resulted in a huge increase in available scrap, which the mini-mills were able to use for smaller-scale production.

In the past, the major companies have always considered mini-mills to be insignificant competition, but today the mini-mills are rapidly becoming a significant threat. In 1960, mini-mills had a 3 percent market share; today, they have over 20 percent. One of the mini-mills, Chaparrel Steel near Dallas, is now the fifteenth largest steel maker in America. The projections are that mini-mills will control 30 percent of the domestic steel market by the end of this decade. The mini-mills are expected to have a total steel-producing capacity of thirty-seven million tons (a 133 percent increase) by the year 2000.

According to some mini-mill executives, their advantage was that they did not know a great deal about the industry when they started up as new firms. They simply scoured the world for the best technology and began to use it. This use and development of state-of-the-art technology is an underlying reason for the phenomenal growth of the mini-mill sector of the steel industry. Along with the technology itself is a philosophy of how to use it that is opposite to the strategy of the big steel companies. While the traditional approach assumes that improved performance is only possible with massive capital expenditures, the mini-mill entrepreneurs seek continuous marginal improvements in operating techniques. They stay on the cutting edge: building tight, quick, and cheap; avoiding excess and unnecessary refinements; and understanding that anything they improve may quickly become obsolete.

The ability of U.S. mini-mills to compete with both domestic and foreign steel producers is heavily affected by their management style and practices. Where the large integrated mills are price makers, the mini-mills are price takers. This forces them to be cost-conscious on the plant floor and in the executive offices alike. They boast of no company cars, jets, hunting lodges, luxurious office suites, or executive dining rooms. Everyone travels economy class. Headquarter staffs are much leaner, further reducing operating costs. An awareness of the overall company cost structure, something that has been difficult or impossible for the big producers to instill in its management, substantially improves managerial decision making in the mini-mills.

Most mini-mill companies have spanned the wide gap between labor and management traditionally found in integrated steel companies. According to mini-mill executives, the managerial advantage of being nonunion lies not in low wages but in greater flexibility and higher productivity. The same flexibility, the same team-oriented corporate culture, is equally possible for unionized companies.

From a business perspective, the bottom line of mini-mill success is profitability. Nucor boasts earnings at 18 percent of equity, which easily beats the average for Fortune 500 companies. The high profit rates of mini-mills attract more investment than the traditional steel industry. This allows for the financing of improvements in technology, thus reducing costs and boosting profits. It is a positive version of the vicious circle in which the big steel companies are trapped.

There are a wide variety of additional innovations worth exploring. Recently, General Motors and the United Auto Workers have joined forces in the Saturn Motor Company—a labor-management partnership to design, market, and manufacture a whole new line of automobiles. At Saturn, a new collective bargaining agreement employs fewer job classifications and merit-based incentives for high performance. This unprecedented program has been so successful in its start-up phase that other auto plants and various other companies in different industries are beginning to talk of "saturnizing" their operations.

A remarkable variation of this theme is the creation of joint ventures with foreign manufacturers. Virtually all American auto companies have now stabilized shared ownership in order to learn from each other and achieve mutually beneficial gains. For instance, GM and Toyota reopened a shutdown facility in Fremont, California, and completely reversed a decade of lost profits and labor conflicts. Combining the best of the American and Japanese ways of running a business, the transformed plant has become a model for the industry. More of this should occur in other industries as well.

As discussed in an earlier chapter, worker buy-outs of troubled factories may also be a tool for industrywide innovation. The trucking, airline, and steel industries all seem to be on the way toward becoming entirely employee owned. Evidence from the steel industry in particular suggests that worker buy-outs may have the potential to rescue the industry. In over a dozen cases, troubled mines and mills have been saved through carrying out a feasibility study, negotiating a buy-out with the owner, designing an ESOP structure, and securing adequate financing for purchase and start-up. Threatened operations have been given a new lease on life through ESOPs at Bethlehem Steel, Eastmet, Continental, Gilmore, Wheeling-Pitt, Armco, and the White Pine mine in Michigan. In the process, thousands of jobs have been saved.

As mentioned previously, perhaps the most successful case to date is Weirton Steel in West Virginia, a mill which was bought by 8,000 steelworkers from the parent company, National Steel. Since the buy-out in 1984, the company has not only preserved jobs, it has also reversed years of steady decline. The mill has pumped over a billion dollars into the local economy, and may well become the prototype of success for the steel industry as a whole. If executives of large steel firms are unable to manage their way out of their problems, and if we are understandably reluctant to let the Japanese acquire an industry so vital to national defense, then perhaps we should turn the mills over to the American worker.

A final form of labor-management cooperation as a way of revitalizing troubled industries is corporate democracy—reforming the board of directors. Some advocates urge opening boardrooms to independent, outside directors who will look objectively at management decisions and the bottom line. Others urge that community and public interest groups be represented on corporate boards to guard against antisocial corporate actions and to encourage the development of healthy products.

The obvious other candidates for a new participation in

corporate governance are the employees. In Western Europe, this democratic approach to economic performance, called codetermination, has been a growing aspect of business for many years. Workers began appearing on boards of directors in France and West Germany shortly after World War II, and by the 1980s there were similar developments in seven countries. Today, workers in Germany hold 50 percent of the board seats in all major companies. In Sweden, any firm with twenty-five or more employees must have board-level representation for its workers. While codetermination is still in its infancy in the United States, a number of companies have followed the lead of Chrysler and the UAW, who first agreed to a labor seat on the board in 1981. If the European experience is any indication, board representation by industry workers promises not only labor peace and heightened morale, but better productivity and profits as well.

STATE-LEVEL POLICY AND STRATEGY

What can state governments do to address the problems of absentee ownership and managerial decline? Policy makers around the country are attempting a variety of practical strategies to meet the economic challenges of the 80's, strategies which have important implications for other regions.

Massachusetts represents perhaps the best model of legislative action for economic development. From the mid to the late 1970s, the state suffered over 600 plant closings and the loss of 150,000 jobs. Two thirds of the factory shutdowns were unionized shops. Out of this crisis, a number of new initiatives were enacted:

- A Mature Industries Act was passed in 1984 based on a "social compact." This compact cushions the blow of a shutdown by extending state unemployment benefits to laidoff workers and enjoining companies to provide advance notice and severance pay.

- A Massachusetts Product Development Corporation was established to facilitate new industrial production, headed by a board of business, union, community, and state participants.

- A new, quasi-public agency, the Economic Stabilization Trust, jointly managed by union and business representatives, provides last-minute financial assistance for firms in crisis.

- A number of incentives have emerged in recent years to lure investors with state and corporate interests to create a dynamic high-tech economic sector. Today Route 128 is as well known as Silicon Valley as a launching pad for many new firms and jobs.

- The state office of labor, along with the United Electrical Workers, has set up the Machine Trust Action Project to revamp the inactive machine tool industry.

Collectively, these various approaches in Massachusetts have clearly mitigated the general industrial decline so common in the Northeast states. Massachusetts now has a vibrant economy and about 3 percent unemployment, the lowest in the nation.

Other states have tried different tactics to reduce runaway plants and capital flight. Some two dozen states have enacted or are considering plant-closing legislation. Maine's law, enacted in 1971, affects all firms with one hundred or more workers, and requires a company to notify the Director of the State Bureau of Labor at least sixty days prior to shutting down. Employees with three years or more seniority must receive one week's wages for every year of employment as a severance.

Other state bills or proposals portray a broad range of approaches designed to minimize the extent of closures and mitigate their negative impact. Wisconsin, for example, requires a 60-day advance notice of shutdowns, and has the power to fine a violating company up to $50 per worker. Michigan is considering a bill requiring companies to put a year's worth of health insurance benefits into an escrow account for laidoff workers, and provide extra paid leave of up to two weeks to facilitate the search for another job.

Obviously states do not have the ultimate power to block industrial shutdowns. But plant-closing legislation at least creates disincentives that may cause absentee owners to think twice before pulling out of a region. Critics worry that business will be unwilling to locate in states with such legislation, but there is no evidence for such a fear. In Europe, where plant-closing laws have existed for decades, there has been no diminishment of investment or decline in plant start-ups.

Another approach is illustrated by the five-year effort to save the Mahoning Valley's steel and manufacturing sectors. The struggle over the years has involved state senators and representatives, community officials, labor and business leaders, religious spokesmen, and academics. Basing their opinion on the Municipal Authorities Act of 1945—which legitimized acquisition of industries by eminent domain for the public good—many people maintain that absentee-owned firms should turn over business to local control, rather than simply shut down and leave regions of the state decimated. They have raised funds to conduct feasibility studies of takeovers and blocked the removal of major equipment in closed plants through court injunctions. In 1986, the Steel Valley Authority, modeled after the TVA, was incorporated by the state of Pennsylvania to further facilitate such developments.

Similar efforts are now taking shape in Ohio and West Virginia. Connecticut has created the Naugatuck Valley Project, a regional coalition of over fifty organizations, to monitor industries and watch for early warning signs of plant closings. Basically a grass roots organization, NVP has confronted company banks about their lack of investment in regional business, passed new legislation to create a state trust fund for worker buy-outs, raised monies for economic impact and feasibility studies, and provided leadership training programs to develop more effective leaders in the region.

Some 17 states have passed employee ownership legislation, many using ESOPs as a central element in strategic economic development plans. The fundamental arguments in favor of this innovative legislation include preserving economic stability, reducing state contributions to welfare and unemployment compensation programs, perpetuating the continuity of local ownership, and avoiding acquisitions by outside interests which drain capital from a region.

Since the first state legislation in 1980–1981, various mandates have been created. Some, such as in Delaware and Minnesota, are primarily expressions of support and advocacy. Others, like New York and Wisconsin, require the state to educate the public on ESOPs through conferences, workshops, brochures, and so forth. A third grouping of laws go further than mere policy guidelines, providing technical assistance (New Jersey and Oregon) or tax incentives for employee-owned firms (New Hampshire). Loans or loan guarantees for buy-outs now exist in California, Illinois, and other states. Michigan has even established an office to assist groups attempting worker ownership.

ESOPs are not the only alternative form of ownership structure currently being advocated by state governments. Maine, Vermont, and three other states have made loans to encourage the formation of producer or worker cooperatives. Recently New York used state funds to help launch a new business venture as a co-op. Massachusetts now has an extensive program for facilitating cooperative ownership, including simple incorporation loans, consultation services and financial assistance to worker groups.

Such efforts could be extended even further by the tapping of employee pension funds or other industrial pools of capital to finance employee ownership. Instead of investing pension resources in out-of-state corporations, we can revitalize industry far more efficiently by maintaining local control and building an employee-owned economy. States could also provide incentives for employee-ownership in Urban Enterprise Zones and show preferences for ESOPs in state procurement policy and practice.

Federal Programs of Economic Revitalization

Some existing national programs designed to curb the effects of economic decline are currently threatened, and we urge their preservation. Other new policies are now being hotly debated. We wish to add to this debate by suggesting several other possibilities for federal intervention.

First, as the nation attempts—during the Reagan administration and beyond—to trim government spending, we must be sure that such efforts strengthen rather than weaken economic development. As we have argued throughout this book, small, locally owned enterprises are exactly what the economy needs; and therefore, we are seriously opposed to current attempts to scuttle the Small Business Administration. We believe that the SBA's budget should be increased, particularly funds for technical assistance programs, education, and loans for entrepreneurs. The best counter to our increasingly monolithic corporations would be hundreds of thousands of successful small firms, and the SBA is a crucial factor in fostering this kind of entrepreneurial economy.

Second, we need a change of priorities in government support for research and development. Today, the vast majority of federally funded R&D goes to large companies, especially in the energy and defense industries. But while America funds research for new weapons, other nations are putting their resources toward developing technologies—including robotics, computers, semi-conductors, and pharmaceuticals—with far more commercial value. The United States needs R&D that will improve our competitive position in a global economy; and we can best do so by giving priority to small enterprises and industries of the future, which create jobs and wages for Americans. In West Germany, the Ministry of Technology limits its R&D grants for large companies to half of the thousands it administers annually, reserving the other half for small and medium-sized companies.

The federal government should also reexamine its role in the current merger frenzy and the accompanying problems of increased concentration of assets, illegal insider trading, and managerial greed. In early 1986, Wall Street was rocked by the news that a respected investment broker with Drexel Burnham Lambert had personally picked up $12.6 million in fifty-four illegal transactions. As it turned out, however, this was only a minor violation of the public trust compared to the spreading scandal centered on arbitrageur Leon Boesky, who made at least $200 million through insider trading.

What is to be done? Congress needs to push through legislation to curb hostile takeovers and mega-mergers. The Federal Trade Commission must perform objective critical analyses and block proposals for big mergers which are in conflict with the best interests of society as a whole. The Securities and Exchange Commission must beef up surveillance and aggressively track down questionable activity. Improved auditing systems and corporate monitoring programs are needed to trace dummy corporations and offshore banking in protected retreats such as the Bahamas and Switzerland. Finally, we need tougher laws to limit managerial self-interest exercised at the expense of stockholders, consumers, employees, and the general public. Insider trading is not merely unethical and bad for Wall Street's reputation. The government must see such activities as what they are: corporate crime.

Furthermore, as we attempt to assist declining industries, there is much we can learn from other nations that suffer similar problems. Japan's Ministry of International Trade and Industry (MITI), for example, is an impressive institution for policy formulation. MITI not only regulates existing business, but also promotes the growth of new products and devises plans for troubled sectors of the economy. France and West Germany are closely pursuing similar institutional practices. There, long-range planning, financial incentives, and global marketing strategies are being coordinated by the federal government in close cooperation with the business community. While the United States continues to debate the need for a national industrial policy, most other Western nations are moving rapidly to phase out obsolete industries, revitalize industrial sectors in temporary trouble, and foster future growth. America needs to recognize that survival in the coming years is not guaranteed, and that the federal government can play an important and appropriate role in restructuring industrial development, stimulating investment, and expanding overseas markets.

There is already tremendous debate in Washington about international trade. The American market share of automobiles, steel, textiles, and many other products has dramatically eroded, yet there is wide disagreement on how to reverse this trend. On the one hand, proponents of free trade advocate a hands-off policy, arguing that natural market forces are operating and that any tinkering would be counterproductive. Others point out that whole sectors of the economy and a tremendous number of jobs are being lost while we wait for free trade prophecies to come true. These doubters point to our record-setting trade imbalance, our growing foreign debt, and the increased acquisition of American companies, farms and banks by other countries; and push vociferously for tariffs, quotas, and other protectionist legislation to help our troubled industries.

We contend that both extremes are missing the point. It would make more sense for the government to combine several different strategic options to achieve both short-term and long-term goals. First, the nearly forty-year-old General Agreement on Tariffs and Trade must be updated. The whole system of international trade agreements needs revision to preserve neutrality and reflect current conditions of economic development. As it stands, the Japanese and Koreans are sinking our basic industries while we merely hope for projected future change and ask for "voluntary" reductions in their market penetration. What we need, however, is not a protectionist lockout of other nations from U.S. markets, but greater openness for our products in their economies—in short, reciprocity. Instead of individual tariffs that protect specific industries and invite retaliation, we need a coherent and fair international policy.

And here at home, we must reverse the current trend that asks workers to accept pay reductions while maximizing compensation packages for top executives. Workers must be better compensated to raise morale and increase productivity. The evidence is compelling that sagging productivity, not rising wages, is the real cause of economic stagnation. So far, the whittling away of blue-collar pay has been practically the only cost-cutting solution to industrial decline. Now we must ask ourselves: do we really want to emulate the Third World and become a nation of $1-an-hour data-entry clerks and machine operators?

CONCLUSION

As reality itself grows ever more complex, business too becomes correspondingly more difficult. We have argued throughout this book that, in effect, our industrial problems are too complex to be left to executives—those elite professionals who manage their absentee-owned companies from distant offices and determine the fate of America's communities while they climb the corporate ladders of wealth and power. The economy is simply too important to be left in the hands of a few at the top of that ladder. To solve our problems, we need reconciliation, cooperation, and the broad participation of all parties to the economic enterprise: workers, consumers, unions, the state and federal governments. Working together, we just might make a difference.

Index